CONTEMPORARY THAI HORROR FILM

Traditions in World Cinema

General Editors
Linda Badley (Middle Tennessee State University)
R. Barton Palmer (Clemson University)

Founding Editor
Steven Jay Schneider (New York University)

Titles in the series include:

Traditions in World Cinema
Linda Badley, R. Barton Palmer and Steven Jay Schneider (eds)

Post-beur Cinema: North African Émigré and Maghrebi-French Filmmaking in France since 2000
Will Higbee

New Taiwanese Cinema in Focus: Moving Within and Beyond the Frame
Flannery Wilson

International Noir
Homer B. Pettey and R. Barton Palmer (eds)

Films on Ice: Cinemas of the Arctic
Scott MacKenzie and Anna Westerståhl Stenport (eds)

Nordic Genre Film: Small Nation Film Cultures in the Global Marketplace
Tommy Gustafsson and Pietari Kääpä (eds)

Contemporary Japanese Cinema Since Hana-Bi
Adam Bingham

Chinese Martial Arts Cinema: The Wuxia Tradition (Second edition)
Stephen Teo

Slow Cinema
Tiago de Luca and Nuno Barradas Jorge

Expressionism in the Cinema
Olaf Brill and Gary D. Rhodes (eds)

French-language Road Cinema: Borders, Diasporas, Migration and 'New Europe'
Michael Gott

Transnational Film Remakes
Iain Robert Smith and Constantine Verevis

Coming-of-Age Cinema in New Zealand
Alistair Fox

New Transnationalisms in Contemporary Latin American Cinemas
Dolores Tierney

Celluloid Singapore: Cinema, Performance and the National
Edna Lim

Short Films from a Small Nation: Danish Informational Cinema 1935–1965
C. Claire Thomson

B-Movie Gothic: International Perspectives
Justin D. Edwards and Johan Höglund (eds)

Francophone Belgian Cinema
Jamie Steele

The New Romanian Cinema
Christina Stojanova (ed) with the participation of Dana Duma

French Blockbusters: Cultural Politics of a Transnational Cinema
Charlie Michael

Nordic Film Cultures and Cinemas of Elsewhere
Anna Westerståhl Stenport and Arne Lunde (eds)

New Realism: Contemporary British Cinema
David Forrest

Contemporary Balkan Cinema: Transnational Exchanges and Global Circuits
Lydia Papadimitriou and Ana Grgić (eds)

Mapping the Rockumentary: Images of Sound and Fury
Gunnar Iversen and Scott MacKenzie (eds)

Images of Apartheid: Filmmaking on the Fringe in the Old South Africa
Calum Waddell

Greek Film Noir
Anna Poupou, Nikitas Fessas, and Maria Chalkou (eds)

Norwegian Nightmares: The Horror Cinema of a Nordic Country
Christer Bakke Andresen

Late-colonial French Cinema: Filming the Algerian War of Independence
Mani Sharpe

Australian International Pictures (1946–75)
Adrian Danks and Constantine Verevis

Film Censorship in a Cultural Context
Daniel Sacco

Liminal Noir in Classical World Cinema
Elyce Rae Helford and Christopher Weedman

Contemporary Thai Horror Film: A Monstrous Hybrid
Mary Jane Ainslie

Please see our website for a complete list of titles in the series
www.edinburghuniversitypress.com/series/TIWC

CONTEMPORARY THAI HORROR FILM
A Monstrous Hybrid

Mary Jane Ainslie

EDINBURGH
University Press

Edinburgh University Press is one of the leading university presses in the UK. We publish academic books and journals in our selected subject areas across the humanities and social sciences, combining cutting-edge scholarship with high editorial and production values to produce academic works of lasting importance. For more information visit our website: edinburghuniversitypress.com

© Mary Jane Ainslie, 2024, 2025

Parts of this book were previously published in [Chapter 1] Ainslie, M. (2014) 'The Supernatural and Post-war Thai Cinema', *Horror Studies*, 5(2), pp. 157–169; Ainslie, M. (2017) 'Post-war Thai Cinema: Audiences and Film Style in a Divided Nation', *Film International*, 80, 15(2), pp. 6–19; [Chapter 4] Ainslie, M. (2009) 'The Monstrous Chinese "Other" in the Thai Horror Movie *Zee-Oui*' in R. Cheung and D. H. Fleming (eds), *Cinemas, Identities and Beyond* (Cambridge: Cambridge Scholars Publishing); Ainslie, M. and Blake, L. (2015) 'Digital Witnessing and Trauma Testimony in *Ghost Game*: Cambodian Genocide, Digital Horror and the Nationalism of New Thai Cinema', in L. Blake and X. Reyes (eds) *Digital Nightmares: Wired Ghosts, CCTV Horror and the Found Footage Phenomenon* (London: I. B. Tauris); [Chapter 5] Ainslie, M. (2011), 'Contemporary Thai Horror: The Horrific Incarnation of *Shutter*', *Asian Cinema*, 22(1), pp. 45–57; [Chapter 9] Ainslie, M. (2015) 'Thai Horror Film in Malaysia: Urbanization, Cultural Proximity and a Southeast Asian Model', *Plaridel: A Philippine Journal of Communication, Media, and Society*, 12(2).

Edinburgh University Press Ltd
13 Infirmary Street
Edinburgh EH1 1LT

First published in hardback by Edinburgh University Press 2024

Typeset in 10/12.5 pt Sabon by
Cheshire Typesetting Ltd, Cuddington, Cheshire

A CIP record for this book is available from the British Library

ISBN 978 1 4744 8445 9 (hardback)
ISBN 978 1 4744 8446 6 (paperback)
ISBN 978 1 4744 8447 3 (webready PDF)
ISBN 978 1 4744 8448 0 (epub)

The right of Mary Jane Ainslie to be identified as the author of this work has been asserted in accordance with the Copyright, Designs and Patents Act 1988, and the Copyright and Related Rights Regulations 2003 (SI No. 2498).

CONTENTS

Acknowledgements and Author Note   vi
Traditions in World Cinema   vii

Introduction   1
1. Post-war Thai Cinema: Audiences and Film Style in a Divided Nation   15
2. After the 16mm Era: Horror and Progressive Social Critique   44
3. New Thai Cinema and *Nang Nak*: Heritage Horror and Economic Crisis   64
4. Thai Horror and the 'Other': *Zee Oui* and *Ghost Game*   88
5. The Monstrous Thai Feminine: *Shutter* and the 'Vengeful Ghosts'   110
6. Horror Beyond the Screen: *Victim*, *The Screen at Kamchanod* and *Coming Soon*   125
7. Village Horror: Continuing a Provincial Film Style   137
8. Middle-class Horror and Urban Modernity: *The Promise*   149
9. Regional and International Success in the Digital Age: Folk Horror and a Southeast Asian Model   167
Conclusion   190

Bibliography   194
Index   205

ACKNOWLEDGEMENTS AND AUTHOR NOTE

The author and publisher give special thanks to GDH559 Company Limited for their assistance with this volume.

The author wishes to thank the University of Nottingham Ningbo School of International Communications and the Institute of Asia Pacific Studies, the Thai Film Archive, Dr Linnie Blake, Dr Katarzyna Ancuta, Dr Kengkij Kitirianglarp, James Nethercote, Dr Filippo Gilardi, F. W. Ainslie, Dr Susan Marsden, Catherine Norris, Dr Jiro E. Kondo and Dr Tracey Fallon and many others for their support throughout the writing process.

Please note: To avoid confusion Thai names and film titles in this book have been transliterated according to the most prevalent English spellings, though such a system inevitably falls short of standardisation. Where possible, both Thai and English titles have been included, with priority given to the most used and recognised title.

TRADITIONS IN WORLD CINEMA

General editors: **Linda Badley and R. Barton Palmer**
Founding editor: **Steven Jay Schneider**

Traditions in World Cinema is a series of textbooks and monographs devoted to the analysis of currently popular and previously underexamined or undervalued film movements from around the globe. Also intended for general interest readers, the textbooks in this series offer undergraduate- and graduate-level film students accessible and comprehensive introductions to diverse traditions in world cinema. The monographs open up for advanced academic study more specialised groups of films, including those that require theoretically-oriented approaches. Both textbooks and monographs provide thorough examinations of the industrial, cultural, and socio-historical conditions of production and reception.

The flagship textbook for the series includes chapters by noted scholars on traditions of acknowledged importance (the French New Wave, German Expressionism), recent and emergent traditions (New Iranian, post-Cinema Novo), and those whose rightful claim to recognition has yet to be established (the Israeli persecution film, global found footage cinema). Other volumes concentrate on individual national, regional or global cinema traditions. As the introductory chapter to each volume makes clear, the films under discussion form a coherent group on the basis of substantive and relatively transparent, if not always obvious, commonalities. These commonalities may be formal, stylistic or thematic, and the groupings may, although they need not, be popularly identified as genres, cycles or movements (Japanese horror, Chinese martial arts cinema, Italian Neorealism). Indeed, in cases in which a group of films is not already commonly identified as a tradition, one purpose of the volume is to establish its claim to importance and make it visible (East Central European Magical Realist cinema, Palestinian cinema).

Textbooks and monographs include:

- An introduction that clarifies the rationale for the grouping of films under examination
- A concise history of the regional, national, or transnational cinema in question
- A summary of previous published work on the tradition
- Contextual analysis of industrial, cultural and socio-historical conditions of production and reception
- Textual analysis of specific and notable films, with clear and judicious application of relevant film theoretical approaches
- Bibliograph(ies)/filmograph(ies)

Monographs may additionally include:

- Discussion of the dynamics of cross-cultural exchange in light of current research and thinking about cultural imperialism and globalisation, as well as issues of regional/national cinema or political/aesthetic movements (such as new waves, postmodernism, or identity politics)
- Interview(s) with key filmmakers working within the tradition.

INTRODUCTION

Contemporary Thai Horror Film undertakes a timely analysis of the form and characteristics of Thai cinema. Often referred to as 'New Thai Cinema',[1] post-1997 Thai film has attracted much popular and academic interest, with recent publications exploring both individual productions and the wider changes enacted upon this industry. It is to this growing body of scholarly work that this book contributes, being the first book-length publication to trace the development of Thai horror cinema through the wider contextual changes of the twentieth century and into the twenty-first. In order to conduct such an in-depth overview, the book focuses upon a significant and dominant characteristic of Thai cinema throughout its history: the Thai incarnation of the horror genre and the central role this plays in Thailand's film industry. The notable success and frequency of this genre in Thai filmmaking makes it a staple and significant cornerstone of New Thai cinema and a strong representative of this industry, film style and wider Thai cultural logics. Indeed, horror has been an extremely popular and prolific genre throughout Thai film history. As this book demonstrates, ghosts and supernatural elements were frequently inserted into early post-war productions up to the present day, and the New Thai industry of the late 1990s even began with (and has maintained) a heavy focus upon such films.

In 2005, Thai scholar Alongkorn Parivudhiphong noted that 'six movies out of 20 top Thai hits of all time are ghost movies' (Parivudhiphong, 2005), and although figures change constantly and are difficult to track down, this is a believable figure. The highest grossing Thai film of 2004 for example was *Shutter* (Pisanthanakun and Wongpoom, 2004) and in 2003, *Buppha Ratri* (Yuthlert Sippapak, 2003) was the third highest. Writing in 2008 Chaiworaporn stated 'horror still fills the Thai screen. A quarter of overall film releases last year fell into this genre, followed by comedy' (Chaiworaporn, 2008: 79). Horror is even purposely deployed as a means to attract audiences, with internationally celebrated auteur Wisit Sasanatieng asked to direct horror story *The Unseeable* (Wisit Sasanatieng, 2006) 'to help his producers, Five Star Productions, as his earlier films didn't make any profit' (Chaiworaporn, 2007: 73), indicating how much of a profit guarantee the genre's popularity is considered to be.

Given the significant popularity of horror in Thailand and the substantial amount of scholarly analysis addressing this genre globally, close attention to Thai horror becomes a vehicle through which to address the complexity that characterises contemporary Thai film. Such complexity can leave global viewers perplexed, being, as this book demonstrates, a product of specific historical, social and economic circumstances that engender different forms of popular entertainment in different periods. It is only through examining this wider context and placing Thai films within such a contextual background that we can begin to understand the form of Thai film today. Such an examination not only outlines a specific style of Thai film but also the wider social forces (both formal and thematic) that have shaped this national industry. To this end the book gives a detailed overview of the industrial, economic and social development that has shaped Thai film, indicating how such an impact is most evident in Thai incarnations of the popular horror genre.

Defining Horror as a Genre

As a means to conduct such an analysis, the book deploys horror theory to explore and define the Thai film style throughout history. Such an approach questions our understanding of 'horror' as a genre category when we move outside of its traditional Euro-American origins and the voyeuristic viewing scenario often associated with this genre. Horror must be deployed as a generic term, and one that can be stretched to encompass Thai films that may not necessarily adhere to mainstream horror conventions as understood by fans and defined by theorists.

The designation of a specific horror genre is difficult and problematic. Horror overall is difficult to define as a category, and indeed Peter Hutchings criticises the practice of reducing such a diverse category of film to a totalising term and set of conventions (2004). Steve Neale indicates that terms such as 'genre' and 'horror' are contested and imprecise. Such vague and unfixed terms have been used 'in different ways in different fields', much of which has 'been governed by the history of the term within these fields – and by the cultural factors at play within them – rather than by logic or conceptual consistency' (Neale, 2000: 28). This lack of logic and the connection to 'cultural factors' indicates the imprecise and problematic nature of genre categories. Andrew Tudor also recognises this when he connects this definition with a set of learned audience expectations that are 'sets of cultural conventions' and will therefore 'vary from case to case' (Tudor, 1974: 18). This again stresses the imprecise nature of categories based upon a set of expectations that are constantly changing. Neale also disputes other imprecise definitions of genre as a system of categorisation, pointing out the difficulty of defining genres, particularly those that lack visual emblems (such as the gangster film and the Western) (2000).

This abstract and imprecise nature of genre as a means of categorisation allows me to refer to Thai films as horror films. Neale indicates that it is important to extend concepts such as genre beyond the limited context in which these categories have traditionally been theorised and this book responds to such a call. Indeed, answering much of the confusion and dispute over genre as a term and set of categories requires 'thinking of genres as ubiquitous, multifaceted phenomena rather than as one-dimensional entities to be found only within the realms of Hollywood cinema or of commercial popular culture' (Neale, 2000: 28).

This overarching conceptualisation also indicates that while genre categories are ever-present and can always exist, attention must be paid not to the 'one-dimensional' defining of them but to the ways in which they are constructed and realised. For example, in encompassing the many diverse and global horror films assessed in her examination of Trauma studies, Linnie Blake similarly chooses to interpret genre as 'a loose and ever-mutating collection of arguments and readings that help to shape both aesthetic ideologies and commercial strategies and that on examination can tell us a great deal about the culture from which such arguments or readings emerged' (Blake, 2008: 6). Both Neale's account and Blake's interpretation indicate that Thai films can be referred to as horror films, yet are 'characteristically Thai' horror films that, this book indicates, differ from many of the specific conventions identified by theorists.

The Abstract 'Ideal' Of Horror

Analyzing how Thai films relate to the recognised structural and thematic characteristics of the horror genre can illustrate the film style and hybridity of Thai productions that this book is concerned with exploring. This analysis not only defines the distinct characteristics of Thai film but also illustrates how these films differ from the stylistic conventions of globally popular horror films. Indeed, examining Thai horror through horror film theory offers a means to distinguish and understand the Thai film form. Such an examination outlines the hybrid nature of the New Thai industry while also connecting this to the wider cultural logics of the Thai context. In this way, the book provides an alternative way to examine Thai cinema, one focusing significantly upon empirical elements such as narrative structure and viewing context, both of which impact upon film form and are particularly notable in the horror genre.

As a means to define the formal attributes of Thai horror films and assess their relationship to this loose and diverse genre, this book deploys a set of key conventions discerned by theorists. Such characteristics have been honed through analysis of significant productions and their themes, films that continue to be regarded (and remade) as 'defining' works of the genre. In doing so it will be informed by what Hutchings calls the 'ideal of horror' (Hutchings, 2004: 7). In his exploration of the many ways in which the genre has been defined, Hutchings argues that critical attempts to define horror have in essence constructed a 'totalising' model that 'exceeds localised uses of the term' (Ibid.: 7). Rather than a specific localised investigation, this definition operates on an 'abstract level' and therefore constructs 'what in effect is an ideal of horror that is seen to lurk behind a whole range of horror films' (Ibid.: 7). Horror films tend to be reviewed and assessed through their relationship to this totalising abstract ideal. Films such as *Psycho* (Alfred Hitchcock, 1960), *The Exorcist* (William Friedkin, 1974), *The Omen* (Richard Donner, 1976), *The Texas Chain Saw Massacre* (Tobe Hooper, 1974), *Halloween* (John Carpenter, 1978) and the various filmic incarnations of *Dracula* and *Frankenstein* are all staple films of critical writing on the genre that crop up again and again in both academic readers and fan-produced histories of horror, so constructing this 'ideal'.

This abstract 'ideal' also begins to recognise film as a global model that takes influence from many different traditions and has been shaped by different models of filmmaking. Reading Thai film through such an 'ideal' illustrates how this industry relates to regional, national and international models of film, so highlighting the specific socio-cultural formation of horror in Thailand. This book therefore acknowledges the relationship between texts on a global, national and regional level rather than reducing such a study purely to that of national cinema. Such a move follows Andrew Higson's argument that cinema cannot be defined purely through the national, a construction that 'imagines the nation as limited, with finite and meaningful boundaries' and so is unable to acknowledge films outside of such an interpretation or incorporate alternative forms of identity (Higson, 2000a: 66).

The book also does not employ concepts such as 'cross-cultural' or 'multicultural', which Willemen argues have been added to the 'standard menu' of analysis in film and media studies (2006: 31). These terms, according to Willemen, are problematic because they 'suggest the existence of discrete, bounded cultural zones separated by borders which can be crossed' and also suggest that there exists some kind of repository of 'cultural authenticity' within miniature replicas of some original national culture (Ibid.). Willemen labels this a kind of 'cultural apartheid' which 'fetishes the separateness of the cultures thus called into being' (Ibid.: 32). Instead, the study of an abstract 'ideal' of horror that underlies the construction of horror cinema in Thailand is one that adheres much more to what Willemen calls 'socio-cultural specificity' and 'national specificity' of film. These terms are different from the reductive concerns regarding national identity and instead address the specific formation of cultural norms which may relate not only to the national but also the various forces within and outside of such boundaries.

Horror and Theoretical Frameworks

As a means to investigate the film style and hybridity of Thai films, this book deploys several recognised conventions of this 'ideal' of horror. On a structural level these include the formation and distinguishing of a separate genre known as horror, the dominant narrative structure employed, the effects horror aims to elicit from the viewer and the primary style of filmmaking employed to do this. For instance I deploy Tamborini and Weaver's (1996) observation that the horror genre was created through a violation of 'Natural Law' (a result of the progress of the Enlightenment) as a means to distinguish Thai horror from such conventions. Likewise I also make use of the question and answer suspense structures that Noel Carroll (1990) calls the erotetic horror narrative, again arguing that Thai films do not follow such structures and instead deploy the concept of 'numbers' (Freeland, 2000: 256) (instances of visceral excess that are unconnected to narrative) to explain the visceral nature of Thai productions. I further utilise Noel Carroll's (1990) observation that horror is defined by the emotions of fear and disgust, indicating that the variety of 'numbers' in Thai productions discount this. Most significantly, I repudiate aspects of Screen Theory that have come to dominate the study of horror films. I use notions such as Miriam Hansen's (2000) 'classical principle' term that describes the voyeuristic scenario in which film must function in order to indicate how Laura Mulvey's viewing paradigm is not appropriate to understanding the shared pleasure of the Thai scenario.

Along with establishing the structural parameters of such films the book also assesses the thematic and ideological perspectives embodied in key Thai productions. This involves investigating the relationship between horror films and social inequality within Thailand, an analysis that outlines the changing political categorisation of Thai horror throughout history. In such an examination I utilise Wood's (2004) now classic model of the horror film as surplus repression, a framework that represents possibly the most notable, recognised and sustained discussion of the horror film and one that can indicate the progressive or reactionary nature of Thai horror at different historical periods.

This is also coupled with Barbara Creed's (1993) deployment of Julia Kristeva's (1982) notion of the abject to analyse the representation of the monstrous female abject within the horror film. Such frameworks are very much part of the abstract horror 'ideal', forming the very basis from which contemporary horror film theory began.

Deploying such frameworks highlights a number of key characteristics in Thai horror, specifically how films respond to and negotiate different structures of inequality in different ways in different periods. This response changes between progressive and conservative depending upon the relationship of the film to both lower-class provincial Thai society and urban-based Thai elites as well as the future generations of Thais and their relationship to the state. For instance, Chapters 1 and 3 address how films depict the repression of female sexuality by patriarchal social forces during key periods of social change. Likewise in Chapter 4 I illustrate how contemporary New Thai productions depict Chinese and Cambodian characters as a damaging Other in order to uphold nationalistic and racist conceptions of Thai superiority.

The book also deploys Trauma studies as a means to explore the structural characteristics that shape the stylistic hybridity of contemporary Thai films. Trauma theory concerns the study and research of the effects of traumatic events upon survivors, working towards formulating treatment for conditions such as posttraumatic stress disorder. Its application to film involves examining how media such as art, cinema and television function to represent traumatic mass events and experiences that may be suppressed and not adequately represented or explored in mainstream discourse. Roy Brand defines trauma as 'an experience that is registered without being processed or experienced in the full sense' and so one that 'cannot simply be expressed or represented due to the fact that there is nothing there to be expressed or represented' (2008: 192). This lack of acknowledgement is one reason why theorists such as Blake (2008) and Lowenstein (2005) have specifically attached the horror genre to this branch of theory. They argue that due to their disturbing and disruptive nature, horror texts are crucially able to engage with traumatic events that are otherwise suppressed and so function as a means to mediate traumatic social events and upheaval for viewers. For instance, Blake posits that horror films are able to engage with and reopen what she calls 'wounds' that are otherwise sealed and suppressed by the process of nation building, a process which seeks to erase any conflict and resistance in its quest for homogeneity and conformity.

Refuting Orientalism Through Thai Cultural Logics

Such formal conventions and thematic motifs are connected to the wider social context of cultural logics that produced such characteristics. Close analysis can therefore both explore and distinguish Thai film as a distinctively Thai cultural product and film style. As mentioned earlier, this book is underpinned throughout by original empirical research that explores both the productions and the wider context. The structural and thematic aspects outlined in the previous paragraph can be traced to the specific Thai circumstances that produced a distinct set of formal horror conventions. These include the communal scenario in which the films functioned, the social position of and attitudes towards the supernatural and the local media and entertainment that is already present.

By outlining the specific film style and origins of Thai cinema, the book seeks to dispute any misunderstanding of Thai film and prevent the disdainful orientalist-inflected attitudes that tend to characterise global constructions of Thailand. Peter A. Jackson (2005) recognises the strong presence of this Eurocentrism in the traditional cultural interpretations and exploration of Thailand. Common Euro-American accounts of Thailand champion the notions of excess, paradox and contradiction. In the non-Thai imagination Thailand has been incarnated as an exoticised land offering a debauched and chaotic lure: an imperfect importation of Western culture fused with the savagery of the Orient. This orientalist ideology involves the comparing and contrasting of a 'superior', 'developed' and 'safe' West with an 'inferior', 'lawless' and 'underdeveloped' East. As Thai film critic and journalist Kong Rithdee comments when exploring filmic representations of Thailand by non-Thai filmmakers, 'the impressions Thailand makes on the world still concern superstition, debauchery and fantastic Orientalism' (Rithdee, 2005).

Such constructions are found in previous filmic representations of and engagements with Thailand: European and American filmmakers have continually used the country as a setting for both exotic locations (as in *Alexander* [Oliver Stone, 2004] and *The Man With The Golden Gun* [Guy Hamilton, 1974]) and as a fantasy land for Western protagonists to experience pleasure, danger and adventure (as in *The Beach* [Danny Boyle, 2000] and *Bridget Jones 2: The Edge of Reason* [Beeban Kidron, 2004]). This reinforced not only an exotic and paradisial depiction of Thailand but also pandered to conceptions of Western superiority over this colourful, childish and simple land where very little meaningful infrastructure, industry or domestic authority is ever represented. The same image is represented in literature; as a popular travel handbook states 'in a world gone increasingly dull, Thailand remains a land of magic and mystery, adventure and romance, a far-flung destination still strange and exciting in a Westernized world' (Parkes, 2000: 1). This colourful description emphasises a chaotic and unorganised element. Likewise, the American filmmaker Seth Grossman (writer and director of feature film *The Elephant King* [Grossman, 2006]) states that 'the Thailand that *farang* (foreigners) see, ... is colorful, foreign and extreme in its pleasures and deprivations' (quoted in Rithdee, 2005). Grossman quite deliberately identifies both 'pleasures' and 'deprivations' in his description of Thailand, two extreme elements that he fits comfortably side by side. This statement seems to signify that inherent in the experience of 'pleasure' within Thailand is also a degrading effect which reduces the Western tourist to a level of 'depravity' in their irresponsible behaviour and, he continues, causes them to 'leave[ing] behind the superstructural domestic authority' and 'abandon their American morals and enjoy the debauchery of booze and "rental" women that are available to tourists in Thailand' (Rithdee, 2005). This statement also implies a certain level of orientalist superiority when contrasting the 'domestic' and 'moral' Western culture with the experience of the 'depraved' and 'debauched' Thailand.

This construction follows from a long historical representation of Thailand, one that Van Esterik illustrates was created 'for the European gaze of the nineteenth century' (Van Esterik, 2000: 126). Thai historian and academic Thongchai Winichakul states 'in the West the place of Siam was predetermined; namely as one among the Others of Western civilisation, although not the barbaric one' (Winichakul, 2000: 541). It suited the colonialist arrogance by exhibiting 'the beauty of simplicity and elegance of the preindustrial age' (Ibid.: 541). Early European accounts, such as this from George Curzon MP (a Conservative statesman who served as Viceroy of India and Foreign Secretary) in *The Manchester Times* in 1893, portrayed Siam and its people as relatively harmless, decadent and excessive: 'The national character is docile, indolent, light-hearted, gay. The Siamese are devoted to the holiday-making and ceremonies and processions which accompany the most important anniversaries or incidents of life, death, and religion, and which cause an infinite amount of money to be squandered and time lost' (Curzon, 1893). In the early twentieth century, British diplomat Sir George Scott also characterised Siam as 'a country rich enough to inspire cupidity, weak enough to tempt ambition, and foolish enough to court embroilments' (1930, quoted in Christian, 1941: 185), a statement that foreshadows the attitudes and continuing derogatory adjectives that were to infuse both anthropological and popular Western accounts. In 1941, the exoticised image of Siam had evidently already been solidified: John L. Christian reported 'the Western world has difficulty in thinking of Thailand as anything but a story-book autocracy where there is still a certain amount of beautiful indolence and convenient corruption' (Christian, 1941: 185).

Such flawed interpretations are what Jackson labels as 'tensions' resulting from the failure of 'Western frameworks' to map the complexities of Thai culture when they are not sufficiently translated or reconstructed (Jackson, 2005: 33). Such tensions can be avoided only through empirical research, whereby we can avoid any residual distortion and instead both recognise and repair the potential power imbalance between 'Western analytical discourses' and Thai cultural logics' (Ibid.). This book builds upon such a perspective, remaining aware of these potential difficulties and seeking to translate theoretical models through empirical 'locally grounded enquiry'. This book seeks to reinsert 'Thai cultural logics' into an analysis of Thai film and define these cultural products as a distinct film form that has evolved from specific circumstances. Such empirically-based analysis also allows me to 'translate' theoretical models that have developed from a different historical and cultural situation into the Thai context.

This Book

This book therefore conducts a timely exploration of Thai cinema's transition from the characteristically Thai subaltern 'cottage industry' of the 1960s through the blockbuster contemporary New Thai industry and up to the recent global success in the 2020s digital era. Through conducting much-needed original research into the surrounding empirical social context and textual analysis of rare and forgotten Thai films, the book substantially contributes to the limited body of knowledge that already exists regarding the development of Thai cinema. The book explores the influence of audiences and viewing scenarios from previous decades, connecting the conventions and development of Thai film with the various social groups within Thailand.

The chapters chart the changing relationship of Thai film to a range of Thai viewers and viewing practices, as well as the wider historical and contextual circumstances that have influenced this development. This includes drawing upon frameworks of current genre analysis and analysis of non-Western film cultures to assess how these interact with both cultural expectations, narrative structure and contexts of viewing. Such hybridity involves both the stylistic and formal influence of previous post-war Thai film conventions and the impact of global horror trends from Europe, America and East Asia. The book identifies key themes and motifs that occur in this genre, analysing a range of films from the contemporary industry. Likewise, by examining Thai horror's growing reputation within the Southeast Asian region, *Contemporary Thai Horror Film* is one of the first works to approach Thai cinema's regional rather than exclusively national scope.

Chapter 1 conducts a crucial beginning overview of Thai film and its formal characteristics; one that is both complex and lengthy yet also indicative of the need to understand the wider contextual development of Thai film and horror in particular. The chapter begins by going back to the significant post-World War Two era of Thai film, outlining the specific circumstances and development that led to the significant period known as the 16mm era. The chapter indicates how this era is deeply embedded within the rural village context and its audiences. It demonstrates how engaging with supernatural entities became an important means to both represent and appeal to rural lower-class viewers, evident in how various spirits and belief systems are woven into this body of films. In particular, it also highlights how this engagement reflects the wider changes experienced in Thai society, ones connected to the encroachment of modernity and rural development.

The chapter demonstrates how such concerns are realised by the many depictions of monstrous women, who take on characteristics associated with modernity, such as heightened mobility, independence and sexual agency. Functioning as a traumatic mediation of this changing environment, these monstrous depictions operate as a patriarchal critique and condemnation of such changes. This is particularly true given the potential for supernatural discourses to provide a form of empowerment for lower-class women in other contexts.

The chapter then moves on to examine how it is difficult to describe such productions as horror films, despite the frequent supernatural and horrific elements, drawing upon wider anthropological research to indicate how spirits permeate rural Thai society and do not constitute a violation of natural law. Likewise, it examines the emphasis upon spectacle and display and the blending of visceral numbers from different genres, highlighting how the corresponding film style becomes appropriate to the rural viewing situation. Attributing such characteristics to the collective nature of rural Thai society and the communal viewing scenario in which film was consumed, the chapter then also indicates how these elements cause Thai film to be constructed as an inferior and lowbrow form of cinema. Such views can be attached to both a condescending colonialist construction of Thailand that is also adopted by Thai elites, as well as a general Eurocentric attitude towards the privileging of emotional affect.

Chapter 2 then continues this overview and analysis of Thai film development. Outlining the political and social changes in Thailand during the 1970s and 1980s, the chapter charts the end of the 16mm era and the standardisation of 35mm with synchronised sound, identifying key productions within this shift. The chapter again outlines the importance of horror and the supernatural as a key means through which films engage with and negotiate the wider context, paying close attention to the 1989 film *Baan Phii Pop* (Srisawat, 1989) as a key production during this period. The chapter then demonstrates how such films offer a different engagement with wider Thai society to that of the 16mm era, operating as a progressive critique of modernity and the exploitive treatment of lower-class women. Again, the chapter highlights how the film form that developed in the post-World War Two era continues to feature in Thai films, and argues that such characteristics are now much more indicative of a cultural preference than a style necessitated by technological limitations.

Building upon the previous two chapters, Chapter 3 then moves into the contemporary post-97 New Thai industry. The chapter charts the development of Thai film into the early 2000s and explores the deployment of heritage as a significant mode of representation in a society coping with the aftermath of the 1997 Asian financial crisis. The section analyses the significant and seminal heritage horror production *Nang Nak* (Nonzee Nimibutr, 1999), a film that was highly lauded locally and internationally, and explores how the film offers an affirmation of conservative social values through the sacrificial peasant woman Nak. However, the chapter then indicates how within this retrograde gender ideology, the film retains the earlier characteristics associated with Thai film. Analysis outlines how Nak does not violate natural law, and how this portrayal is in keeping with continuing social attitudes and function of the supernatural, which remains a significant part of Thai society into the new millennium. The chapter also explores how the film style and narrative structure of *Nang Nak* is again indicative of a film form made for a collective society, so highlighting the continuing presence and significance of the rural and lower-class viewer into the New Thai industry.

In the same way, Chapter 4 analyses another key thread and reactionary portrayal in the New Thai industry. The chapter indicates how seminal horror films *Zee Oui* (Nida Sudasna and Buranee Ratchaiboon, 2004) and *Laa Thaa Phii/Ghost Game* (Sarawut Wichiensarn, 2006) mobilise a monstrous Other through which to construct a unified version of Thai-ness. Exploring the demonisation of Chinese-ness and Cambodian-ness in these two films, the chapter examines how these two non-Thai minority races become a vehicle to demonstrate the superiority of Thai-ness during the post-economic crisis time of turmoil. The chapter deploys Wood's (2004) famous concept of surplus repression to highlight this reactionary and nationalistic agenda, one that becomes particularly disturbing given the attempt to both target minorities and hijack Cambodia's tragic history. However, as with *Nang Nak*, the chapter then also indicates how these films become stylistic hybrids which still bear evidence of the lower-class preferences associated with the collective audiences of the 16mm era. Furthermore, the chapter argues that this film form can offer a potential means to undermine this nationalistic depiction and disrupt such bourgeois ideology.

After two chapters examining the conservative ideological position of New Thai horror films, Chapter 5 then takes a different perspective. The chapter explores films that offer a progressive critique of contemporary Thai society, relating this to the wider context of post-1997 economic crisis. The Vengeful Ghost films are a corpus of productions that depict an abused women using the supernatural to take revenge upon those who mistreated her. Usually targeting upper-class men, this motif reflects the dialectical position of the female regarding the supernatural, whereby such powers can not only demonise but also offer a means to articulate a female perspective in this patriarchal context. The chapter conducts a close analysis of the very successful 2004 film *Shutter*, indicating how the film engages with and gives voice to this traumatised position. However, the chapter then indicates how the film also replicates the film style of hegemonic East Asian ghost films, and so paradoxically erases the evidence of the lower-class origins of Thai cinema.

After outlining the various ideological positions of horror films in the New Thai industry, Chapter 6 moves on to explore the blurring of boundaries between the film and the audience, a phenomenon known as (self-)reflexivity. The chapter examines the history of such direct involvement and acknowledgement of the audience in Thai film, drawing upon the presentational style and communal audience explored in Chapter 1. The chapter argues that this phenomenon should be seen as a separate tradition to that of the 'found footage' and digital horror sub-genres recognised today, and instead is more akin to the 'Cinema Spiritualism' recognised in early film. Horror in New Thai film therefore becomes a means to assess the relationship between society and the supernatural in the modern context, and one that can be explored through the cinematic technology. The chapter then finally indicates how these films depict spirits as accosting the cinematic technology to critique wider Thai society, a critique which again gives voice to an abused and marginalised perspective akin to that of the vengeful ghosts explored in Chapter 5.

Chapter 7 then moves on to outline how despite the development of the big-budget New Thai industry that seeks international recognition, there is still a body of Thai films that continues to target provincial viewers. Fully embracing the characteristics designed to appeal to this communal audience, these films deploy a presentation film style akin to that of the post-war 16mm era productions, all of which are most evident in visceral slapstick horror productions. The chapter indicates how within a wider context akin to that of 'class war' during the late 2000s, these films function as both a recognition and reassertion of the marginalised provincial Thai perspective. This film style distinguishes such productions in the contemporary age, with films appearing very different to the global conventions associated with horror as a genre. Such a style is indicative of the unequal and divided nature of Thai society at this time, circumstances that engender the collective and objective style of filmmaking in the immediate post-war era which is still very much a part of Thai entertainment in the twenty-first century. That such different models of filmmaking can exist within the same nation and, indeed, the same industry, is testament to the differing lifestyles within this nation.

Moving to examine Thai horror in the 2010s, Chapter 8 begins to place Thai popular culture within a wider context of regional economic development. Seeing Thailand's social changes as part of a wave of modernity across the Asia region at this time, the chapter addresses how such turbo-development is represented in horror films. This includes examining the problematic position of the Thai middle-classes, a social group that has grown significantly across the region, yet has become increasingly politically isolated in Thailand. The chapter examines how Thai horror in the 2010s depicts socially isolated individuals responding to economic pressures, drawing upon existing analysis of wider East Asian models of horror such as that in South Korea. The chapter pays particular attention to the key production *The Promise* (Sophon Sakdaphisit, 2017), indicating how the film engages with the precarious, isolated and anxiety-inducing position of the new Thai middle-class, offering both a critique and a potential way forward for society.

The final chapter in the volume moves beyond the Thai context and explores how horror has become an important signifier of Thai popular culture within the wider Southeast Asia region as well as a rare example of pre-digital inter-Southeast Asian cultural exchange. Through close analysis the chapter points to a 'cultural proximity' based upon a shared experience of modernity and an emphasis upon blended visceral numbers (particularly comedy-horror numbers) that is appropriate to the diverse audiences of the Southeast Asian nations. It argues that this combination has been most successfully realised in Thai horror, which also circulated at a crucial period when regional authorities were (and still are today) busy forming and promoting the notion of ASEAN identity. This national genre then potentially offers a form of regional cultural identity, evident in examples such as the phenomenally successful Pee Mak, a film that enjoyed significant popularity and success around Southeast Asia.

After examining such regional success however, the chapter moves on to explore the introduction of Thai horror onto international streaming platforms in the digital era. It outlines how the fast-growing digital infrastructure in Thailand has impacted upon the horror genre, creating new forms of episodic horror designed for these platforms. The chapter addresses the wider thematic and stylistic changes adopted when trying to appeal to both local viewers and the newly accessible international audience. This includes how Thai horror has paradoxically moved to embrace older spirit beliefs that now appeal to an international and middle-class Thai audience seeking 'authenticity', a notion that is realised in 'folk horror'. The chapter finally illustrates how this change has led to a potential resurgence of disdainful attitudes from middle-class viewers towards products that do not seek to construct such 'authenticity', comments that are reminiscent of previous constructions of the 16mm era films.

Note

1. This term is somewhat misleading however. Chaiworaporn and Knee note that despite the enormous boom in filmmaking, 'this is not to claim that there was suddenly a clear-cut "new Thai cinema" movement at that moment' (Chaiworaporn and Knee, 2006: 60).

1. POST-WAR THAI CINEMA
Audiences and Film Style in a Divided Nation

To launch our examination of Thai cinema and Thai horror in particular, this book begins by focusing upon what may seem to be a rather obscure era of Thai film history. This period has been singled out as a key moment in the development of cinema and film culture in Thailand. The extant critical literature concerned with Thai cinema history contains lengthy reference to this period and its lasting influence upon the Thai film style. Often called the 'Golden Age' of Thai cinema, Thai film historian and archivist Chalida Uabumrungjit labels this key stage – from around the mid-1950s to the early 1970s – the '16mm era' and dedicates it a specific slot in the history of Thai cinema due to its honing of a distinctive narrative style and appeal to a particular section of Thai society (Uabumrungjit, 2003b). Udomdet refers to this period as 'restoration through the 16mm silent film', an indication of how crucial it was to the development of film in Thailand (Udomdet, 1990: 57). In her PhD thesis, Thai academic Patsorn Sungsri (whose assistance has been much appreciated in my research for this volume) understands this post-war period as signaling the emergence of the 'Conventional Thai film style', arguing that this was largely popular in rural areas, taking inspiration from indigenous forms of entertainment which spoke to Thai people in a way that Hollywood could not (Sungsri, 2004: 53–57). In another rare academic study of Thai cinema history, former actress-turned-scholar Parichat Phromyothi also refers to this period as 'Classical Thai Cinema' (Phromyothi, 2000). Even after the era drew to a close (a result of specific industrial, economic and technological developments that I will discuss at length in Chapter 2), Phromyothi still recognises this narrative formula with its blended 'attractions' and repetitive staple stories that hold little ambiguity as 'the prominent characteristic of Thai films' (Phromyothi, 2000: 25).

Despite this recognised importance, a detailed scholarly analysis of the productions of this era has really yet to be conducted. Inevitably, most existing research on Thai cinema focuses upon the now readily available contemporary films and specific genres. Academic work on Thai cinema is still marginal within film studies (though growing fast) and there is a particular lack of in-depth empirical historical analysis; many academic sources are as yet unpublished though still offer crucial insight into the development of early Thai film. This chapter will attempt to fix such an omission and to demonstrate that if we want to truly understand the form of Thai film and its complicated relationship to the horror genre, we must begin by going back to its contextual, stylistic and formal beginnings.

The Beginnings of Thai Cinema

The long and varied history of Thai cinema begins in Bangkok with the showing of early short films in June 1897, less than two years after the famous Lumière Brothers showcase in Paris. Before long, cinemas had begun to appear in urban Thailand, with the first crude buildings set up by Japanese entrepreneurs and then various other companies who established more permanent buildings from 1919 onwards. Mirroring cinema's evolution across the globe, this new form of entertainment grew quickly: in the 1920s cinemas are recorded to have spread outside of Bangkok to outer provincial towns, and by the late 1930s it is estimated that there were around 120 cinemas in Thailand, mostly located in Bangkok (Boonyaketmala,1992: 65). What is considered to be the first Thai production, *Nang Sao Sawan/Miss Suwanna of Siam* – actually directed by Henry MacRae, an American, though starring only Thai performers – appeared in 1923; the first completely indigenous Thai production, *Chok Song Chan/Double Luck* (Manit Wasuwat, 1927), followed a few years later. As is the case with much early cinema, the vast majority of Thai features produced in this period are now lost, including a number of co-productions between Western filmmakers and the Thai elite that were concerned mostly with state propaganda.

It is during the immediate post-war era that Thai cinema began to grow significantly as a recognisable industry. The Japanese occupation of Thailand prevented the influx of Hollywood productions that fed the very healthy exhibition industry which relied upon such imports. In light of this absence, indigenous Thai entertainment enjoyed an upsurge as it had to fill this exhibition space. The industry then begins to carve the beginnings of a locally orientated form of entertainment and film style, close analysis of which allows insight into the origins of contemporary Thai film.

Due to financial and technological constraints, Thai filmmakers had to work in 16mm filmstock, which was then dubbed by two live narrators in cinemas. Previously, a few (mostly American-backed) Thai production companies had begun making 35mm synchronised sound productions before World War Two. After the war, these few Thai sound studios were forced to close due to the halted supply of imported filmstock and the chemical solutions needed to produce it. Crucially, however, the smaller film companies and independent producers that had not been able to afford the technology involved in the switch to sound were able to survive by using 16mm filmstock that was available during and immediately following World War Two. Both portable and quick and cheap to develop, this frugal stock also did not need to be sent abroad to be developed. In the late 1940s *Supab Burut Suatai/Thai Gentleman Bandit* (M. C. Sukrawandit Ditsakul and Tae Prakartwutisan, 1949) was produced on 16mm silent filmstock and released to huge domestic success, inspiring other entertainment entrepreneurs and businessmen to finance cheap 16mm live-dubbed colour productions of popular cinema. Film production therefore grew from ten per year in the immediate aftermath of World War Two to around fifty in 1956. This new 16mm industry was so successful that it then continued despite the reintroduction of Hollywood imports after the war. Due to Thailand's proximity to the Communist-influenced countries of Laos and Vietnam, American and Thai authorities established extremely close relations immediately after World War Two. The major American film companies set up representative offices in Bangkok and funded 1,000-seat air-conditioned cinemas during the 1950s and 60s. The 16mm Thai films, however, were able to survive by continuing to target the rural lower-class agrarian workers outside urban Bangkok society. This division is reflected in analysis of Thai society at the time. Writing in 1962, Wilson comments:

> Thai society is (still) characterized by a gross two-class structure, in which the classes are physically as well as economically separated ... The rural agrarian segment is separated geographically from the urban ruling segment. The agrarian segment is, in the main, land-owning and survives by a quasi-subsistence economy. The ruling segment is salaried (when its members own property, this is usually urban or sub-urban) and lives on a cash economy (Wilson, 1962, quoted in UNESCO, 1982: 38).

Such divisions created a two-tiered audience: while the more affluent urban Thai viewers enjoyed impressive Hollywood productions in state-of-the-art cinemas in Bangkok, rural and lower-class viewers were the primary audience for silent, dubbed, 16mm era local affairs.

The 16mm Era and the Horror Genre

Close attention to these successful early productions suggests there is a strong thematic link between Thai filmmaking and the horror genre. Overwhelmingly, the 16mm era productions display a frequent and significant insertion of supernatural elements into the diegesis, a key iconographic association with horror as a genre, albeit one that is necessarily problematic as a definition. This characteristic is connected to the upcountry rural Thai audience, an environment in which supernatural animist belief systems were (and still are) deeply embedded. Thai elites have historically associated spirits and superstition with the rural village and its occupants, who are often referred to by the somewhat derogatory term *chaobannok*. The *chaobannok* are physically distant from the location of political and religious authority – the centre of dhamma – and their existence outside of this 'umbrella of merit' places them alongside the *Pa* ('the domain beyond normal social and political power' [Winichakul, 2000: 537]) that is 'inhabited by wild animals and spirits' (Ibid.: 537). The *Pa* exists alongside the dangerous realm of the spirits known as *Phii*, understood as 'invisible supernatural beings' (Kitiarsa, 1999: 56) that can be ghosts of the dead, spirits of the living, free-floating spirits or spirits of sacred objects (Suwanlert, 1976). These can be benevolent, malevolent or simply indifferent, and many require offerings in order to pacify them or elicit protection and good fortune. The distance of the rural village from the centre of dhamma also lessened the spiritual quality of people, making them more susceptible to interference from *Phii*. Indeed, medical anthropologist Suwanlert notes that *Phii*-possessed hosts are not only village-dwelling but 'are characteristically of low educational and socioeconomic status' (1976: 120), and later ethnographic studies still link such beliefs strongly to people in rural areas (Burnard, Naiyapatana and Lloyd, 2006: 745).

Engaging with this supernatural subject matter was certainly a significant means for Thai filmmakers to target rural lower-class Thai viewers; those outside the push towards globalisation and modernity in the post-war years. Close analysis of such depictions also begins to reflect the wider social upheaval experienced in rural post-war Thailand, demonstrating that the supernatural in the 16mm era performs a very similar social function to that which theorists note in horror today. One common motif in productions is the depiction of female characters as monstrous and fearful and having a distinctly unsavoury connection to the supernatural. This is evident in just about all 16mm era films that engage with the supernatural and the monstrous. In *Nguu Phii* (Saet Thaa Phak Dee, 1966) the terrifying and seductive snake spirit is female; in *Nang Prai Taa Nii* (Nakarin, 1967) the spirit Taa Nii is female; and in *Phii Saht Sen Haa* (Pan Kam, 1969) it is the young woman Karaket who is taken into the afterlife and her mother who exists as a spirit and controls minions to protect her daughter. Finally, *Mae Nak Prakanong* (Rangsir Tasanapayak, 1959) follows the endlessly remade Thai ghost story of Mae Nak, versions of which continue to be remade in the contemporary industry. A devoted wife and mother, Nak returns to be with her husband after her death in childbirth, becoming a terrifying ghost (and rotten corpse) that refuses to pass over to the afterlife.

Such a motif is all too familiar to those studying horror texts and the supernatural, linking back to Barbara Creed's famous Monstrous Feminine framework (Creed, 1993). Attaching monstrous and supernatural elements to dangerous and uncontrolled female characters is indicative of a patriarchal need to exercise dominance and control over women. Indeed, in Thailand female sexuality has been specifically linked to notions of supernatural destruction and 'the power of female sexuality to harm the spiritual potency and physical wellbeing of men is a feature of cultural beliefs in many parts of Thailand' (Mills, 1995: 255). Virtually all scholars researching spirit cults and spirit mediums note the distinct attachment of this frightening and ancient animist realm to the female sex (as opposed to the official Buddhist order, which is nearly always coded as male). Tanabe (2002) notes how Thai patriarchy positions women as weak, with an unstable and inferior *khwan* to that of men. Pattana Kitiarsa even states that 'the main difference between Buddhist monks and spirit-mediums is that the mediums are predominantly women' (Kitiarsa, 1999: 2).

Yet such cinematic depictions are not only indicative of patriarchy, but also demonstrate how these films respond to the radical changes in post-war Thailand, changes that particularly impacted upon social constructions of gender. The close proximity of Thai and American government interests led to their continued close cooperation against the Communist threat in Southeast Asia. Richard A. Ruth even labels the 1960s as the 'American era' due to the vast influx of American culture (Ruth, 2011). In its war against Communist forces, the US not only financially supported the deployment of Thai troops but also stationed around 45,000 American troops throughout the country. This transformed Thai society and particularly for rural people (Ruth 2011: 31). American money contributed to rural development in building roads, machinery and other infrastructure that Ruth states transformed both the 'physical landscape and social and economic systems' of rural Thailand in the 1950s and 60s along with its people (Ruth 2011: 5). This changed the relationship between rural and urban Thailand as the transition between the two spheres became much easier. The need for workers in urban areas also resulted in a flood of migrant workers into cities, thus constructing an 'exchange between two formerly antithetical geographical cultures' (Ruth 2011: 6).

This not only altered the make-up of urban Bangkok (previously an almost exclusive haunt for richer citizens), but also impacted rural areas. The improved infrastructure and movement of workers introduced new possibilities into rural and lower-class consciousness for the first time, ones that were intricately linked to the American influence that had caused them. As Ruth states:

> The newly mobile brought back the ambitions, ideas and perspectives of the capital city. These men and women became a migratory population whose outlook was simultaneously rural and urban, traditional and modern, settled and restless. (2011: 6)

The increased mobility of women in society became a significant issue connected to the encroachment of modernity in rural Thailand. During this time Thailand shifted from a largely subsistence economy to that of market Capitalism, with the first five-year development plan implemented after 1961 (Pongsapich 1997: 25). Such industrialisation brought about radical changes in family and community settings: at first, it was only men who migrated in search of work, while the domestic domain of children and the home was left to women. However, with the development of a full cash economy, women also had to leave home in search of work to substitute this income (Ibid.: 26). This new ability threatened to undermine both patriarchy and the core construction of this gender (much was which was actually an adoption of notions favoured by the European powers in the colonial era, see Reid 2014), particularly in light of the traditionally inferior designation of women by the religious order.

These social changes are reflected in the 16mm era productions, and these films become a reactionary response to social developments that could present new opportunities and possibilities for rural Thai women. In his seminal scholarship on the horror film first published in 1979, Robin Wood refers to this relationship as the 'political categorisation' of horror (Wood, 2004). Horror films can be politically reactionary or progressive and over time this categorisation can change; something Wood calls the 'evolution' of the horror film (Ibid.). At the time when Wood was writing in 1979, he argued that horror was dominated by a reactionary agenda, giving the examples of *Alien* (Ridley Scott, 1979) and *Halloween* (John Carpenter, 1978), which in their regressive attitudes towards sexuality 'seal' the possibility of 'social revolution' that had been awakened by wider contextual events and instead seek to restore the previous status quo. The model of horror displayed in the 16mm era productions can be generalised as a similar reactionary response to anxiety over social developments affecting the traditional construction of gender.

If the association between women and the supernatural reflects how Thai patriarchy naturalises female subordination (as it makes natural the presence of the supernatural realm and its unquiet *Phii*), then the 16mm productions allow a working through of the horrors of female empowerment in an era of rapid social change. The supernatural in these films can be interpreted as what Blake titles a 'cultural attempt' to 'bind those wounds in the interests of dominant ideologies of identity' (2008: 2), with these 'wounds' being the trauma inflicted upon Thai patriarchy by the wider social upheaval of increased female autonomy. The evil snake-woman from *Nguu Phii*, the murdering sky spirit Taa Nii in *Nang Prai Taa Nii* and probably the most famous ghost in Thailand, Mae Nak, all perform such a social function: they are interpretations of cultural beliefs that are mobilised to seal the wound that has been ripped open during this turmoil and must be addressed.

Such empowerment is critiqued through constructing mobile and independent women as monstrous and/or dangerous. When outside of a family environment, women are overwhelmingly associated with the supernatural and this uncontrolled femininity becomes dangerous and destructive to social wellbeing. The female spirits are all at first harmless when integrated into the family environment, only becoming powerful, destructive, monstrous and dangerous when they are forced outside of this. When the previously loving wife Nak dies in *Mae Nak Prakanong*, she exists outside of the family and becomes a monstrous and powerful abject (her husband runs in fear from her animated corpse). In *Nguu Phii*, the evil and monstrous femininity of the snake-women is positioned deep in the forest away from the family and home. Initially harmless when adopted into a local family, the snake-woman's full monstrosity becomes apparent when she exercises sexual desire and agency by bewitching and seducing the hero and imprisoning him in a cave far away from any familial or village influences. Her deviant femininity tempts men when she appears as a beautiful half-naked young woman yet then changes into a horrific gruesome monster (abject) and kills them. This ability to exercise such mobility and desire is depicted as destructive and terrifying in its control and manipulation of men. Similarly in *Nang Prai Taa Nii*, Taa Nii falls from the sky, a supernatural means to enter the village rather than a modern means. The character is rendered immediately harmless when she is adopted into a local family, and the full extent of her monstrous capacity only becomes apparent when she later finds her adopted parents murdered and so is detached from the family-sphere. This destruction of her family surroundings then sets off the narrative train of events in which this now independent and mobile woman embarks on a monstrous supernatural killing rampage of revenge, mercilessly pursuing the men responsible for murdering her adoptive parents and killing them horribly.

Other 16mm era films place strong emphasis upon a status quo that highlights the female connection with the home and the masculine as mobile. In *Yort Gaen* (Amnuai Kalatnimi, 1968) the heroine is a tear-away tomboy who first views the hero from the top of a tree. She meets him when he arrives into her environment in a shiny modern car. The Pygmalion-esque story follows that of the hero trying to teach and tame the wayward young woman with whom he eventually falls in love; lessons that primarily seem to involve decreasing her free-spirited mobility by taking her out of the tree and into the home. In contrast, male heroes can travel freely outside the home and village, achieving movement through modern and technological means. This independence is evidence of virility and attractiveness, illustrating the different construction of the sexes in Thailand. The hero often arrives into the rural village as an outsider from the city: he can travel both into and outside the community while the heroine originates from within it and remains there. In the films *Nguu Phii*, *Praai Phitsawat* (Chaluay Sri Rattana, 1968) and *Jaawm Khon* (Daen Krisada, 1969), the hero's first introductory shot depicts him as moving. In *Jaawm Khon* he rides into the town as a cowboy on a horse, in *Nguu Phii* he arrives in the village on the back of an ox-cart and in *Praai Phitsawat* he is driving a car filled with nubile attractive women. In *Phii Saht Sen Haa* he even makes a trip to India and becomes the very personification of a jazzy new urban lifestyle, symbolised by his shiny tight suit, sunglasses and briefcase. Such a depiction is unthinkable for the virginal heroine, whose purity would be compromised by such a solo trip. If a female character must travel, then it is only through the supernatural that she is able to acquire this mobility and autonomy, a process through which she becomes monstrous, dangerous and threatening. For instance in *Phii Saht Sen Haa*, the heroine is bitten by a poisonous snake put into her room by her evil stepmother. She then uses supernatural means to appeal to the hero for help, becoming a voice from beyond the grave as he wanders around the streets of India and the Taj Mahal.

This depiction is also particularly reactionary given the potential for the supernatural to provide an unofficial means of empowerment for disenfranchised women under the patriarchal system in Southeast Asia (Karim 1995). As anthropologists understand, the connection between the female and the supernatural can be subverted to provide a means of empowerment in a staunchly patriarchal society that otherwise denies women agency. In Thailand, women may achieve a degree of autonomy and empowerment due to the distinct connection forged between the female's weak *Khwan* and the *Phii*. In 1971 Sangun Suwalert documented the *Moh Lum Phii Pha*, a traditional healing method from the Northeast conducted by a special ceremonial shamanistic team. It involved the possession of the leader (the *Kog*) by the benevolent *Phii Pha* sky spirit, who must then remove the spirit or ghost that is causing the illness in the client (Suwanlert, Sangun and Vissuthikolsol, Yupha, 1980). Notably, the *Kog* can only be a woman, because it is only the female qualities of being 'warm, gentle and empathetic' (Suwanlert, Sangun and Vissuthikolsol, Yupha, 1980: 237) that can engender the folk songs and 'welcome atmosphere' that will reassure and persuade the patient to name the spirit or ghost that possesses them. This spirit medium can communicate between 'the human world and the spirit world or between the living and the dead' (Kitiarsa, 1999: 53), and therefore carries a significant amount of authority in society. Their weaker *Khwan* allows them to identify, interact and even become voluntarily possessed by the offending spirit, so removing it from the affected patient who has approached them for assistance. Tanabe identifies this as a dialectical process, in which the inferiority of the female under the patriarchal Buddhist order is subverted to become a source of power and authority through the older pre-Buddhist animist beliefs. Although dealing mostly with the transference of this phenomenon in the modern contemporary context, Tanabe still states that 'even before the 1970s–80s, this dialectical transformation was a general condition underlying spirit mediumship during the sporadic emergence of semi-professional mediums in village settings' (Tanabe, 2002: 54).

The supernatural and the spirit mediums not only provided a means of lower-class female empowerment, but also a degree of social recognition of this inferior and increasingly difficult status. Virtually all of the possessed participants in Sangun Suwanlert's research into spirit possession in the 1970s were lower-class rural women, indicating not only their perceived susceptibility to this condition but also how it provides a means of negotiating the difficulties of living under patriarchy. The possession was often preceded by a disruptive or abusive incident and its cure required a degree of attention and respect not previously awarded to the subject. Incidents such as the infamous 'widow ghost phenomena' documented and analysed by Mary Beth Mills provide an illustration of how the supernatural constitutes 'an alternative, largely counterhegemonic discourse on modernity' (Mills, 1995: 244) within sections of Thai society in which the experience of rapid modernity and rural migration had merely produced a new form of oppression and control. This source of power and legitimating of female authority with its 'alternative' discourse to that of the state-sanctioned authoritative religion is regarded with disapproval and suspicion by authorities (Kitiarsa, 1999: 1).

The 16mm era Thai films therefore mediate the trauma of wider social change in lower-class society by demonising both this newfound ability of women in the modern age and the dialectical means by which women deal with such subordination. They respond to anxiety around potentially challenging social advances and developments with depictions that confirm the inferiority of and so the need for control over the female.

Such an overview and analysis begins to outline the strong historical link between Thai filmmaking and the horror genre. This rests largely upon a liberal insertion of and reliance upon the supernatural, often a key ingredient in creating horror, as well as its wider function as a form of traumatic mediation in a rapidly changing and unstable environment. While these stories and the wider discourses they represent are certainly reactionary in their social implications, this body of films still remains a distinctly rural and lower-class entertainment that functions within this context, responds to it, addresses lower-class viewers and negotiates it for them. The conservative reaffirmation of gender relations is one way in which these successful films function as mass entertainment at a time when the stability of social norms was challenged by uncontrollable and unaccountable outside influences.

Defining Horror: The Supernatural as 'Natural Law'

Such texts can lend themselves well to existing theoretical frameworks analysing the cultural function and significance of horror. However, addressing the formal parameters of horror begins to outline some significant differences which problematise the description of post-World War Two Thai films as horror. In particular, the lack of a clearly defined separate horror genre in this era means that the 16mm era films can seem very different to the formal textual characteristics associated with horror by theorists.

Indeed, defining such films as 'horror' becomes less appropriate (and more difficult) because these texts do not create a separate horror diegesis, but instead mix and insert the supernatural alongside other genres. In 16mm era productions, the supernatural can interject into the narrative quite legitimately without stretching credibility or even necessitating the creation of a separate and distinct supernatural diegesis. Ghosts and spirits often appear among characters and village life as merely an addition to, not the subject of, the narrative and can be inserted alongside other genre motifs quite comfortably. For instance, while characters may express fear at the actions of malevolent spirits, they do not exhibit much surprise regarding their actual existence. This is again connected to the wider environment: in rural Thailand beliefs in the supernatural realm and spirits are a very natural and physical part of life, to the extent that they can significantly influence social organisation and personal wellbeing on an official level. Buildings, businesses, politics and many aspects of human behaviour are designed around and conducted in accordance with the existence of the *Phii* and their supposed preferences.

Due to such beliefs, the supernatural in post-war Thai cinema appears to occupy a similar social position and function to that which Tamborini and Weaver afford to pre-eighteenth-century archaic horror in Europe before the Industrial Revolution (1996). European fables, fairy tales and myths functioned as a means to explain and organise the ambiguity of the wider world, in a similar way to that exercised by spirits in rural Thai society. The eighteenth-century 'Age of Reason' involved 'a growing disbelief in things that could not be observed' (Tamborini and Weaver, 1996: 6) and a scepticism and rationalism which ensured that the fantastic must now be explained empirically or curbed. The supernatural then became a monstrous and frightening violation of what Tamborini and Weaver call 'natural law' (it is important, however, to note that the supernatural did not disappear from society at all – rather the opposite is true – despite its new classification). Yet this historical division does not appear so clear-cut in rural Thailand. The very concrete presence of *Phii* clearly indicates the existence and influence of a supernatural 'reality' that need not be a violation of any law and so need not necessarily be 'horrific'.

For instance, after the spirit Taa Nii falls from the sky in *Nang Prai Taa Nii*, she is adopted by a childless older couple in the local village. Notably there is no attempt to explain this strange opening event and instead the film launches straight into the story of Taa Nii's escapades within the village. Likewise, in *Phii Saht Sen Haa*, the heroine's dead mother tries to protect her daughter from the murder attempts of the evil stepmother, an action that is not depicted as unusual. The film even begins with two bumbling comical characters in a graveyard discussing their fear of ghosts before a phantom suddenly appears and scares them. There is no explanation or further reference to this incident, so illustrating the presence and acceptance of this element within everyday society. This can also be applied to the orphaned snake child of *Nguu Phii*, who the audience must merely accept is the child of a snake spirit that was killed. Likewise in *Mae Nak Prakanong*, the ghostly Nak is certainly horrific in her corpse-like appearance, yet she does not appear to violate any natural codes or laws. Her actions, while they are wrong and need to be corrected, are depicted as logical and understandable.

Supernatural entities are also accepted without any significant fear or surprise: in *Phii Saht Sen Haa* the hero does not appear frightened by the heroine's voice contacting him from beyond the grave after she has been killed by her stepmother; he only grieves at her new predicament and is motivated to help her. In the same film, the sudden appearance of the heroine's dead mother as a ghost in the final showdown scene is also not cause for fear: even when she strangles the evil stepmother in front of everybody this is instead regarded as a moral (even happy) conclusion to the episode. The existence of the spirit itself is not an event that requires an extended reaction, and this supernatural number sits right next to and does not interfere with the final marriage of the leading couple, Kangwan and Karaket. Indeed, the evil stepmother's own daughter Eau (Karaket's stepsister) even falls in love with another male character immediately after witnessing her mother's extraordinary and brutal death. All of these elements illustrate a very different relationship of the productions to the supernatural world. It is only when spirits are depicted as being deliberately disgusting (as in the rotten corpse of Nak in *Mae Nak Prakanong*) or commit malevolent acts (as in Taa Nii's bloody and violent revenge upon the men who killed her adoptive parents in the film *Nang Prai Taa Nii*) that their presence and actions are challenged at all, both aspects that are not necessarily explicitly connected to their supernatural nature.

The 16mm Era Film Form

This blending of genres results in a film style and a model of horror that can be attributed to the diversity of the Thai audience, the financially precarious position of the industry, the communal viewing scenario and the collective nature of Thai society. Such influences led to the development of a particular film style and format, one which places emphasis upon engaging with what this book will call 'spectacle' and 'visual excess', notions that begin to attach Thai film to a particular model of horror. In his seminal study of horror film narratives, Noel Carroll refers to the dominant structure of the horror film as the erotetic narrative, suggesting that this suspense narrative of question-and-answer fulfilment is held to be a dominant and aspirational norm for this genre. Carroll believes that this dominant form permeates horror to such a degree that it is in fact the main method of connection for the vast majority of popular narratives (1990: 134). Tan also agrees with this, stating 'suspense is a quality of the stimulus: it is a narrative procedure, the result of which is an increase in interest in the viewer' (1996: 101). For Carroll, it is ultimately these 'processes of discovery' that make the horror narrative pleasurable. Yet this process of discovery is largely absent as a source of engagement from the ghost and spirit films of the 16mm era. Instead of engaging the viewer through Carroll's proof and discovery structures, emotional display takes precedence as a source of engagement over that of posing questions as to what the characters will do next or what solution will be constructed for the situation.

Patsorn Sungsri refers to this popular style of emotional display and blended genres as the 'conventional style' (2004). She takes this term from an interview with renowned Thai film researcher and historian Dome Sukawong, who considers the 16mm era's defining characteristic to be the blending of many different genre traits to elicit a range of emotional states from the viewer. Sukawong uses the metaphor of Thai food (a staple ingredient in many Thai idioms and allegorical phrases) to illustrate this cultural phenomenon:

> Dome Sukawong explained the conventional style as Krob Touk Rot which means 'full of flavour'. He declares that Thai film is like Thai food, which blends a lot of flavour in one meal. The conventional Thai film blends emotions and emotional states such as melancholy, excitement, arousal and romance. (Sukawong quotes in Sungsri, 2004: 54)

Sungsri links this blended, generically and tonally hybridised format to the wide-ranging audience, stating that '[t]he varieties of genres are created to satisfy the demand of different audiences' (Sungsri, 2004: 15–16).

Such analysis is similar to Miriam Hansen's explanation for the global appeal of American cinema (Hansen, 2000: 340). Hansen argues that one reason Hollywood enjoyed worldwide success from such an early age was because its format and style was already designed to cater for a wide-ranging variety of indigenous and immigrant communities within America itself. There is also evidence that early Thai filmmaking was certainly influenced by early Hollywood, with theorists recognising that this set a 'global' standard to which it aspired in both technique and style during the pre-war period. This enables us to draw a useful parallel between early US and Thai filmmaking: although Thai cinema was certainly in a very different financial and technical position to that of Hollywood, films were similarly designed to bridge barriers and engender the widest appeal among a diverse population. While such observations may point back to Tom Gunning's oft-cited 'cinema of attractions' thesis, it seems more appropriate to parallel this with the evolution of US narrative filmmaking. Early Hollywood made films for audiences who were often illiterate and/or non-anglophone speakers, hence its strong melodramatic tradition and emphasis upon affect and emotion over more 'literary' pleasures.

In the high-risk conditions of early Thai cinema, lavish spending on expensive sets and equipment was certainly not a viable option and so instead it was an emphasis upon attraction and excess that could engender the productions to the wide range of audiences across this diverse nation. In the 16mm era, Thai filmmakers received no official financial support, to the extent that Boonyaketmala describes the era as effectively a 'cottage industry' (1992). In order for these financially insecure productions to be a success, the films had to reach an audience that was starkly diverse and physically and culturally divided. Thailand has a widely differing population with many different traditions, distinct communities and cultural groupings which had been merged together into a single nation. Wanni Wibulswasdi Anderson describes it as an important location for the convergence of many different cultures and traditions from across Asia, a multi-ethnic society combining elements of Islam, Mahayana Buddhism, Brahmanism, Christianity and the belief systems of several other ethnic and tribal groups. Anderson then illustrates the numerous cultural traditions that exist:

> Just as Indian epic, 'The Ramayana,' and Chinese novel 'The Three Kingdoms,' and the Javanese literary hero, Panji, have become parts of the Thai literary and artistic traditions, so are the folklore and folklife of Thailand enriched by the mosaic of these diverse cultural traditions. (Anderson, 1989)

Accounts from those involved in Thai film around this period also illustrate the need to rely upon spectacle in order to cultivate wide appeal. Seiji Udo, a Japanese man married to a Thai woman and living in Thailand during the 1970s, gives an account of his observations of his wife's family shop in

Bangkok's Chinatown, which operated as a film wholesaler to supply the showmen who would travel to the outer provinces and show films. He distinctly connects the format of Thai films to the differing audiences the films must appeal to:

> [F]rom the standpoint of film production, it is necessary to produce films on a low budget that appeal to the general public in both cities and rural villages. As a result, their material is so full of different elements that the overall point becomes unclear (Udo, 1990).

The many thrills and emotional states which Sukawong refers to as 'flavours' (*Rot* in Thai) I henceforth refer to as 'numbers'. 'Numbers' are graphic and visceral instances of excess that do not appear to contribute to an overall narrative structure, but rather are standalone affective instances that produce physical reactions such as disgust, wonder, shock and laughter. The term is taken from the musical sequences that Linda Williams uses in her analysis of pornography to refer to the instances of sexual acts (Williams). When deploying Williams' term to explore the visceral instances of the contemporary horror film, Cynthia Freeland defines genre numbers as:

> sequences of heightened spectacle and emotion. They appear to be interruptions of plot-scenes that stop the action and introduce another sort of element, capitalizing on the power of the cinema to produce visual and aural spectacles of beauty or stunning power. (1989 in Freeland, 2000: 256)

Woofter and Stokes define such responses as 'representations of human experience rendered less through appeals to positivism, logic and moral allegory, and more through a desire to see and to feel' (2014). These 'seeing' and 'feeling' emotional affects do not necessarily contribute towards a cause-and-effect linear narrative, but rather exist as episodes in their own right, which aim to elicit strong physical emotions from the viewer. Freeland also recognises that 'numbers' can offer an alternative to suspense or mystery structures as a means of eliciting emotional affects from the viewer, wherein 'narrative and emotions are subordinated to spectacle as a goal in its own right' (2000).

In the 16mm films, the varied emotional 'numbers' fit into a very broad and recognisable narrative structure in which there is little ambiguity around the outcome of 'answering scenes'. Films such as *Jaawm Khon*, *Nguu Phii*, *Nang Prai Taa Nii* and *Phii Saht Sen Haa* tell the story of a brave, clever and strong yet also kind and gentle hero who arrives into a village and falls in love with a shy or immature village woman. At the same time, there is a disruption to village equilibrium caused by bandits, supernatural entities or other scheming women who want to marry the hero themselves. The story follows the couple, moves onto their courtship and then eventual marriage or engagement, which is also entwined with their defeating of the force that threatens them and finally ends with the restoration of harmony and order.

This spectacle/narrative debate implicitly relates back to Bordwell and Thompson's original notion of narrative 'excess': instances that bear no narrative function and exist outside of advancing a story (Thompson, 1981; Bordwell, 1985). Hansen also builds upon this, constructing classical forms of narrative as a scaffold, matrix or web that hosts 'aesthetic effects and experiences' (2000). Yet such analysis also positions spectacle as complimentary to narrative structure, implying that 'attraction' has moved from the foreground in early Hollywood melodrama to merely a supporting role in the contemporary era and is now supposedly secondary or even entirely redundant in the progression towards an ideal linear classical form. Current analysis questions this division, pointing out that in the contemporary era such an organic involvement of the audience with the text may be part of dramatising difficult and morally complex questions. Lowenstein talks of the 'allegorical moment', when temporal spectacle combines with historical trauma and becomes an invocation of past traumatic events, an analysis that is overwhelmingly attached to debates around post-9/11 horror films and the contentious texts that are popularly known as 'torture-porn' (2010). In his analysis of the contemporary Hollywood Action film, Scott Higgins embeds spectacle and narrative closely together, arguing that what he terms 'situational dramaturgy' is 'part and parcel of a kind of narrative construction that favors sensational situations' rather than a rejection of narrative as a source of stimulation (2008).

However, the scholarly analysis of Indian cinema, another non-Western cinema, offers an alternative explanation with regards to this relationship. The formalist comparisons between Thai cinema and Indian cinema seem yet to be made, which is surprising given the similarities between the metaphors of the 'Masala' film and Sukawong's reference to the blended nature of Thai food when referring to Thai film's narrative structure. Likewise, the religious, cultural and historical traditions across Thailand are historically very much connected to South Asia. This lack of connection in film analysis can probably be attributed to both the lack of song and dance sequences in Thai films (which are such a staple part of defining Hindi cinema) and the inclusion of Thai cinema in scholarly analysis and collections of East Asian cinema (rather than South Asian cinema). South Korean, Japanese and Hong Kong cinema are associated more strongly with the horror genre (in both scholarly literature and the popular imagination), while the analysis of horror in South Asian and Hindi cinema is a much more recent phenomenon (despite the long history of this genre in such industries).

In an analysis of Indian cinema, Schneider connects the excessive emotional nature of 'Bollywood' film with classical Indian aesthetic traditions that place emphasis upon the merits of such aesthetic engagement (2009). This suggests that when moving outside of the Euro-American context, spectacle and narrative may not seem so separate and emphasis upon spectacle is also not so surprising. Certainly, the song and dance sequences within Hindi cinema require 'less cognitive effort and awareness than verbally communicated themes' (Birr 2009, 45). While scholars connect this very much with music in particular, it can be stretched to include sequences which perform the same function as narrative interludes and can also act as junctures between different parts of the story (Hogan 2008). While such instances are therefore important on a narrative level, they also function to 'generate' and 'intensify' the emotional response of the viewer (Birr 2009, 45).

The emphasis upon spectacle and numbers is also a general characteristic in the artistic products of collectivist societies and can be attributed to a prevalence for affective empathy over that of cognitive empathy. In collective societies such as rural Thailand in the post-World War Two era, social connections are highly significant and people possess a much more interdependent self-construal whereby defining the self is strongly dependent upon others (Kastanakis and Voyer, 2014). This holistic, as opposed to analytical, cultural perspective then shapes the aesthetic products of nations (Masuda et al., 2008b).

While film analysis often tends to separate out cognition and affect as separate variables of (cognitively affective) narrative and (emotionally affective) spectacle, it seems more productive to address cognition and affect as different forms of empathy which can be correlated with individualist and collective societies. Studies focusing upon collective societies record strong affective empathy for other people, with feelings of concern and compassion for the state of others, and ones that are generally more accurate than those in individualist Western societies (Realo and Luik, 2002). However, cognitive empathy, the adoption of another person's psychological perspective and understanding of another's intellectual processes is low, with one study even ranking this as specifically low among Thai participants (Errasti et al., 2018).

Artistic products in collectivist societies also tend to place emphasis upon the wider context over that of the perspective of individual objects and people (Nisbett and Masuda, 2003). Correlating with diminished cognitive empathy, the emphasis upon context over that of personal perspective and experience means that individual psychological perception is less important. Stories from collective societies therefore value conformity and harmony over that of personal achievement and self-direction (Imada, 2012).

This preference for affective empathy can explain the strong reliance of entertainment products such as the 16mm films upon aspects such as spectacle, character types and stock narratives, all of which can be connected to emotional affect rather than the psychological perception associated with cognitive empathy. Certainly, within the 16mm films we see a strong emphasis upon background and context, with characters defined by their positions within social groups and their conformity to such norms and rules. Emotional display and the desire to 'see' and 'feel' then takes precedence as a source of engagement over any cognitive process of questions, answers and resolutions.

For instance, in *Mae Nak Prakanong* there are plenty of horrific elements. This includes the horror of the husband Mak when he first sees the rotten corpse of his wife instead of the beautiful woman he thought he had been sleeping next to, the monstrous elongated arm of Nak in an infamous scene where she extends it to reach out and the murders committed by Nak herself in order to maintain her secret. However, alongside this there are also numerous scenes of comedy, such as slapstick numbers performed by a fool. Together with these comedic and horrific numbers there are also heavily exaggerated romantic numbers, such as the early shy and flirtatious courting and then marriage of Mak and Nak. These diverse 'numbers' are also accompanied by the opening action-packed joyous communal temple celebrations, at which Mak and Nak meet and the unrestrained mass fistfights which ensue from fighting gangs after the celebrations. Finally, the film ends in a tragic separation scene, when Nak and Mak must be parted and Nak climbs sobbing into a pot sealed with sacred cloth to be forever separated from the world of the living.

This final ending separation scene is melodrama in a nutshell: the body is caught in the intense sensation or emotion of the sort of text that Williams terms 'the weepie'. The scene is drawn out to include the two lovers calling to each other from across the divide, extending the tragic moment into a number that is intended to elicit strong sympathetic emotions from the viewer. While it may be a long and emotionally draining episode it communicates very little in terms of advancing a story. It does not contribute towards the construction of a cause-and-effect linear narrative and creates neither suspense (the delaying of the affect) nor mystery (the obscuring of the cause). Indeed the histrionic and drawn-out tragic separation of the two lovers seems similar to Rick Altman's observations on the final generic 'reversal', in which order is restored, the wrong is righted and the pleasure derived is proportional to the distance/effort that must be traversed (1999). The action merely restores a final state of equilibrium (Nak climbing into a sacred pot and so signifying her, and Mak's, acceptance of their necessary separation and her new status as 'the dead') and is secondary in significance to the emotional elongated number (their separation).

Such exaggerated and elongated emotional scenes are also evident in other 16mm era films. In *Phii Saht Sen Haa* the hero and heroine meet at the local graveyard when she is laying flowers for her dead mother. When their courtship begins, the heroine's stepmother (her father's evil second wife) encroaches upon this equilibrium by killing the heroine in order to have the hero marry her own daughter. The 'number' in which it is revealed to the hero that the heroine has been killed takes second place as a story event to the spectacle of an exotic foreign location (the Taj Mahal in India). When informed by the ghostly voice of the heroine that she needs his help, the hero stops walking instantly and calls her name while putting his hands to his face and looking shocked, an action that is repeated and continues for some time. Rather than setting up a situation that disturbs the equilibrium and engages viewer curiosity as to how this will be restored, the scene in fact functions as a number, celebrating the spectacle of India and emphasising the hero's romantic devotion to the heroine.

Thai Film as 'Lowbrow' Horror

Crucially, this emphasis upon spectacle and emotional affect removes Thai film from the parameters of respectable and acceptable 'high-class' horror and its associated conventions. Despite questioning this division, scholars note that an emphasis upon spectacle and an overly emotional response is generally positioned as less intelligent than the cognitive processes involved in following a story. Williams attaches spectacle to the category of 'the sensational', in which she places horror, pornography and melodrama, genres awarded a 'low cultural status' due to both their physical emotional effects upon the viewer and their concentration upon the female body (Williams, 1991: 4). Leon Hunt notes how horror films that appear to privilege spectacle over that of plot are considered 'lowbrow': overt and graphic low-budget incarnations that exist on the fringe of 'good taste' and so are judged accordingly (Hunt, 2000: 326).

This may shed much light upon the disdainful attitudes towards the 16mm era films. Despite the impressive evolution of this frugal 'cottage industry', the 16mm productions were quickly designated as an inferior and unsophisticated model of film by both Thai and non-Thai viewers. Writing in 1983, Ian Buruma describes Thai cinema with disdain, pouring scorn upon these characteristics: 'most Thai melodramas, starring the same tired idols and directed by company hacks, are not worth serious attention' (1983: 53). He highlights two factors as the cause of what he terms the continuing 'mediocrity' of Thai cinema: the habitual use of the same 'exhausted' stars and over-familiar narrative formulas. Within Thailand, Patsorn Sungsri also indicates that conventional Thai films were regarded disdainfully, being described colloquially as *nam nao*. The *nam nao* term was first applied to a genre of popular literature that consists of 'escapist stories of melodrama, comedy and action' that the 16mm era freely borrowed from (Sungsri, 2004: 234). These 'escapist stories' emphasise the aesthetic of attraction and a generic hybridity of stimulating 'numbers', both attributes of the 16mm era film style. This term refers to dirty or stagnant water, implying a low level of imagination and sophistication and reaffirming the stereotype of the 16mm era film form as crude, inferior and – to all intents and purposes – abject.

This attitude was not just confined to film critics. A 1982 UNESCO Transnational Communication and Culture Industries report also passes judgement upon Thai film. One of the many basic problems facing Thai film, it suggests, is 'the unprofessional approach to film-making and a desire to become rich quickly among the producers' (UNESCO, 1982: 41).[1] The description of this 'unprofessional approach' laments the position of filmmakers as business entrepreneurs instead of artists that are part of (and possibly struggling against) a clear-cut industry, as if uniquely in a commercial medium they were wrongly placing the pursuit of profits above that of 'art'. The report concludes that 'faced with so many basic difficulties, the Thai film industry has very little prospect of expanding in a socially meaningful way' (Ibid.). UNESCO does not define what it means by 'socially meaningful', though it appears to involve removing the pursuit of profit as a primary goal of filmmaking. This fails to note not only that the vast majority of films worldwide are made in pursuit of profits, but also that this status can be correlated to the Thai government's lack of support for the industry, not the personal preferences of Thai filmmakers.

Thai elite views echo the Euro-American colonialist gaze that constructs Thailand as somehow inferior, as both conveniently occlude the specific logics that have shaped popular culture products in Thailand. They neglect to take into account the context that has shaped the Thai film industry, specifically the audience preferences and the situation of Thai filmmaking itself, and instead designate it as inferior against a putatively superior Natural Language of film. Such disdain can also be attached to a Eurocentric hierarchy of a civilised and ordered West that is opposed to a chaotic and emotional East. Sneja Gunew argues that while affect theory has grown as a discipline within the humanities, it is still dominated by 'the Eurocentric assumption that cognition (or thought) is superior to feeling as a form of intelligence' (Gunew, 2009: 11). This begins to explain the disdainful attitudes towards Thai filmmaking from within and outside Thailand. Scholars specialising in Thai studies argue that Thailand has long been subjected to constructions of inferiority. As outlined in the Introduction, common Euro-American accounts of Thailand champion notions of excess, paradox and contradiction (Jackson, 2005: 30).

Thongchai Winichakul argues that the views of Thai elites echo the Euro-American colonialist construction of Thailand as somehow inferior and backwards (2000). The adoption of and preference for Euro-American models of behaviour and dress in Thailand has been a documented phenomenon since the colonialist era, when the adoption and conversion of the country to 'civilisation' (or siwilai in Thai) was the concern of King Mongkut and Thai elites. The attainment of this vague and unspecified term became entwined with the adoption of 'Western ways' (Winichakul, 2000). This was part of authorities' attempt to model Thailand upon international concepts of nationhood while grappling with the 'regional and minority cultures' it was encountering within the state, a form of internal colonialism (Reynolds, 2002: 5). Winichakul interprets the attempt by Thai elites to incorporate this siwilai into everyday life as a means by which to retain dominance within its geographical region and keep up with the new European world powers, as it came loaded with ideas of progress and development. However, this came at the expense of minority and lower-class culture, which was designated as inferior and backwards.

Such a hierarchy is, of course, reminiscent of Bourdieu's theorisation of 'highbrow' and 'lowbrow' taste, a model that is relevant given the rigidity of the social divisions in Thailand at this time (Bourdieu, 1979). Associating oneself with the highbrow taste of Europe and its siwilai, thereby rejecting 'local' culture, demonstrated that one possessed the cultural capital to understand it and so was able to associate with and exist alongside these elites. With its out-of-date technology, village settings, hokey ghosts and emphasis upon crude 'numbers' and staple plots, the 16mm era must have seemed particularly opposed to the modernity and 'progress' represented by the sophisticated Hollywood productions shown in state-of-the-art 1,000-seat urban cinemas in Bangkok. Accounts indicate that the film form, with its repetitive visceral thrills, was discursively constructed as trashy and unsophisticated. Indeed, this inferior designation of 16mm film was strongly attached to the upcountry audience and lower-classes who avidly consumed such films. It is evident in statements such as this, which was recorded by journalist Bernard Trink in 1968: '"Thai motion pictures," according to a university student in Bangkok, "are directed at, and seen by, the people upcountry, the old women in Bangkok, and servants on their day off"' (Trink [1968] cited in Boonyaketmala 1992: 82). The derogatory nature of the quote gives an indication that Thai film was judged through its appeal to a viewer labelled as both unsophisticated and undesirable. Certainly, Ian Buruma notes that 'many members of the urban middle-class profess indifference to the point of contempt for Thai films' indicating how those at the bottom of the social hierarchy such as the poor, the aged, rural provincial people or those who work in the service industry are suggested to be uneducated and unintelligent, and their popular entertainment products likewise embody these characteristics (1983: 53).

The 16mm Era Viewing Scenario

The style of filmmaking employed by the 16mm era is also influenced by this viscerally-orientated film form, and so becomes quite different to the cinematic structures associated with 'high-class' notions of horror and its suspenseful narrative. Cinematography and editing is integral to creating a suspenseful narrative of question and answer fulfilment. A familiar structure is that associated with what Brannigan calls the 'classic POV shot'[2] (1975: 55), when the spectator is positioned within a particular character's point of view. Point-of-view shots encourage the viewer to follow a single character's subjectivity, so aiming to create an individualised immersive experience similar to that of first-person narration in literature. Horror films such as *Jaws* (Steven Spielberg, 1975) or *Halloween* place the camera and spectator in the position of the Killer and/or Monster's point of view, and also in the perspective of the unaware or escaping victim in order to raise questions that contribute towards the construction of the suspense narrative. Suspense is created through a 'disjunction in knowledge' between the audience and the character whose POV they are experiencing. According to Neale, this involves 'suspending' 'the spectator's knowledge, position, and sense of certainty' (2004: 359) as the viewer does not know what the action will be or the motivations behind it or even who or what exactly they are. This raises questions that need answers, ones that combine with the larger overarching suspense narrative.

However in keeping with Sukawong's conventional narrative structure and the privileging of the aesthetic of attraction over that of a suspenseful narrative, the cinematography and editing of the 16mm era Thai films does not display the POV shot and the corresponding structural characteristics that are associated with the horror genre. The 16mm era's concentration upon the aesthetic of attraction over that of a suspenseful narrative is reflected in the style of filmmaking. The 16mm films do not favour the point-of-view shot and the corresponding continuity editing structures. Instead they take the ethos of a drawn-out 'display' through a series of objectively presented numbers and a presentational style that is appropriate to decreased phenomenological proximity between the viewer and text. They deploy what Tom Gunning calls 'independent automate shots' that consist of wide-angle shots and lengthy takes directly in front of the characters that create a perspective similar to that of a stage audience (Gunning, 1991: 66). The viewer's attention is guided by performance (the exaggerated histrionic gestures of the proprietor and her customers) rather than the roaming 'eye' of a camera edited together through different shots. Within these shots it is the histrionic movements of the performers that draw the viewer's attention in the same way as with a stage audience: the viewer's 'eye' moves within the shot, rather than being framed by it, again reminiscent of a stage performance or display.

This film style can also be attributed to the communal viewing conventions of the lower-class and rural upcountry audiences who were designated as so 'inferior' by Thai elites. Despite its empirical focus, the viewing scenario is an element that film analysis rarely seems to take into account. While there are many historically and culturally different contexts of cinema viewing, these conventions are still heavily associated with those of the novel: a solitary singular relationship between the reader and text that must occur without distraction or interruption. Within dominant film theory, particularly that from the tradition of psychoanalytic screen theory, the film viewing scenario is predicated upon an isolated silent viewer and an immersive experience with the screen. While analysis of early cinema seems to recognise the significance of the cinematic environment (see Gunning, Eisenstein et cetera), Linda Williams states that 'classical' theories of spectatorship tend to be predicated upon a docile and mute viewer who must now enter 'the spell of a unified place and time' (Williams 2002: 366). While the assumptions made about the relationship between viewer and screen have recently been critiqued by those who argue that this scenario and the viewer positioning/response is actually much more complex and significant, the cinema itself is still most often constructed as (and assumed to be) that of a darkened space with a silent isolated viewer.

Historically, film theory and analysis demonstrates a general lack of attention towards 'the experiential effects of co-present viewers' (Hanich, 2022: 593), meaning that the 'social affordances' (what the environment can offer a person) of communal viewing are often ignored (Ibid.). Reminiscent of a lingering Eurocentrism, alternative viewing situations and behaviours are mostly considered to be exceptions to this rule. This is deeply flawed: investigations into the post-colonial audiences of Hollywood point to a chaotic and rowdy viewing context far different from such assumptions, while classical Hollywood itself, with its 'distracted viewers wandering into theatres at any old time' (Williams 2002: 366) rarely delivered this scenario and/or spectator.

The horror genre in particular is so entwined within the silent immersive scenario of the multiplex that even recent studies addressing cinematic affect that directly reference the viewing scenario tend to remain primarily within this when considering the genre. For instance, Julian Hanich recognises the significance of the viewing context in his analysis of the horror film, which begins to illustrate a key difference between Thai cinema and the globally dominant horror models. While acknowledging that cinematic norms do vary, Hanich argues that the cinema 'owes its attractiveness, among other things, to its ability to partially relieve us from the burden of social interaction' (Hanich, 2010: 63). Hanich further argues that this viewing context creates a high degree of 'phenomenological proximity' between the text and viewer as they become immersed in the fictional diegesis. This invokes a singular relationship between the viewer and film that Hansen alludes to as 'institutionally regulated' due to its ability to control the viewer. The cinema becomes a 'private space' in which the viewer is supposedly isolated within a darkened room and closed off from other influences, including the presence of other viewers. They are compelled to remain silent and passive and enjoy an intense private and psychological relationship with the events unfolding on the screen, a process that Hanich calls 'individualized absorption' as it 'allows the viewer to relate more strongly to the film' (2010: 57).

Yet targeting the rural Thai audience involved functioning within a different type of society with a different kind of cinema and viewing context, one that that may place such productions beyond these assumed characteristics of spectatorship. The films were very consciously designed to function within a shared public space and cultivate an atmosphere of communal pleasure that Gerald Fouquet describes as 'specifically Thai' (2006: 53). Discussing the period roughly between 1960 and 1990, Fouquet states that Thai cinemas are divided into four categories. He begins with 'First class theatres', which are large and expensive and all located in Bangkok. Below this category are 'Second and Third class theatres', which occupy the surrounding provinces of Bangkok and other major cities such as Chiang Mai. Finally he described 'Itinerant cinema', which involves temporary showings by travelling cinemas in the upcountry provincial villages and small towns. In these, Fouquet notes the terrible quality of the showings: reels snapping, catching fire, getting lost, running too slowly or too fast, and stresses how this does not seem to bother the audience, who actually rarely stay seated for long and are instead constantly talking, laughing, eating and socialising. This was a social occasion designed to create communal shared pleasure. The atmosphere was one of informality and communal enjoyment and 'resembles more that of a local fete or fair than that of a film projection such as we usually know it', thus actually adding to the cinema-going experience (Fouquet 2006: 54).

The communal scenario Fouquet describes seems to create a version of Bakhtin's 'carnivalesque' atmosphere, suggesting that film-going functioned as a form of transgressive pleasure for lower-class audiences who were subjugated by the authority of urban (and/or colonial) elites. Thai researcher Juree Vichit-Vadakan, writing in 1977, provides a description of this:

> The atmosphere of the film showing is carnival-like. Some theatres have microphones blasting away advertisements and announcements in a style comparable to a temple fair. Hawkers and blackmarketeering of tickets (which theatre managers seem to endorse, mainly as proof of the popularity of their films) are markedly aggressive and active. Before and during the film show, a quantity of food is consumed as evidenced by the symphony of chewing, nut cracking, and popping of melon seeds. (Vichit-Vadakan 1977: 41)

In the Thai context, such a scenario can perhaps be related to the creation of what is termed *sanuk*, a Thai word most often translated into English as 'fun' but which actually covers a range of emotions and feelings emanating from a notion of 'shared pleasure'. This required a different aesthetic attitude towards film-going, one evident in Juree Vichit-Vadakan's early observations of Thai cinema audiences. Vichit-Vadakan states that the many interruptions of children or chattering viewers throughout the showing are not a distraction from the events on-screen but instead 'the sharing of feelings and emotions is implicitly recognized' (Vichit-Vadakan 1977: 40). The audience actually enjoys the many comments and communal interactions with the film:

> A crowded movie house is not a passive viewing of the actions which take place on the screen, but an 'event' where casual and also very emotional comments are made; where outbursts of emotions (laughing, crying, cursing, screeming [sic]) are given free rein; and where exchanges of opinion are common. (Vichit-Vadakan 1977: 41)

The show is a social event in which the audience enjoys freedom to behave as it wishes, turning to and from the screen at will. Its actions are an extension of the show, as Vichit-Vadakan understands: 'a Thai film showing allows its audience to be actively involved in an event which is culturally, socially, and psychologically meaningful and comprehensible to the Thai audience' (Ibid.).

Analysis of Indian cinema provides a template for a similar viewing scenario, in which audience interactions always take precedence over the film itself. The film must be interwoven with this communal interaction and must appeal to everyone (Srinivas, 2016). As Birr states:

> Indian audience behavior is usually described as involving spirited participation. Activities such as cheering loudly, singing, or talking along to dialogues and song lyrics are considered quite normal during a film screening, underlining the overall impression of a rather animated experience. (Birr 2009, 46–47).

Post-war Thailand therefore requires an alternative model of consumption in keeping with what Hansen called 'institutionally less regulated viewing situations' (Hansen 1994: 136). Hanich labels this a 'socialising theatrical experience', and offers the rowdy lower-class early Nickelodeon picture houses of early twentieth-century America as an example (Hanich, 2010). Indeed, the early Nickelodeons and Indian cinema would appear to have much in common with the communal scenario typical of the rural upcountry viewing context. Thai films therefore developed characteristics that could both function within and contribute towards an atmosphere of 'shared pleasure'.

Yet the 16mm era viewing situation should not necessarily be seen as socially transgressive in the same way as early Hollywood. In contrast to Bakhtin's carnivalesque, the communal viewing of 16mm era films is in keeping with and can be attributed to the collectivist nature of rural Thai society. It is therefore unlikely that this activity offered much 'relief' from social and behavioural norms. Film analysis honed from more individualistic societies attributes part of the pleasure of 'fearful cinematic encounters' to the collective nature of the cinema and its ability to alleviate loneliness. The reassuring presence of others provides needed relief from the fragmented and isolating existence of urban modernity, a unique part of the cinematic pleasure of horror in particular (Hanich 2010). This problematises our understanding of the pleasures and appeal of films within collective societies, specifically those associated with the horror genre. While such film viewings were enjoyable and entertaining, the cinema reinforced social cohesion and collectivity as it already existed in society, rather than providing a 'relief' from everyday existence. 'Fearful cinematic encounters' instead reaffirmed the collective nature of society, social bonds and, therefore, a degree of social conformity. Unlike the darkened multiplex of urban modernity, norms are not suspended but reaffirmed by the 16mm screenings.

Instead, just as the cinema (and horror films in particular) functions as a 'tonic' to relieve the individual isolation of modernity in individualist societies (Hanich 2010), film (and spectacle in particular) may function as a 'tonic' for emotional response in collective societies which generally suppress such expression, one that is able to operate freely within this safely demarcated space. Indeed, emotional arousal level is strongly influenced by culture, with collectivist societies favouring low arousal emotions and the suppression of emotional response and processes (both positive and negative) as a means to maintain group harmony (Chiang 2012; Lim 2016). The function of film as a 'release' from such restraint can explain why collective societies which may not favour such individual emotional expression actually have more raucous and expressive cinema audiences and make films that engage strongly with emotional affect (largely through spectacle) over that of cognition.

Certainly, the emphasis upon spectacle and the aesthetic of attraction was designed to function within a far less regulated scenario and cultivate shared pleasure. The visceral 'numbers' and the wide range of emotional affects invoke very physical responses that make the experience a communal one. The action, horror and comedy built around a loose plot with familiar characters and story developments engendered this communal atmosphere, ensuring that viewers can turn away from the screen to indulge in other activities (talking, eating) without diminishing the viewing experience. Major events in the narrative are also often stretched over long scenes: in *Phii Saht Sen Haa* a scene where the heroine is bitten by a snake placed by her evil stepmother is drawn out and elongated to over four minutes. Likewise, these films are also excessively long (an element that Seiji Udo criticises): *Nguu Phii* lasts for two hours sixteen minutes and *Praai Phitsawat* for two hours thirty-two minutes. The audience is sustained through the varied distractions in the communal situation of shared pleasure. While this does not engender any suspense or mystery, the scene's length ensures that it can still be appreciated and absorbed in an environment where the film must function in the midst of a rowdy and distracted audience.

There are also very few shot transitions in a single scene, and the few cuts used are jerky and disjointed, so disrupting the diegetic world for the viewer and inadvertently reinforcing the artifice of the film. This disjointed editing, while likely the result of technical flaws, ensures that it would be very difficult to construct Hanich's 'phenomenological proximity' between the text and viewer. Many of the 16mm era productions display these disjointed shot transitions, so suggesting that this was not a concern or disruption for the audience and that 'immersion' in a diegesis was not necessary to Thai viewing pleasure in this context. Critiquing the construction of an imagined perfect film style by film theorists, Brown (2015) comments that 'as long as audiences are primed regarding how they should receive a film … then you don't need to care about and can even love the stylised acting, the ropey *mise-en-scène*, the unmotivated camera movements, the strange edits and the story loopholes' (Brown, 2015). These 'primed' expectations seem particularly strong in the conventional Thai film narrative with its stock plots, genre numbers and characters, while continuity editing and a strong sense of realism are not expectations held by the audience.

Most notably, the lack of synchronised sound and the oral commentary of the dubber also contributed towards this shared pleasure. Fouquet cites live dubbing in the 16mm era as a means through which a bridge was constructed between the text and audience, one that sought to make the film relevant to the immediate world of the viewer (2006). Dubbers also offered up their own informal commentary upon the text and inserted references to popular (or even local) culture (that could also be conducted in the local dialect of the audience). As Sukawong understands, the dubbing would sometimes bear little connection to the original story, with dubbers choosing to reference local events or create humorous situations themselves that were not necessarily synchronous with the actual events unfolding on the screen (2001).

Despite the unusual nature of the 16mm era and its films, this form of entertainment is perhaps not as 'specifically Thai' as Fouquet observes. The films are more accurately attributed to the collective nature of rural Thai society, in which collective gatherings would have been (and indeed still are) a very staple part of everyday entertainment. Film screenings occurred alongside other forms of mass entertainment such as boxing matches, village fairs and religious festivals. As such, the 'social affordances' of film viewing are not an added bonus but a crucial part of the film itself and even the main reason for watching. 'Shared pleasure' is so crucial that if we question what effect the fellow audience members have upon one's experience of the film, then this is not actually an 'effect' per se for the 16mm viewer, but an integral part of the film itself, without which it would not function as an entertainment product (Hanich, 2018: 4).

Certainly, this collective atmosphere of shared pleasure can also be found in other older forms of entertainment in Thailand. The design of the films reflects the dominance and popularity of communal entertainment in Thailand and the rural and lower-class cinemas resemble the festivals and fetes that play an important role in traditional indigenous entertainments. Indeed, to a certain extent this space is a shared one: after 1952, when stage performance decreased in the face of renewed filmic competition, 'several founders of drama troupes turned to producing films' (Phromyothi, 2000: 21). Literature was not a popular medium in the country and instead theatre, puppetry and radio, all forms based upon communal rather than individual enjoyment, were, for various reasons, popular much earlier than the novel among the general population. With the spread of modern media and entertainment, it was radio in particular, then film and later television, which was the popular medium throughout the country. All of these forms notably engender shared pleasure and involve a communal scenario of consumption. The presence of a dubber providing voices for so many different characters was also familiar and well established in Thai entertainment, being 'similar to the method of narration used in Thai classical masked drama, in which a narrator was used because face masks prevented the actors from speaking for themselves' (Sukawong, 2001: 10). Shadow puppetry is another medium which operates as a communal event and from which Thai film even takes its Thai language designation: that of Nang. It also shares the necessity of a narrator and Koanantakool identifies the oral commentary – another possible origin for the dubbing convention in 16mm era films – as absolutely crucial to the success of this entertainment, as this improvisation allows a direct communication between the puppeteer and the audience through dialogue and jokes (Koanantakool, 1989: 43).

Conclusion

Such analysis begins to track the development of a cinematic model of horror that is relevant to understanding the contemporary incarnation of this genre in Thailand today. Thematically, this chapter has demonstrated that the post-World War Two 16mm era offered a generally reactionary and conservative model of film. These films respond to anxiety around social advances and developments that challenge gender norms with depictions that build upon the sociological link between the female and the supernatural. This subject matter 'makes safe' that which could be threatening social order, so becoming somewhat reactionary in nature by reinforcing rather than challenging social boundaries. This traumatic response to destabilisation of traditional gender roles by encroaching modernity serves to affirm both the inferiority of and so the need for control over increasing female autonomy.

However this response is essentially reactionary in a specifically Thai way, one that I have indicated possesses a particular style and conventions that at times seem to run counter to the definition of horror as a genre. The chapter has demonstrated that such characteristics are related to the post-war development of Thai film and its primarily lower-class rural audience, in which spirits and ghosts are an important part of society and social organisation. Within the 16mm era productions, this subject matter is not a violation of natural law and can interject into the diegesis without the creation of a separate horror genre. Traits from different genres are therefore 'blended' into a single production and film style is also correspondingly different. Films lack the POV shots typically found in horror, and long takes and shots take the place of edited sequences. The analysis attributed such characteristics to the rural Thai communal viewing scenario and the need for 'shared pleasure', a crucial element of entertainment in collectivist societies. Indeed, the communal nature of cinema seems to reaffirm collectivist social norms, while also providing an outlet for (usually repressed) emotional expression.

The chapter further demonstrated how this blended film style also pushed 16mm era films into a 'lowbrow' and sensationalist model of horror that places emphasis upon spectacle, 'numbers' and 'emotional effect' within a scaffold of stock narrative structures and character types. Such a construction adheres to an elitist Eurocentric image of Thailand as an uncivilised, chaotic and imperfect imitation of a global (largely Western and East Asian) model. Further causing these films to be viewed as inferior, the era becomes a lower-class film form that functions within the lower-class context, responds to it, addresses lower-class viewers and negotiates this environment for them.

The next chapter addresses the development of Thai film after the 16mm era and up into the post-97 New Thai contemporary industry. It tracks the continued existence of the formal characteristics I identified, assessing the extent to which these are still visible in a context in which the cultural logics that engendered such conventions have progressed in line with Thai social developments and global film influences. Given the changing social context after the 16mm era, the chapter also investigates the common horror motif of monstrous femininity. Through this it explores the political relationship of Thai film to the wider social context, so illustrating the ways in which the Thai horror film continues to mediate such discourses for the contemporary viewer and how this viewer was now beginning to change.

Notes

Parts of this chapter have been previously published as Ainslie, M. (2014) 'The Supernatural and Post-war Thai Cinema', *Horror Studies*, 5/2, pp. 157–169.

DOI: https://doi.org/10.1386/host.5.2.157_1 and Ainslie, M. (2017) 'Post-war Thai Cinema: Audiences and Film Style in a Divided Nation', *Film International*, 80, 15/2, pp. 6–19. DOI: https://doi.org/10.1007/978-3-319-66344-9_17

1. This also disregards a number of highly regarded artistic Thai films that actually were made during this period.
2. This is 'a shot in which the camera assumes the position of a subject in order to show us what the subject sees' (Brannigan, 1975: 55).

2. AFTER THE 16MM ERA
Horror and Progressive Social Critique

As the second analytical chapter of the volume and the final section to focus upon outlining the historical context necessary to explain and understand Thai horror today, Chapter 2 is concerned with the development of Thai film after the 16mm era and into the early 1990s, finishing this overview just before the teen era of the early 1990s and the post-97 New Thai contemporary industry. The chapter ultimately argues that despite some significant changes, the characteristics associated with the 16mm era films and their provincial audiences are still evident in Thai film, indicating how the marginalised subjectivity of provincial Thailand impacts upon and shapes Thai entertainment and cultural products. This chapter identifies some key moments in Thai cinematic development, including the watershed production *Tone* (Piak Poster, 1970), the culturally significant Social Problem films and the international ambitions of renowned Thai auteur Ratana Pestonji.

Moving on to address the B-grade productions, a phenomenon from the late-1970s to the mid-1990s, the chapter offers a close analysis of horror and the significant horror film *Baan Phii Pop* (Srisawat, 1989). It outlines how the preferences of this lower-class and provincial audience continue to cause Thai film to deviate from the characteristics (both formal and theoretical) generally associated with horror films and so problematise the construction of a separate horror genre. Finally, the chapter indicates how horror becomes a means of articulating and engaging with the trauma of an exploitive wider context, particularly the abuse and mistreatment of lower-class Thai women throughout the 1980s and 1990s economic boom. This results in a very different ideological engagement from that of the conservative and reactionary position of the 16mm era films of earlier decades.

The End of the 16mm Era: *Tone*, The Social Problem Films and the 'Culture Of Dissent'

The 16mm era eventually came to an end in the early 1970s. Chalida Uabumrungjit singles out the success of the films *Monrak Luktung* (Rangsi Thatsana Payak, 1970) and *Tone* as contributing towards standardising the use of 35mm filmstock with synchronised sound in Thailand (2001). Both films were very successful and lie at a transitional point when Thai film begins to develop from the 16mm era 'cottage industry' into something much bigger and better organised. *Monrak Luktung* was by far the bigger phenomenon and occupies primary place in Thai film history, with a long and lasting impact upon Thai cultural memory. A nostalgic portrayal of rural life starring the 16mm era's top performers Mitr Chaibancha and Petchara Chaowarat, this film capitalised upon the popularity of Thai country music (luk thung) and deployed this as a means to engage with the trauma of rural displacement over the post-war period. However, overwhelmingly it is *Tone* that Thai film historians note as being the crucial turning point that forged a new direction for Thai cinema after 1970, offering a radically different engagement with wider social changes. The film tells the story of Tone, an orphaned temple boy who saves the visiting city boy Aod from a group of bullies. Tone is invited to stay with Aod while they study together in Bangkok. There Tone meets Aod's sister Dang, a sexy young woman who is always going out with men. When Dang gets in trouble with some gangsters, Tone saves her and the couple begin to fall in love.

Tone marked a dramatic developmental turning point and a shift in Thai film's relationship to its surrounding context by incorporating and responding to elements of American popular culture that had impacted upon Thailand in the post-war era. The 1960s saw an increased questioning of and opposition to the military rule and political oppression endured by Thailand since 1948, with growing dissatisfaction towards the authoritarian and repressive regime of Field Marshall Sarit Thanarat.[1] While the influx of American pop culture was largely a result of American and Thai collaboration against leftist discourse that the Thai government was eager to suppress (both internally and externally), this imported pop culture nevertheless provided a vehicle for radical and rebellious Thai youth. Modern and consumerist American pop culture and infrastructure came to represent new and radical social developments, and this was taken up by Thai youth culture. Associated with self-expression, freedom and opposition, this became a radical alternative 'counterculture' for hungry youths eager for the urban modernity that was so opposed to the traditional rural life of their parents' generation.

Indeed, the 1970s turned into a period of dramatic political and social turmoil in Thailand. A growing dissatisfaction with the military rule Thailand had endured since the end of the war and a push in favour of democracy culminated in huge demonstrations. The discontent brewing from Thailand's military rule eventually culminated in the October 1973 revolution, in which the ruling Junta was forced to step down after firing upon a mass student demonstration. A brief period of democratic rule ensued, under which Thai artists enjoyed freedom and creativity. This was crushed in the bloody coup of 1976, in which around 100 demonstrating students were brutally murdered and many more injured when both police and anti-Communist vigilantes of the Red Gaur organisation stormed the gates of Thammasat University and brutally lynched, beat, raped and burned a peaceful group of 4,000 students and workers staging a sit-in. Military rule again ensued and anti-leftist rhetoric swept the country.

Close attention to *Tone* indicates how Thai film continued to respond to and mediate its social environment. Indeed, as a fantasy and wish-fulfilment of a fully Americanised Thailand, *Tone* is saturated with the ideology of global corporate Capitalism that (understandably) represents freedom from the conformist village environment of the 16mm era productions. Indeed, *Tone*'s success was related to 'the influence of Western youth counterculture in Thailand generally' (Chaiworaporn, 2001: 142) as the film mediates young Thai citizens' desire and ambition for this foreign lifestyle.[2] Demonstrating the adaptation of Thai film to a rapidly changing social environment, *Tone* targeted younger Thai film-goers by incorporating American popular culture into Thai cinema, performing a mediation of these new and modern elements at a time when they fed into a politically radical discourse.

Embracing youth-orientated 'counterculture' points to a socially progressive text, and one that is very different to the conservative affirmation of social norms seen in the 16mm era films. As part of this 'counterculture' *Tone* self-consciously rejected the conventions of the 16mm era, instead embracing the new and modern consumer culture that was transforming Thailand and arguably creating opportunities and lifestyles for Thai citizens. The film embraced these freedoms formally and ideologically, so shifting the parameters of Thai film away from the 16mm era. Attributes such as the village setting and the 16mm era film style became diametrically opposed to the freedoms and excitement offered by this new foreign discourse of modernity, and were rejected in favour of American cultural conventions and this form of filmmaking.

For instance, Tone contains far more shots within a scene and takes are much shorter, with conversations broken down into shot-reverse-shot sequences and high and low angles used. This is also coupled with a new urban and

Americanised *mise-en-scène* as the film rejects the familiar setting of the Thai village and instead changes its location to the city of Bangkok. The experiences of the main character, who migrates to the city and eventually mediates his own position in this new urban Americanised Bangkok, are exciting, attractive and dangerous.

The narrative, themes and characters of *Tone* are also starkly different to the 16mm era conventions, particularly the portrayal of women, which challenged dominant gender constructions and was so radical that it 'rewrote the way of representing Thai women' (Chaiworaporn, 2001: 142). Instead of a reactionary relationship to potentially radical social elements such as uncontrolled femininity seen in the 16mm era productions, the depictions in *Tone* are very different. Rather than demonising female mobility, *Tone* presents this new Americanised culture of flares and mini-skirts, Pepsi logos and rock'n'roll music as attractive and liberating to both men and women.

This is particularly evident in the character Dang, the streetwise sister of Aod. With her modern clothes and sharp tongue, Dang appears almost the polar opposite to Tone and the more traditional female character Kularb. Dang exercises a far greater degree of autonomy than female characters in the 16mm era, controlling her own movement, dress and talking back to male characters. She is first introduced in a point-of-view shot that depicts only her hand putting on a rock'n'roll record, then the camera moves slowly up her body as she dances, revealing her skimpy clothes – bright coloured flares and cropped top – and her bare midriff. As Tone stands transfixed, Dang scolds him and then asks him to help fix the zip on her clothing, something that Tone is shocked by. Throughout the film Dang is also extremely mobile; she climbs in and out of cars with men and drinks in bars. On their first date she also takes Tone to a bowling alley, indicating her familiarity with popular American culture, a modern, urban and foreign activity. Posters of The Beatles and Petula Clark from the musical *Finian's Rainbow* (Francis Ford Coppola, 1968) (an illustration of the popularity of musicals within Thailand at this time) also cover Dang's bedroom wall, further associating this new and radical depiction of femininity with a non-Thai model of popular culture.

Narrative conventions of the 16mm era would also have demanded that Dang's fraternisation with 'bad' gangsters should cause her to be rejected and punished. Yet Dang's lifestyle throughout the film is here presented as fun, exciting and desirable, and she is personally complex. This plot is one that Chaiworaporn describes as 'anti-formulaic' (Chaiworaporn, 2001: 142): although Tone must save Dang from the gangsters she becomes involved with, they still become a couple in the end, a development that Chaiworaporn labels as 'groundbreaking' for a Thai film plot.

The radical modern aesthetic and cinematography of *Tone* together with its *risqué* story pulled politicised and rebellious Thai youth into the cinema in droves, reflecting the changes enacted upon Thai society at this time and the transformations in the viewers' own lives. *Tone* fed into the 1970s 'culture of dissent', of which the release of a number of Social Problem films were also a significant part (Chaiworaporn, 2001: 143). These films were a direct product of directors from this socially conscious era, who were able to capitalise on the success of *Tone*, both in terms of its more technically competent film style and unconventional storylines. These productions are noted by film historians for their socially conscious themes: they deal with issues in Thai society such as poverty, corruption, prostitution and inequality. Chaiworaporn (2001) singles out films such as *Khao Chue Karn* (Chatrichalerm Yukol, 1973) and *Talad Phromajaree* (Sakka jarujinda, 1973), both socially critical films about struggling lower-classes and corruption of authorities, as being directly influenced by the style of *Tone* in this way. They appealed to the young, educated and politically aware urban viewers, continuing Tone's audience shift from the traditional audience of the 16mm era to modern urban youth. Indeed in the 1970s, for about the first time in Thai film history, Thai productions began to appeal to intellectuals, an indication of the changing state of film in Thailand.[3]

The Lasting Effect of the 16mm Era Film Style

However, despite these radical ideological and stylistic changes, a close examination of *Tone* indicates that the film still displays the conventions of the 16mm era film style and still adheres to this film form. This is crucial, as while *Tone* and the Social Problem films may represent a politically progressive movement, in rejecting the 16mm era they shift away from the preferences of the marginalised lower-class rural viewers. Such productions would ultimately remove the subjectivity of provincial Thai culture, ironically while leftist intellectuals celebrated the representation of a marginalised Thai point of view and a new perspective on Thai society.

Ultimately, the conventions nurtured in the 16mm era did not vanish and while Thai film changed in its political response to wider social upheaval, it continued to do this in a distinctly Thai way, one that still engages with and bears the legacy of rural Thai society and its entertainment preferences. The identification of the characteristically Thai framework within a production seen as so revolutionary in its impact upon the Thai film industry also indicates how prominent and popular these nuances continued to be in Thailand. The fact that such influences are still present illustrates how this audience and its preferences continue to influence Thai filmmaking and betrays the origins of post-war Thai film as the lower-class entertainment that Thai elites so disliked. The preferences of the lower-class spectator still 'haunt' Thai film and cannot be entirely erased. While viewing situations, audiences and Thailand itself have all changed therefore, this film style had a continued relevance to Thai viewers and an ability to adapt to new and changing circumstances.

For instance, *Tone* places great emphasis upon musical numbers, placing spectacle and emotional effect as a source of stimulation over that of narrative and cognitive effect. The many musical numbers, with characters singing and dancing throughout, are largely separate from narrative events and function as spectacles in their own right, especially given their incorporation of contemporary American influenced rock'n'roll tracks. Along with this music, the modern 1960s costumes and hairstyles also function as spectacles, with the camera often deliberately singling out dancers who have no contribution to the narrative. The narrative itself also follows the familiar prior-known story of a couple who will get together at the end, in particular a love story involving a shy boy and outgoing girl – one very similar to 16mm era productions.

To add to this conventional story structure, performance style is also suitably histrionic and presentational. Many of the characters are also recognisable types, including the handsome hero, the beautiful heroine, the odd-looking comedian and the seedy villains all still adhering to the physical construction of these character types. The film also blends many genres, most notably the ending action number of a fight on a moving vehicle, the crime shoot-out number with the gangsters in the end, the musical numbers and of course the romantic numbers between Tone and Dang. Likewise, although the cinematography is certainly more complex than that of the 16mm era, there is still a great use of long shots and takes, especially when depicting the musical performers and fight sequences.

Ratana Pestonji

We also see the influences of this film style in post-war Thai auteur Ratana Pestonji's productions. Pestonji is regarded today as the grandfather of Thai film and was the recipient of a lifetime achievement award by the Bangkok International Film Festival in 2004. Pestonji attempted to improve Thai film through pushing for governmental support and technically modernising the medium, founding one of the few 35mm production companies after the war. Pestonji is also particularly admired for competing artistically on the international stage at a time when Thai cinema was very much a domestic affair.

Pestonji's attempts to cultivate both international and national appeal during the post-World War Two era result in a distinct blending of international filmic influence and the 16mm era stylistics. Again, similar to *Tone*, Pestonji's films still adhere in many ways to the 16mm era style of filmmaking, highlighting how these conventions are such an integral part of Thai filmmaking that they are still found in the work of a filmmaker who can be very much set apart from the 16mm era. Pestonji himself was very conscious of the dominant stylistics of Thai film, as Uabumrungjit states: 'He intended to make a popular film by including songs, dances and sex, but in fact it became a kind of satire on the popular film at the time, which always included songs, comedy and sex appeal' (2001: 137).

Pestonji's most famous production, *Prae Dam/Black Silk*, blends 'numbers' from a variety of genres into a single production, privileging spectacle. Although *Black Silk* appears dark, ruthless and tragic with its story of murder, lost love and psychological torment, it also includes a surprising selection of music and dance numbers along with fight sequences, all of which are depicted in an array of bright primary colours. For instance, despite its tragic story, which involves a gangster trying to stand up to his boss and be with the woman he loves, the film also alternates scenes of music and dance. Uabumrungjit labels these as 'elements of entertainment' that exist alongside the unconventional elements of the film that set it apart from the 16mm era productions (such as the urban street scenes of 1960s Bangkok and the fact that it is shown on 35mm film with synchronised sound).[4] These various 'entertainment' elements of 'songs, comedy and sex appeal' (Uabumrungjit, 2001: 137) are similar to the emotionally stimulating 'numbers' of the 16mm era. Likewise, while Pestonji's use of unknown actors was also pioneering at a time when star images were a major draw, these performers still retain the histrionic performances and character types associated with the 16mm era productions.

Responses to Pestonji's films also then begin to emphasise how the disdainful attitudes towards the 16mm era and these '*nam nao*' films from urban and upper-class Thais are not based upon the quality of the productions themselves, but ostensibly upon denigrating and marginalising the provincial Thai audience and its cultural preferences. This is evident because despite the similarities between Pestonji's productions and the 16mm era productions, critics continued to praise Pestonji's films partly due to their supposed difference to this era. Contemporary Thai film critic Kong Rithdee, who writes film reviews of Thai productions for English and Thai language Bangkok newspapers, lauds Pestonji's dedication and passion for filmmaking as this, Rithdee believes, made his films very different to the mass-produced repetitive 16mm era and its profit-motivated entrepreneurs, which had acquired a reputation as being 'rowdy entertainment for the masses, a gaudy distraction' (Rithdee, 2008). Instead Pestonji's productions qualify as 'serious art' due to his technical innovations and his desire to make films that are more than mere entertainment. The presence of the 16mm era conventions within the productions of such a prestigious filmmaker therefore emphasises not only how profound and pronounced this was within Thai society, but also how the wider derogatory attitudes towards this film form were concerned not with the lack of 'quality' or 'art' in the 16mm productions but rather the targeted audience.

The B-Grade Productions and *Baan Phii Pop* – Continuing the 16mm Era

Despite the success of *Tone* and the Social Problem films, another model of Thai film continued to thrive among lower-class urban and provincial audiences and their cinemas. Existing alongside the celebration of Americanised modernity seen in *Tone*, the international ambitions of Pestonji, and the intellectualist Social Problem films, this was an informal independent sector of what Chaiworaporn titles 'B-grade productions' (Chaiworaporn 2001: 156). This sector was the result of major developments that occurred in the Thai film industry that significantly altered the production of film in Thailand. In 1977 the tax on imported foreign productions was increased, resulting in somewhat of a boycott by foreign distributors. The lack of foreign imports resulted in what Chaiworaporn labels the post-1976 'boom period' of Thai cinema, when up to 160 productions were made annually and many new filmmakers emerged (Ibid.). Crucially, this opportunity allowed a greater level of organisation in the industry, with several influential production companies founded. In a model echoing that of vertical integration in the US, these not only made films but also controlled their own distribution and even cinemas (Dome Sukawong, 2001: 14). As with the American system of big studio dominance, this inevitably caused the smaller independent producers from the 16mm era to disappear (Ibid.). This brief boom was to end in the early 1980s, when, with the return of Hollywood productions and increased availability of videocassette rental, 'more than 700 cinemas and 1000 open-air screens disappeared' (Ibid.). However, the groundwork for a viable filmmaking infrastructure with established filmmakers and audiences had now been established, and this continued into and up to the mid-to-late 1990s (with the arrival of the post-97 New Thai Film industry, covered in the next chapter).

These films targeted provincial viewers who had been both neglected and exploited in the post-war push towards economic prosperity and largely excluded from the celebration of urban modernity seen in *Tone*. Throughout the 1980s and the early 1990s, scholars note how Thailand had 'plunged headlong into a postmodernist global economy' (Hamilton, 1994: 142) following 'an export-orientated ("neo-liberal") growth model promoted by the World Bank' (Bell, 1997: 56). Inspired by the shining examples of nearby Singapore and Hong Kong, rapid economic growth occurred throughout Southeast Asia during this period, with Thailand's being the highest of all. Modernity, business and economic investment was promoted by Thai elites as a positive step forward and a form of growth for the nation. Specifically this involved a high level of non-Thai Euro-American investment, partly, as Pasuk Phongpaichit and Chris Baker have argued, because 'foreign investors liked Thailand's combination of relative political stability and relatively cheap labour' (Phongpaichit and Baker, 1998: 312).

Thailand thus followed a growth model promoted by the World Bank (and based upon a Western system) that actually 'intensified regional, class and gender biases in the society' (Bell, 1997: 56). Through such exploitation the Thai economy was able to grow substantially, particularly between 1985 and 1995, but despite such economic prosperity little changed for the ordinary Thai citizen. Little of the newly created wealth actually filtered down to the 'cheap labour' that generated it, and Thailand became one of the most unequal countries in the world in terms of wealth distribution. This enormous social change also reorganised the ways in which families and villages were structured, leaving many rural families heavily dependent upon the sons and daughters who had been sent to work in factories and cities. The discrepancy between upper and lower-class living standards grew. While cities such as Bangkok grew enormously and spectacularly, with air-conditioned cinemas in luxury shopping centres showing Hollywood blockbusters, life in the outer provinces and the villages within them changed little: rice farming continued to be the main source of income and the mobile *Nang Re* touring cinemas continued to cater for a communal form of viewing appropriate to village life.

Baan Phii Pop is the production that Chaiworaporn uses as synecdochal of the B-grade industry and its provincial audience. This film was 'so popular that thirteen subsequent sequels have been made, all with the same actors and characters, and specifically targeted at rural audiences' (2001: 156). The film also demonstrates the continued primacy of horror in Thai filmmaking and its specifically Thai incarnation at this time. Released from 1989 and continuing until 1994, this popular series ended around the time that urban cinemas came into existence as a significant phenomenon. The franchise has clear significance in the history and development of Thai cinema, underlined by the original's many sequels and its 2008 remake starring the same lead actress, Nattanee Sitthisaman.

The story begins with a grandmother who is possessed and attacks people around the village. This old woman is nursed and helped by a good and pure young woman called Pra Preung. A group of doctors visiting from the city is then attacked and chased at night by the Phii Pop, and Pra Preung saves them. The head doctor, Dr Ret, is immediately attracted to Pra Preung, but when the village sends a shaman to exorcise the grandmother he stops them, thinking that the woman is merely old and sick. Later in the night the Shaman is killed by the Phii Pop. The village headman's daughter Kradeung is also attracted to Dr Ret and jealous of Pra Preung. Throughout the film a group of three badly dressed buffoons/fools are also frightened by the Phii Pop grandmother and crack jokes continuously.

Baan Phii Pop indicates how different the B-grade productions were to the celebration of urban modernity depicted in *Tone* (as well as Pestonji's international ambitions). The stories, settings and characters of these films are set in and focus largely upon rural village life and its provincial inhabitants. This echoes the situation of the lower-class audience for whom this urban capitalist dream is not so accessible and far less viable. The film is set in a rural provincial village whose inhabitants are terrorised by a Phii Pop ghost, a malevolent spirit that can possess a person and force them to come out at night to eat raw animal and human entrails. While *Tone* depicts a shy village boy travelling to the city and experiencing the wonders of modernity, this B-grade production depicts the reverse: an educated urban doctor comes into a rural village environment and falls for a good-hearted and chaste village girl, a scenario similar to 16mm era productions.

Not only the story but the *mise-en-scène* of *Baan Phii Pop* remains embedded within the rural environment. Wooden village houses feature prominently, and the structures of the dwellings – high up off the ground on stilts with slats for walls – physically inform the story, with people leaping in and out when scared by the ghost. The traditional walls of wooden slats also help create an eerie *chiaroscuro* effect, casting shadows across the setting. Perhaps most prominently, the forest outside the village is a crucial setting in which much of the narrative takes place, with the frequent use of long shots highlighting the importance of situating the characters within this.

In targeting the provincial audience, the film not only shares a similar story and a *mise-en-scène* with the 16mm era productions, but even depicts identical scenes. We see the main female character, Pra Preung, bathing in a river wearing a sarong and the comedic buffoons spying on her. This is very similar to the female character Taa Nii in the 16mm era production *Nang Prai Taa Nii* (Nakarin, 1967), in a scene that depicts a man spying upon her while she is bathing wearing a sarong. That this very similar scene should exist in two films that are decades apart illustrates how this significant production targets the rural provincial audience rather than the 'modernity' of American Capitalism and the economic development transforming urban Thailand: bathing in the river is an everyday activity undertaken by village inhabitants, and women wear a sarong to conceal their modesty, a situation ripe for voyeurs to exploit and so a staple source of slapstick comedy (indeed in both of these films decades apart it is used as a source of comedy). Even during the late twentieth-century period of economic growth and the corresponding impact of modernity upon wider social norms, such depictions indicate how little has changed in the everyday reality of the viewers consuming these texts: people still bathe in sarongs in the river, still construct their own wooden houses and still live alongside dense untamed jungle.

Like the 16mm era productions, the supernatural interjects into the diegesis liberally and still does not appear to violate 'Natural Law'. Again this continues to problematise the definition of horror as a genre; *Baan Phii Pop* treats the supernatural as a frightening yet natural element in society, one that occurs automatically and elicits little dispute or protest from characters. For instance, despite the characters' horror and fear at the Pop ghost, they readily accept the existence of this entity. In the opening scene a woman gives birth and a man is immediately told to hide the umbilical cord lest a Pop entity find it and eat it, so it is hardly a major disruption to the natural order when exactly this happens. The ghost is also not used to establish a dilemma or mystery that will drive the narrative, indicating the continued lack of mystique attributed to the supernatural. Visually the Pop ghost is fully revealed in the pre-title opening scene and so there is little process of discovery by either the viewer or the characters, removing suspense as a source of narrative stimulation. When the man who is instructed to hide the newborn's umbilical cord is discovered murdered the next day the cause is immediately apparent, indicating that the presence of the Phii Pop is almost accepted as an element of village life. There is little investigation and even less attempt to explain the presence of the ghost in the village: the old woman is simply targeted and then revealed to be a host for the Pop ghost.

Along with this depiction of the supernatural, these films still retain many of the formal characteristics that can be attributed to the post-war 16mm era audience and its communal viewing context. Despite the economic and social changes of this time, provincial Thailand remained very much a collectivist culture and entertainment products were designed for this social environment. The B-grade productions were shown in Fouquet's second and third class suburban and provincial cinemas as well as the mobile itinerant theatres, all of which continued to engender the communal viewing scenario and the shared pleasure atmosphere in which the 16mm era functioned. The primacy of this audience within Thai film continued even long after the demise of the 16mm era and up into the late 1980s, with filmmakers recognising 'the prevailing wisdom that Thai films needed to cater to the nationwide provincial market' (Ingawanij, 2006: 152). In 1992, *Asian Advertising and Marketing Magazine* mentioned the 'outdoor movies' and 'mobile movies' that toured the provinces outside Bangkok, and in which companies were able to place commercials, giving the example of the Nestle Company that 'achieves brand awareness upcountry by buying commercial time in outdoor movies' (Hamid, 1992: 40–42).[5] Thai film therefore remained within a film form that is outside of the individualised immersion that global models of filmmaking and film theoretical analysis are built upon.

In keeping with the 16mm era productions and highlighting how Thai film adheres to the entertainment products associated with collective societies, the B-grade productions also privilege context and emotional affect rather than individual psychological perception and the associated cognitive affect. Instead of a suspenseful narrative, therefore, this prior-known structure and type of characters continue the 16mm era tendency to engage with emotional affect by placing emphasis upon emotional and visceral 'numbers' as a source of stimulation. For instance, films such as *Jolokay Phii Sing* (Rit Ti Narong, 1993) (which is about a crocodile monster) and *Phii Saat Meng Mum Sao* (Wan Chana, 1990) (about a spider monster) largely consist of numbers connected to their central monsters. Again this results in a film style that still adheres to forms of horror constructed as 'lowbrow', reminiscent of Bourdieu's High Culture/Low Culture divisions and Gunew's identified Eurocentric preference for 'cognition' over that of 'feeling'.

This is evident in *Baan Phii Pop*, in which we see an emphasis upon 'numbers' that do not necessarily contribute towards creating dilemmas or situations that propel the film narratively. At times these are even disconnected from the actual story, and the overarching loose narrative therefore comes second as a source of engagement to the aesthetic of attraction. Similar to the 16mm era productions, the film blends a variety of emotions within a single production, again making it difficult to define a specific horror genre by not emphasising the key emotions (fear and disgust) associated with this genre. This blended narrative is evident in accounts of Thai films from this period: observing the Thai films available to rent in the late 1980s, Hamilton mentions an abundance of 'gangster films, melodramas and ghost stories' (1993: 529) and that 'there was a strong preference, particularly in provincial areas, for Thai movies, closely followed by Chinese costume-history dramas (usually made in Singapore), and Hong Kong gangster movies' (Ibid.: 523). Chaiworaporn also indicates of the second-class suburban/provincial cinemas: 'most movies shown in these venues fall into four genres: ghost stories, slapstick, drama and action, and soft porn' (2001: 156).

For instance, in *Baan Phii Pop*, slapstick comedy is created by the antics of the group of buffoons. These feature prominently throughout the film despite contributing very little to the overarching narrative. This group tends to surface after a narrative event in scenes that most often involve them reacting outlandishly to the situation; for instance, just after Pra Preung visits the old grandmother, they appear out of the background foliage to comment upon the possibility that she is possessed. Likewise, horror numbers are cultivated in the close-ups of the Phii Pop's face licking her lips while she searches for victims, the visual effects of her glowing eyes, her slaughtered victims, the gory moments of her eating entrails and her flying across the screen when chasing the doctors in the forest.

Alongside horror and comedy, romance and melodrama also pepper the narrative, especially in the interactions between the Bangkok doctor Ret and the village girl Pra Preung. A sequence in which they enjoy a boat trip together along the river accompanied by non-diegetic soothing music functions as a romantic number that again contributes little to the story as a whole and outside of these conventions would seem a somewhat surprising addition to a horror film. There are even tinges of soft pornography and eroticism when Pra Preung is bathing and being spied upon by the fools. All of the exploits, such as the buffoonery of the fools, the comedic histrionic encounters between the villagers and the ghost, the disgust from the eating of entrails and the fear elicited by the Pop ghost chasing characters across the screen act as a series of numbers.

Together with an emphasis upon 'numbers' as a means of cultivating wide appeal and emotional affect through spectacle, the character types and stock narratives of the B-grade productions are characteristics that must conform to existing wider systems in order to maintain the social and structural harmony upon which collectivist culture depends. Similar to the 16mm era, films follow a familiar prior-known narrative structure and the characters are yet again 'types' to which the performers conform through their physical appearance and behaviour. In *Baan Phii Pop* this stock narrative includes the handsome male outsider Dr Ret, with all the signifiers of modernity and urban life, arriving into a rural upcountry village and falling for the beautiful traditional poor and chaste maiden Pra Preung. He is also pursued by the less-pure conniving and sexually voracious headman's daughter. Alongside this love triangle is the ghost story of the Phii Pop's possession of the old grandmother and her gory exploits of killing, chasing and eating entrails.

These *Baan Phii Pop* characters are defined largely by their physical attributes and outward exaggerated behaviour, attributes that can be matched to characters from Thai traditional performance. This includes the beautiful good-hearted heroine Pra Preung (the *Nang Ek*), the handsome outsider love-interest doctor Ret (the *Phra Ek*), the jealous scheming 'other woman' Kra Deung (the *Toa Itcha*), the wild-haired, absurdly mismatched clothed comedic buffoons (the *Toa Talok*), the drunken father, the cavalry villagers running around chasing the ghost and the flying screeching ghost herself (the Phii Pop possessed host). Notably, there is no inner psychological depth to these characters: the film is not driven by their personal desires and motivations nor questions constructed by them. They instead fulfill roles and actions that are pre-determined. For instance Pra Preung and Dr Ret must eventually fall in love despite Kra Deung's scheming to keep them apart. Kra Deung herself must be punished, and indeed the film eventually depicts her as the next person possessed by the Phii Pop ghost.

Baan Phii Pop also deploys a film style very similar to that recognised in the 16mm era productions, and one which again points to the continued positioning of the Thai audience as a communal group. Designed specifically for the provincial cinemas rather than the urban multiplexes, the cinematography of *Baan Phii Pop* follows the ethos of an objective display similar to a theatrical scenario and is again opposed to the voyeuristic point-of-view shots associated with the horror genre. Instead of POV shots, the cinematography of *Baan*

Phii Pop favours long shots and takes together with a performance style of exaggerated and histrionic gestures, best illustrated through scenes of the slapstick comedy of the band of buffoons, the grotesque Phii Pop herself and the extreme hyperbolic portrayals of fear from those reacting to her. The Phii Pop possessed grandmother, who sneaks up, jumps and even flies down upon her victims, is rarely given a POV shot and/or depicted through the subjective gaze of another character. When Dr Ret and his sidekick are being chased around the forest by the flying Pop, there is only a split second of a close-up subjective shot when she pounces. Everything else is in long shot. During the chase sequence the camera barely moves; the shot is instead all based around a histrionic performance.

Adding further weight to such analysis, the retention of the 16mm era stylistics at this time is also particularly significant given the increased technical ability of Thai film and the lessening of the financial risk involved in making films. New equipment was now much more readily available and filmmaking was no longer a 'cottage industry' that had to guarantee instant returns (due to the demand during the previously mentioned Hollywood boycott). Smaller and more mobile cameras and 35mm synchronised sound meant that Thai film was able to experiment more and no longer had to exclusively stick to the rigid formula and established conventions of the 16mm era and prior-existing indigenous media.

Arguably, *Baan Phii Pop* was capable of emulating the dominant characteristics of horror, which would have been much more difficult for the earlier 16mm era productions. This suggests that much of this film style was a conscious decision, rather than a necessity brought about by the lack of technology or a need to adhere to indigenous entertainment forms already present (both of which – as I have illustrated – played a part in shaping the 16mm era). The B-grade productions are more technologically inventive than the 16mm era, as filmmaking was now more technologically capable and so could be more inventive in its use of cinematography. In *Baan Phii Pop*, for instance, the camera is far more mobile than in 16mm era productions and can follow actors by panning across the scene to record their movements. There are also more camera set-ups within a scene.[6] The fact that the film does contain *some* subjective shots also indicates that this means of representation *can* be used, indicating that the filmmaker instead deliberately chooses a presentational style similar to that of the 16mm era productions. Also, although there is a crude continuity structure of shot-reverse-shot in the scene from *Baan Phii Pop* (with the opening long shot serving as a crude establishing shot), this scene still contains an overwhelming amount of group shots and objective shots, indicating its adherence to this Thai style of filmmaking. It is significant therefore that such characteristics continued to survive in Thai filmmaking despite the wider changes, becoming cultural preferences rather than contextual necessities.

The Changing Political Categorisation of Thai Horror: A Progressive Depiction

In film style and subject matter, *Baan Phii Pop* and the B-grade productions rejected much of the modernity of American Capitalism depicted in *Tone* and, similar to the 16mm era films, addressed the preferences and concerns of provincial Thailand. In this way the B-grade productions articulate the traumatic experiences of this marginalised audience, mediating the corresponding social upheaval and exploitation of lower-class rural Thailand that followed such post-war development. However, thematically these films possess a very different relationship to wider cultural concerns than that of the reactionary position of the 16mm era. Again, similar to the 16mm era productions, this perspective is best articulated in horror, specifically through the familiar connection between women and the supernatural. While these productions still retain the thematic link between women and the supernatural, the depiction has now evolved[7] to portray women taking legitimate revenge upon men who abused them in life, rather than simply serving their own bloodthirsty interests or lusts.

Repeatedly in the B-grade productions, women who have been ill-treated victims of patriarchal abuse use the supernatural to inflict violence upon those who mistreated them. This is a familiar trope in the horror genre – Carol Clover regards the rape revenge narrative as a classic and staple plot in modern American horror films (Clover, 1993: 115), and together with other theorists regards this recurring motif as a traumatic mediation of an exploitive, abusive and ultimately unaccountable wider social context. Blake also argues that the ghostly Japanese *onryou* figure became prominent as a cinematic discourse in the 1960s as a means of demanding retribution for previous historical crimes against Japan in general and Japanese women, specifically against those who remained unpunished (Blake, 2008: 44). These repulsive, undead female corpses 'return from the dead to demand retribution for the hitherto concealed wounds inflicted on the nation for hitherto unpunished historical crimes' (Ibid.: 44) and become in the process the 'political unconscious' of the 'cultural life of the nation' (Ibid.). As a figure, the vengeful female *onryou* thus served in Japan to undermine the masculine and militaristic *Bushido* code, a purpose also echoed in the 1998 film *Ringu* (Hideo Nakata, 1998), when Blake argues that Sadako, the undead and vengeful victim of male aggression, becomes 'that which will not be eradicated by US colonialism in Japan or the Japanese refusal to acknowledge the sins of its own past' (Ibid.: 54). Transplanted to America in Gore Verbinski's 2002 remake *The Ring* (Hideo Nakata, 1998), the punishing *onryou* figure then also undercuts the validity of the conformist capitalist ideology of American national identity and their supposedly superior cultural status (Ibid.: 63).

The vengeful women emerging in the B-grade productions function as a response to the abuse and mistreatment of Thai women. Such abuse was a key part of the rapid 1980s push towards modernisation, with economist Peter Bell even going as far as to state that 'Thailand's economic miracle has been built largely on the backs of women' (Bell, 1997: 55). The 1980s produced what Bell terms 'the feminisation of production', a process of rapid economic growth and one that rested ultimately 'upon the patriarchal subordination of women in factories, commercial sex work, and unpaid agricultural and household labour' (Ibid.: 56). Throughout the late twentieth century and particularly the early 1990s, the push towards modernisation (in this case a fast-track model of Western style Capitalism) resulted directly in women being exploited along with the rural poor and ethnic minorities, who benefitted the least from this so-called 'miracle' and also suffered the most as a result of its downfall in the 1997 economic crisis.[8]

In Thailand at this time, the supernatural was also a very important cultural means of assimilating the traumatic experiences of social stratification and rapid modernisation into 'an established framework of understanding' (Levi and Rothberg, 2003: 189). The plethora of productions at this time that contained vengeful female spirits who (in common with the earlier 16mm era female spirits) maintained a destructive and dangerous amount of power can be attributed to the growth and prominence of female-run spirit cults. In this period female spirit cults had become an established and legitimate means of negotiating the wider context and experience for disillusioned and marginalised female urban workers. Animist traditions were still prevalent within Thailand, in this period and even in the 1990s the upcountry village continued to be placed in close proximity to the outer edges of karma. However, with the movement of many citizens from rural to urban areas in search of employment, the supernatural changed from a discourse associated with a backwards and superstitious rural viewer to a legitimate means of addressing, incorporating and possibly commenting upon the social experience of urban and rural Thais.

For instance Mary Beth Mills (1995) documents and analyses an outbreak of 'hysteria' in a Northeastern village in 1990 around a spate of supposed attacks by 'maurauding' and 'sexually voracious' widow ghosts who were reported to be attacking sleeping men. This she interprets in part as a traumatic mediation of the villagers' awareness of their own exclusion from new and modern comforts enjoyed by urban and upper-classes, indicating how the supernatural still functions as a vehicle for wider social disillusionment. Likewise, Paritta Kitiarsa (1999) documents the popularity of spirit cults amongst modern urban Thai people over that of the official Buddhist temple order. This continues despite opposition and suspicion from the dominant state and Buddhist order towards these female leaders, who are outside of state control but nevertheless invited to participate in and comment upon society due to their importance and high standing to ordinary people (Ibid.: 2).[9] While Paritta Kitiarsa gives the familiar reason behind the domination of popular and supernatural social elements by women as one connected to the exclusion of the feminine from state and Buddhist discourses due to their inferior status, the dissatisfaction of ordinary Thais with the dominant order also certainly increased their popularity. This unofficial order had begun to appeal to the stressed and overworked urban population, for whom the dominant order and its exploitative economy no longer held answers.

Echoing this use, films depicting ghostly women as vengeful and righteous can be understood as a progressive response to the exploitation of women and the lower-classes throughout the post-war economic boom. This occurs in productions such as *Phii Sam Oy* (Nai Gaay, 1990) (a title that translates roughly as 'Sympathy Ghost'), which tells the story of a young *sam lor* driver, Nat Ti, who lives separately with two young women: first with Ja rit yaa, and after that, with Jit Taa. Upon discovering this betrayal Ja rit yaa commits suicide, her spirit then returning and acting violently, killing many shamans who attempt to remove her. Similarly *Phuu Ti Sa Ney Haa* (Supasith, 1987) tells the story of a young woman returning as a ghost to take revenge upon the three men who killed her.[10] Many of these productions also involve characters moving from rural to urban areas to try and make better lives for themselves and their families, moves which inevitably lead them into prostitution and tragedy, indicating how these lower-class women are not only victims but also subject to a traumatic process of cultural dislocation and isolation.

Such depictions are in opposition to the 16mm era productions' conservative and reactionary depiction that punishes women for possessing such a means of autonomy. As noted by Wood (2004) in his exploration of various American horror cycles, the 'political categorization' of Thai horror films has now 'evolved', adopting a very different view of this new but still avowedly patriarchal social context and ideology. Rather than working through patriarchal horrors about female empowerment and liberation at a time of instability (as did the 16mm era films), the B-grade productions engage with the trauma of exploitation and voice encoded demands for social justice in the face of an unjust system that specifically mistreats women. Horror is once more the genre through which this traumatic upheaval can be acknowledged, as the female *Phii* avenge themselves, in effect, on the negative aspects of the impact of capitalist forces upon rural provincial Thailand during the economic growth of the 1970s, 1980s and early 1990s, and specifically the injustice and exploitation of female workers during the 1980s economic boom. They represent, I argue, the unacknowledged and unrepresented trauma inherent in such mistreatment.

While the 16mm era productions demonise the feminine through their supernatural connection (depicting them as screeching ghosts, rotten corpses and bloodied repulsive monsters), and fear this power attributed to them in a kind of patriarchal warning against uncontrolled femininity, many of the later B-grade productions seem to attribute not only more sympathy to the women's plight, but also view these actions as justifiable in the face of exploitation by unjust men. Horror had now become a vehicle for anger at the lack of social rewards and the continual denial of lower-class marginalised groups who were forced outside of the sphere of urban affluence they had worked to create. The supernatural is still a source of empowerment for lower-class provincial women, yet one that is now treated as legitimate and righteous. In the 16mm era, traditional family values were being reaffirmed through demonising independently mobile and actively desiring women, who then functioned as a vehicle through which these repressed desires and behaviours could be deposited and destroyed in order to keep alienated labour and the patriarchal family safe. However, the women of the B-grade productions now appear to function as a warning to society that there are dangerous consequences to this mistreatment and abuse: these barbarian 'others from within' are no longer irrational and Thai society is now a corrupt institution associated with oppression and unjust treatment (Winichakul, 2000). Rather than a means to promote patriarchal structures of control at a time when the construction of gender roles is changing within society, this suggests more a need for a just treatment of this exploited and vulnerable sex.

In *Baan Phii Pop* specifically, the narrative of an educated urbanised outsider coming into a village and falling in love could be seen as a patriarchal fantasy of 'rescuing' provincial women. It also continues the association of modernity and mobility with masculinity and a chaste homeliness with femininity, so mediating wider changes by potentially reaffirming traditional constructions of gender, similar to the 16mm era productions. Yet in a reversal of the reactionary position of the 16mm era productions, the film rejects the modernity of the male doctor, instead advocating for this otherwise marginalised female and provincial agency. The supernatural is much more powerful than the technology of the urbanites, and the villagers must save and educate these outsiders. The uncanny forest in which the Pop ghost flies through the air and chases the doctors acts as a powerful antithesis to the modern domain of Bangkok and Dr Ret, while it is the villagers who understand the correct means to deal with this very legitimate supernatural threat. Dr Ret, the urban Bangkokian outsider, finds the existence of the Phii Pop very difficult to understand and even tries to stop the shaman's exorcism. This ignorant interference in village life prevents the *mor phii* (spirit doctor) from exorcising the Pop ghost from the old grandmother, and this misunderstanding causes both the later killing of the *mor phii* by the Phii Pop and the continued existence of this threat in the village. It is ultimately the rural village girl Pra Preung who must rescue the supposedly educated and 'superior' doctors from the ghost.

Conclusion

This chapter has tracked the continued existence of the formal characteristics identified in Chapter 1, assessing the extent to which these are still visible in a context that has progressed in line with Thai social developments, technological and industrial changes as well as global film influences. Ultimately, apart from advances in film quality (most notably the addition of synchronised sound) and an increased viewership amongst urban audiences (increased by immigrant workers from the provinces), this chapter has indicated that there is little formal means to distinguish between the 16mm era productions and later productions of Thai cinema. We see the 16mm era characteristics surfacing in productions such as *Tone* and those of Ratana Pestonji, all of which are differentiated from this earlier period in terms of both audiences, technology and wider contextual engagement. Likewise, in the B-grade productions this connection is evident in narrative structure, the privileging of emotional affect, the blending of genres and the corresponding cinematography, all of which caters for a collective society and engenders a communal environment of shared pleasure. Again, as in the 16mm era productions, such characteristics remove many of the recognisable traits associated with this genre, and instead adhere to the 'lowbrow' models identified in the previous chapter. This also continues to problematise horror as a distinguishable category in Thai filmmaking, an issue which, as the next chapter will indicate, bleeds through to the contemporary industry.

The chapter then also indicated how horror continues to mediate wider discourses for viewers, in particular the wider context of social trauma and upheaval experienced in provincial Thailand, particularly the exploitation of lower-class women. The depiction of the supernatural had now changed thematically to become a progressive acknowledgement of such treatment, a representation that follows the wider use of the supernatural as a practical means of expression for otherwise marginalised voices. The next chapter will now explore the birth of the contemporary industry and the way in which these big-budget productions continue this hybrid model of film style along with exploring the political categorisation of these films in terms of social engagement and position.

Notes

1. Sarit came to power in 1959 through a rigged election and then a military coup. He ruled until his death in 1963 and was both immensely wealthy and extremely corrupt, banning any dissent. After his death, power transferred to his generals and the repressive undemocratic regime continued until 1973 when an uprising forced democracy to be restored.
2. Rather than concentrating upon the apprehension and disapproval from within Thailand towards the uninhibited cooperation with US forces and the influx of such a large amount of American soldiers into Thailand.

3. Significantly, and similarly to Pestonji's body of films, the relatively small 'social problem' movement was also noted by the intelligentsia for its contrast to characteristically Thai popular entertainment productions, therefore keeping alive the two-tiered audience in Thailand and contributing towards the cultivation of a disdainful attitude towards the lower-class characteristically Thai films.
4. Uabumrungjit labels *Black Silk* as 'the film that pulled Thai film up to an international level in terms of both photography technique and substance' (2003a: 45). This is due to its location shooting and first ever use of Cinemascope to make widescreen possible.
5. As regards the popularity of the vast number of 'open-air screens', the magazine also gives an indication of their importance to the cinema and advertising business when stating that 'The medium has proven to be an effective tool in product distribution and promotions in rural areas' (Hamid, 1992: 42). The notability of this audience and its viewing method to multinational companies as a means of advertising indicates both how widespread and how significant a presence it was towards communicating with the outer provinces. It is significant that this is the most noted method for reaching the outer audience – the article mentions many methods of advertising, but this is the only one linked specifically to the 'upcountry'.
6. Notably, however, there is virtually no tracking, indicating that the movement of the actual camera apparatus was still beyond the technical capabilities of the filmmaker's equipment, or was perhaps too difficult in such an environment.
7. The connection between the supernatural and the feminine still exists in these later productions, indicating that for all the progressive gender discourse they now represent, the feminine is still considered spiritually weak and incomplete and deemed susceptible to supernatural influences in line with a patriarchal Thai system. The production *Baan Phii Pop*, for instance, invokes a connection not only between the old grandmother who is possessed by the Pop ghost, but also the heroine Pra-Preung's ability to save the urban dwelling hero Dr Ret from the ghost and the bad-girl Kra-Deung's later possession.
8. This later effect will be explored in the next chapter's analysis of the post-97 New Thai industry.
9. The power of this subaltern status inevitably attracts a negative portrayal: 'In Thailand, the urban spirit-medium cult is portrayed as an "outlawed religion" by official authorities and the Sangha order. It is also labeled as an anti-Buddhist cult, a black magic movement. Or even a criminal gang under a religious cover' (Kitiarsa, 1989: 1).
10. These revenge narratives are not exclusively limited to female characters however: *Phii-Taa-Bo*, in 1981, is centred around the ghost of a man whose eyes have been removed by a corrupt doctor, trying to steal them back from beyond the grave. Again similar to other horror films from this time, the film implies both the corruption of officials and the importance of respecting the dead and the spirit world.

3. NEW THAI CINEMA AND *NANG NAK*
Heritage Horror and Economic Crisis

As the third analytical chapter in this volume, Chapter 3 moves into the primary topic of study: the contemporary Thai film industry. Building upon the previous analysis, this chapter first charts the growth of the teen industry of the 1980s and 1990s, demonstrating the industrial and stylistic significance of this period and its new urban teen audience. Moving onto the creation of the big budget and internationally savvy New Thai industry, the chapter then indicates how Heritage became a key form of representation within this industry. The chapter interprets such a motif as part of a conservative response to the wider context of economic crisis, exploring the key internal Thai discourse of Localism as part of removing blame from societal elites' responsibility for this wider devastation.

As a case study, this chapter examines the seminal Heritage horror production *Nang Nak* (Nonzee Nimibutr, 1999). While this film may seem similar to earlier decades of Thai horror (given its setting in provincial Thailand and age-old story), analysis indicates that *Nang Nak* actually represents a new socially reactionary form of horror. Such a model promoted social conformity during a period of instability, negotiating a traumatic wider context through the nostalgic evocation of an idyllic past. Such a depiction seeks to pacify those who suffered the most in this economic downturn, namely provincial Thai citizens and women. The film encourages acceptance of the status quo and promotes a retrograde gender ideology while simultaneously affirming the inferiority of such citizens in the contemporary age.

However, the chapter then demonstrates how despite such ideological inclination, *Nang Nak* retains characteristics from earlier eras of Thai film that now become indicative of the continuing divided nature of Thai society. The chapter demonstrates how characteristics such as the communal viewing scenario and the blended visceral causal narrative structure of the post-war era continued to permeate filmmaking and influence the form of New Thai horror. Such punctuations disrupt the narrative structure of Thai film and potentially undercut this nationalistic portrayal, operating as a reminder of the social and cultural diversity (and inequality) within Thailand. Finally, the chapter illustrates how *Nang Nak* still depicts the supernatural as a natural part of society and not a violation of 'natural law', attributing this continuing construction to the resurgence of the supernatural and spirit cults as a recognised by-product of 1990s modernity.

The Teen Cycle

The New Thai industry and its Heritage productions emerged directly after a much-derided yet crucial period of Thai filmmaking that Ingawanij refers to as the 'Thai teen movie cycle' (Ingawanij, 2006). This short but highly significant era was the last major stage of evolution before the creation of the New Thai industry. These productions are separate from the New Thai industry, yet the audience, subject matter and political categorisation of the later big-budget New Thai productions are a direct outcome of the industrial and social changes that stem from this earlier cycle.

Notably, the teen cycle was designed for a different audience to that of the earlier decades of Thai film. In 1985 the newly founded Tai Entertainment Production Company recognised the merits of directly targeting the new generation of urban teenage audiences and the potential of this market. Its creator Visute Poolvoralaks was attached by family to the exhibition industry and so was able to access the urban market for this filmmaking business venture. The success of their first pioneering production *Suam Noi Noikalon Mak Noi* (Wataleela and Jitnukul, 1985) pointed to the existence of a stable Bangkokian-based teen audience for filmmakers and distributors (Ingawanij, 2006), who subsequently began to target this profitable niche audience rather than the upcountry public in general (Chaiworaporn 2001: 154). The first run urban market proved much more profitable than the outer provinces and suburbs, and so after recognising the potential of this specific spectator group 'Tai entertainment revolutionised theatre standards, moving from old stand-alone cinemas and run-down mini-theatres, to the deluxe culture of multiplex cinemas located in shopping complexes' (Chaiworaporn, 2001: 154). The urban cinemas in which the contemporary industry was to thrive were therefore born.

In subject matter and style, these productions responded to the lived environment and experiences of this new audience of urban teens. Thailand in the 1980s was entering the most prosperous final stage of over three decades of economic growth that had utterly transformed the country and increased access to global texts, products and commodities. The audience for the teen productions was mainly under seventeen and had been the first generation in Thailand to grow up amidst the continued presence of the American popular culture that had been seen as so foreign, exciting and modern in *Tone* (Piak Poster, 1970). These urban-situated children of the 1960s and 1970s were born into and so defined themselves by such a system.

Productions therefore tended to address 'teen or classroom drama, comedy and romance' (Chaiworaporn, 2001: 155), and stories mostly follow a group of teenagers in Bangkok who are friends or housemates. For instance, the *Boonchu* series which ran from 1988 until 1995 (with a remake in 2008) follows a rural boy moving to study in Bangkok. It depicts his interactions with his comedic circle of friends, his preparing for university exams, his university life and eventually starting his working life. This was an unprecedented success, to the extent that it was even remade in the contemporary industry. Similar to *Boonchu*, the narratives of *Chalui* (Adirek, 1988) and *Suam Noi Noikalon Mak Noi* follow 'graduates, (mostly) young men, setting out to find their true vocations in the real world' (Ingawanij, 2006: 153), much of which tend to be associated with rock stardom (Ibid.: 153). Indeed, many of the adolescent characters in these films were played by recognisable teen popstars, such as Rewat Phutthinan in *Phuan/Friends* (Apitchaat Pothipiroj, 1986), Saharat Sangkapreecha in *A Couple in Two Worlds/Khu Thae Song Lok* (Udom Udomroj, 1994) and Champagne X and Tata Young in *Red Bike Story/ Chakkrayan Si Daeng* (Euthana Mukdasanit, 1997).

The film style of these productions is again reminiscent of the 'numbers' and excessive presentational style identified throughout Thai film history. Yet the teen productions also engaged largely with a *mise-en-scène* and subject matter drawn from Hollywood films and American music videos, appropriating numbers and stylistics from a global vernacular of popular teen culture that were relevant to this young urban Thai audience. The parodies, songs and comedic moments become a series of 'numbers' that 'serve as a generic frame supporting the real attraction of the music video intervals' (Ingawanij, 2006: 159). The fast paced and frantic nonsensical nature of the teen films bespeaks the final insertion of Thailand into a global 'aesthetic economy' (Ingawanij, 2006: 155) though the allusion to and parodying of 'an array of global filmic and pop cultural references' (Ibid.: 153) interspersed into a narrative of teenage life. Films such as *Chalui* and *Rorng Ta Lap Phlap* (Prachya Pinkaew, 1992) revel in their display as a copy and parody of teenage icons such as Michael Jackson, Marty McFly and a range of American genre film references. Later films such as *Loke Thang Bai Hai Nai khon diaw/Romantic Blues* (Rashane Limtrakul, 1995) also place greater emphasis upon the incorporations of the music video and popstar performers, becoming a vehicle geared to 'maximise the consumption of the multimedia pop-film product' (Ingawanij, 2006: 161). This 'stylistic borrowing' and 'intertextual allusion' relies upon a 'knowingness' of its specific viewers to 'get' 'an international array of generic pop cultural references' (Ibid.: 155) which spoke to Thai teenagers as a specific group, singling out their lived experiences specifically. Through such pop-culture references, music videos, young stars and their friendships and aspirations, the films of the teen cycle respond directly to the experiences of urban teen youth in the 1980s and early 1990s.

Most tellingly, this 'imitative' quality resulted in a condescending denigration of this period and its productions (Ingawanij, 2006), resulting in a paternalistic dismissal of productions that were nevertheless very successful within a particular group of viewers. Despite its significance in the development of Thai film, the teen era remains critically marginalised and has been largely dismissed by both Thai and non-Thai historians and academics as a 'culturally impoverished period in Thai film history' (Ingawanij, 2006: 1). The practice of viewing Thai film as an inferior model of cinema by those outside of its targeted audience therefore continued, and was once again based upon constructing Thai films as crude productions that appealed to an unsophisticated marginalised audience.

New Thai Heritage Cinema

In the late 1990s, Thai cinema then built upon the establishment of this network of urban cinemas and finally became a 'respectable' addition to metropolitan life, with the arrival of the lavish, big-budget productions that Chaiworaporn calls 'New Thai Cinema'. The industry was able to grow through the recognition of a new profitable urban audience and the corresponding emerging network of cinemas launched by the teen cycle. The return of many future key directors from film schools abroad also ensured that there was a local talent pool familiar with the conventions of international filmmaking, ensuring a new level of international festival success and critical respect. Then, the wider-than-expected appeal of the teen-orientated 1950s-set action film *2499 Antapan Krong Muang/Daeng Birley and the Young Gangsters* (Nonzee Nimibutr, 1997) demonstrated that an older urban viewer was now both accessible and economically viable as a target audience. *Daeng Birley* told the story of a real-life young gangster (who was killed at the time) and depicted teenagers and teen life in the 1950s. This film also positioned itself as both an action number and a nostalgic diversion into living memory (Ingawanij, 2006), and the production's success indicated that engaging in nostalgia had a particular cultural resonance at this moment.

Indeed, after *Daeng Birley*, New Thai Cinema continued to construct depictions that placed emphasis upon nostalgia for an idyllic previous era and the representation of an authentic Thai-ness within this (Chaiworaporn, 2002; Ingawanij, 2006; Seveon, 2006[1]). This phenomenon lasted until around the mid-2000s and was a defining attribute of this new industry. Ingawanij (2006) refers to this corpus as 'Heritage films', and this style forged a definite turning point in the development of Thai cinema by demonstrating the success of deploying such a depiction at this time. Along with *Nang Nak*, films such as *Bang Rajan* (Thanit Jitnukul, 2000), *Khang Lang Phap/Behind the Painting* (Cherd Songsri, 2001), *Hom Rong/The Overture* (Ittisoontorn Vichailak, 2004), *Jan Dara* (Nonzee Nimibutr, 2001), *Fan Chan/My Girl* (Vitcha Gojiew et al., 2003) and *Suriyothai* (Chatrichalerm Yukol, 2001, the highest grossing Thai film for at least another decade) all fall into this category. These productions depict a very broad range of Thai history from traditional stories (*Nang Nak*), key historical battles (*Bang Rajan*) and legendary figures (*Suriyothai*), to a remake of the classic 1930s love story *Behind the Painting* and *Fan Chan*'s simple coming-of-age tale set in rural 1970s Thailand.

This corpus of Heritage films was crucial to solidifying a very different industry to that of decades past and was part of targeting a new viewer as well as responding to a very different set of economic circumstances. As a discourse and style, Heritage is not a critical examination or political analysis of the past, but rather should be understood as an inaccurate distortion and restructuring of historical actuality to suit the present point in time. In his famous examination of English Heritage films, Andrew Higson defines Heritage as a selective preoccupation with the past, being what a particular individual or group takes from this in order to define itself in the present. This gives a particular group an identity, being what '*we*' are happy to regard as '*our*' heritage, so explaining who we are through reference to the past (2003: 50).

The deployment of Heritage discourses in film is interpreted as a cinematic response to social upheaval as this depiction promotes a unifying and nationalistic construction of the nation. As Higson states:

> When heritage culture is mobilised on a national scale ('our shared national heritage'), it is in this spatio-temporal grid that 'the nation' emerges as a unique, organic, meaningful community (Ibid.).

This 'meaningful' construction can be seen in British Heritage films and culture of the 1980s and 1990s. This phenomenon was a response to the decline in British economic stability, global influence and mass unemployment during the Thatcherite 1980s. The retreat into and fascination with the historical past, the idyllic rural and the 'simpler times' operated as 'a form of retreat from the present, providing satisfactions which the present does not provide or compensations for what it lacks' (Hill, 1999: 74). Such a response compensates for the destabilisation of society during traumatic contexts of uncertainty and anxiety. Yet such a 'retreat from the present' becomes a decidedly reactionary move as this 'nostalgic and escapist flight' (Higson, 2003: 51) notably ignores and does not address the causes behind the corresponding social upheaval.

This reactionary construction of a nationalistic 'identity' and a retreat from the present was particularly relevant to the Thai nation in the late 1990s. In July 1997, Thailand's four decades of unprecedented post-war growth, and the boom experienced specifically between 1987 and 1997, collapsed in what has come to be known as the Asian Financial Crisis. When jittery foreign investors began to pull money out of the country, the resulting effects triggered a devastating economic crisis, in which companies and personal fortunes disappeared overnight, children were pulled from university, unemployment soared and half-built skyscrapers stood abandoned. The Thai stock market dropped by as much as 75 per cent, shattering the consumers' materialistic dream as 'Thailand became entrapped in its own desire to look like a fully developed country' (Corera, 1997). The promises of freedom and prosperity through economic growth and capitalist expansion that were earlier championed in productions such as *Tone* had now come crashing down. The push towards modernisation, rapid economic growth, and the adoption of the neo-liberal models designed to transform Thailand into the next Hong Kong or Singapore had fallen through, and so had the brimming confidence in this future prosperity, in particular that of 'national pride' (Hewison, 1999: 8).

Thai elites responded to this context of devastating economic collapse by promoting nostalgia for a purer and simpler time, one encapsulated within the image of the pre-modern impoverished hardworking and sacrificing peasant. A new nationalistic discourse was taken up based upon the concept of 'Localism', a belief in self-reliance that was already in existence among those who had been isolated from the economic boom (mostly impoverished rural rice farmers) (Phonpaichit, 2001: 162). Localism functioned as a means to deflect attention from the elites and their business interests that had ultimately caused such devastation and also fostered a degree of nationalistic social control over a disillusioned and suffering population. After the crisis of 1997 it was no longer profitable for the state to define Thailand and Thai-ness in terms of a global consciousness of progression and modernisation. Localism instead stressed the values of community, locality, self-reliance and indigenous culture, all of which were to be found in the model of the rural village and the hardworking peasant. This movement 'back-to-basics' involved a retreat inwards to traditional Thai values when the global scheme had seemed to fail. As Hewison states: 'Globalisation, consumerism and westernisation are identified as the new colonialism. All threaten Thai values' (Hewison, 1999: 11).

Discourses instead began to focus on Thai society internally, representing Thai culture through the creation of internal myths and traditions focused upon the agricultural sector which was 'seen as providing the cultural foundations of Thai society' (Ibid.). In order to construct its 'imagined community' (Higson, 2000: 64), Thailand turned inwards, and in particular towards an idyllic version of the self-sufficient rural poor. As the previous ideological drive towards modernisation and a consumerist lifestyle was no longer socially, culturally or economically appropriate, an emphasis upon community and self-sufficiency took its place, one envisioned through an idyllic rural scenario. This 'back to basics' return placed an emphasis upon rural simplicity, the family unit and the hardworking peasant, all of which can be located in a pre-modern historical setting before contact with European imperialism of the nineteenth century and so before the forces blamed for the contemporary economic devastation. The hardworking rural peasant became the ultimate symbol of individual freedom and integrity championed against the depersonalised ruthless policies of international economics and globalisation;

> The suggestion is that a self sufficient nation does not need the outside world and may choose its links rather than be forced into international markets and trade. Self sufficiency also builds self-reliance, for it constructs strong communities with the confidence to resist external pressures. (Hewison, 1999: 9)

This philosophy was applied to the nation as a whole, as Hewison understands, 'solutions to the country's economic problems were to be found in a return to community based agriculture' (Ibid.). King Bhumibol himself even legitimated this new ideology at an official level in his Birthday Speech of December 1997, affirming: 'we need to move backwards in order to move forwards' (Phongpaichit, 2001: 161).

Despite its supposed championing of the neglected rural poor and their unfair treatment under the previous capitalist expansion, Kevin Hewison (1999) criticises the Localist response as a profoundly conservative and reactionary discourse that does not tackle the unfair and growing gap between rich and poor in Thailand. While Hewison notes its opposition towards the damaging neo-liberal policies that had caused such a disaster from those who advocated this discourse of self-sufficiency (who at first included NGOs, Buddhist monks, 'workers opposing privatisation' and Hewison himself), it is ultimately, he understands, a conservative discourse that 'does not provide the robust alternative analysis required of a critique of neo-liberal globalisation' (1999: 11). Mirroring the reactionary nature of Heritage as a phenomenon, Hewison regards Localism as 'negative, reactionary, and a dangerous mix of populism and nationalism' (Ibid.). The idealisation of the rural scenario simultaneously ignores and denies the exploitive nature of conservative and patriarchal hierarchies. This feeds into a profoundly right-wing discourse of 'nationalism and chauvinism' (Ibid.: 12), so neglecting to challenge existing hierarchical systems of exploitation that have been partly responsible for the crisis in the first place.

An examination of this term as applied to film therefore begins to highlight the generally reactionary political categorisation of a body of films that were initially so important to establishing Thai film as a viable urban-based and internationally-savvy industry. Instead, film became a means through which to transmit a model of conformity to Thai viewers that assists in upholding the inequality responsible for economic collapse in the first place.

The New Thai Heritage productions specifically adhere to this reactionary localist discourse by restructuring the past to promote a nationalistic vision of conformity and identity at a time of social crisis. Localism is evident in the *mise-en-scène*, stories and themes of the New Thai Heritage films. Many productions consist of traditional stories or reference true people and events interspersed with intertextual references specific to Thai culture, history and people as a means to reinforce an identity based upon nationalism. Each also takes place in a setting that is able to foreground landscape, settings, costumes and props of historical Thailand, presenting an idyllic vision of the nation and the unique traits of Thai-ness.

For example, *Suriyothai* places an emphasis upon (perceived) historical verisimilitude and the authenticity of Thai-ness through the portrayal of luscious, aristocratic settings and figures. Indeed, due to its royal connections, shooting was permitted in official historical locations which would otherwise have been extremely difficult to access. The tale of the sixteenth-century queen who sacrifices herself in battle to save her husband and country was the grandest and costliest Thai film ever made and continues to be regarded as one of the highest grossing Thai films of all time.[2] Research conducted by Knee and Chaiworaporn even illustrates how the visual presentation of this fantasy life history (which has been taken up as a part of Thai culture so strongly, yet about which little empirical evidence actually exists) was a significant factor in the film's appeal for many viewers (Chaiworaporn and Knee, 2006).

Likewise, films such as *Fan Chan* offer a comforting picture of belonging and identity in the construction of an idyllic rural 1970s childhood enjoyed by Jeab, who is the young son of the local barber. This small family-run business and its friendly low-key competition with another village barber shop are worlds away from the ruthless Capitalism of the 1980s boom. The friendship between the son and daughter of the opposing barbers feeds into the construction of a shared experience of growing up in 1970s rural Thailand, as does the deployment of small-town village life with its children on bicycles riding through gentle country roads and deserted rice-paddies.

As in *Suriyothai*, *Bang Rajan* also recreates a shared historical experience, one achieved through the use of historical myths and characters and the display of the corresponding *mise-en-scène*. The film depicts a group of rural villagers attempting to defend their village against Burmese invaders in a depiction of the eighteenth-century invasion that eventually resulted in the siege and then ruin of Ayutthaya (then the capital of Thailand). Notably, the villagers are abandoned by the rulers of the city and left to fend for themselves with little defence against the Burmese army, and are eventually all massacred. However, the film depicts this as a necessary and heroic sacrifice, noting how the various characters refuse to leave their posts and flee, seeing their actions as vital to the defence and future survival of Thailand, a notion they place above all others in importance, including their own lives.

A comparable ideological agenda can be seen at work in *Behind the Painting*. This is the adaptation of a famous Thai novel that depicts an older aristocratic woman falling in love with a young male student. The Marxist sympathies of the original novel (which was written by a left-wing intellectual who was later imprisoned by the post-war military regime for his radical beliefs and can be interpreted as representing the necessary death of the aristocracy in favour of a new and radical age) are notably forgotten in this adaptation (Siburapha, 1990). The film instead focuses upon the sacrifices made by the angelic female character in order to comply with family needs and notions of tradition.

Nang Nak and New Thai Heritage Horror

This reactionary status and its rejection of the lower-class perspective is evident in a close examination of *Nang Nak*, one of the most notable and successful Heritage films of New Thai cinema. A seminal horror production, the film was a contemporary remake of the traditional ghost story previously analysed in Chapter 1 in its 1959 incarnation *Mae Nak Prakanong* (Rangsir Tasanapayak, 1959). Together with *Daeng Birley*, *Nang Nak* was also one of the first New Thai films to achieve widespread international acclaim, winning twelve awards at a variety of international festivals,[3] and was a founding production in this cycle of Heritage films.

The film tells the well-known traditional Thai story of Nak, a young pregnant peasant woman devoted to her husband Mak. This version begins when Mak is called up to fight in a war and so is forced to leave his wife Nak, who then dies during her husband's absence in a difficult and graphically depicted childbirth. However, Nak's love for her husband is so strong that when Mak returns, Nak refuses to pass on to the afterlife. Instead Nak remains as a ghost bringing up her ghost baby, deceiving Mak as to her true nature. Finally, after her tormenting of the villagers who try to warn Mak about his wife, Mak discovers the truth and flees. A confrontation ensues in which the villagers burn down Nak's house and a shaman digs up her corpse to perform a violent exorcism. Finally, the high monk convinces the spirit of Nak to leave her worldly life. She agrees, and as penance for her behaviour, must go to serve the monk. The couple then say a tearful last farewell in an extended scene before they are parted forever.

A familiar story that has been remade throughout Thai film history, this key work of Heritage horror and the New Thai industry is certainly similar to earlier depictions in that it locates events within a provincial setting and the rural scenario of the *chaobannok*. Certainly, heritage films often did turn to depicting poorer rural Thailand and the agricultural sector. As the previous chapter indicated, this section of Thai society was largely ignored during the nation's push towards modernisation, and it was horror productions that had articulated and negotiated the traumatic (and inequitable) socio-cultural marginalisation of lower-class provincial Thailand.

However, close examination of *Nang Nak* reveals a very different style of horror film to that of previous decades, with a different political relationship to wider society. Although Heritage productions do appear to champion the lower-class scenario, this is a mythic idealised world of self-sufficiency and one that must be preserved rather than challenged. In Heritage films, marginalised rural Thais and their situation are positioned as the 'real foundations of its [Thailand's] society, economy, and culture' (Hewison, 1999: 9). As such, this ideology seeks to preserve rather than challenge an unequal and unfair situation. In horror films, this means that the repressed forces that return to disrupt and challenge the unfair status quo are dismissed as illegitimate and are pacified.

While earlier horror cinema therefore offered a means for viewers to negotiate a radically changing environment, articulating social injustice and the abuse of marginalised citizens at the hands of economic development, this is not a part of the Heritage productions. These films do not address the gripes and injustices of living in such a socially and economically unequal nation, but in fact actually erase these problems and instead propagate pacification, acceptance and conformity. Rather than challenging the status quo, Heritage champions self-sacrifice as a means to uphold the very system that has propagated inequality and suffering. Such a depiction therefore neglects the marginalised perspectives addressed in the 16mm era, the B-grade productions and, later on, the teen movie cycle. Films are not concerned with representing such a community to itself, but instead appropriate this depiction to affirm the inferiority of this scenario in the contemporary age.

The 1999 incarnation of Nak follows such an ideology. *Nang Nak* rejects the anger from marginalised individuals and social groups articulated by earlier incarnations of horror. Instead this film follows the New Thai Heritage productions and the localist discourses promoted by elites. Rather than a means to negotiate the trauma of a rapidly changing wider context for those living through this upheaval, the film affirms the need to passively accept the status quo. The story of *Nang Nak* promotes obedience to a natural, social and religious order that may not necessarily lead to personal happiness but represents a greater good. The narrative is one of personal sacrifice, suggesting that individuals must give up their desires and even their lives in order to maintain and defend the status quo of historical Thailand in all its glory.

The film constructs its *chaobannok* characters and the rural context as far away from the urban centre of modernity and instead part of the dangerous, archaic and pre-modern animist spirit world that must be forcibly pacified and controlled. Protagonists are deep in provincial pre-modern nineteenth-century rural Thailand (though the actual date and era is not explicitly stated) at the mercy of unaccountable forces beyond their control. This includes the hardships of agricultural work and difficult living conditions, including depicting a pregnant Nak struggling to plough rice fields while husband Mak endures the horrors of combat on the battlefield as a soldier. Such deprivations are portrayed as part of a necessary submission for rural Thai people, who must suffer in order to preserve the status quo.

Yet while life is depicted as difficult, the historical setting adheres to the ideology of Localism and Heritage culture as an idealised pre-modern rural status quo. The purity of Thai-ness is very much embodied in the innocent and simple rural-situated relationship of Mak and Nak. This tranquillity must then be willingly sacrificed in order to maintain the natural order of life and death; Nak must give up her pursuit of Mak and their life together by accepting her unfair death. The film sympathises with Nak's desire, showing her longing for the idyllic previous world she was happy in before uncontrollable outside forces cruelly shattered and destroyed her union with Mak. However, this idealised rural situation must be preserved and upheld through sacrifice. Indeed, if the film has a moral message, then this is one of acceptance regarding situations beyond the individual's control and adherence to a dominant order.

The depiction of Nak as submissive and sacrificial also reflects the conservative remodelling of female historical figures throughout Southeast Asia. Depictions of semi-mythical historical female figures from the pre-modern (and pre-patriarchal) past that could potentially challenge patriarchal notions of female domesticity were often reconstituted to demonstrate that women were capable of great sacrifice in service of the nation and its status quo (Reid, 2014: 9). This reflects both the continuing patriarchal nature of modern Thailand as well as resistance to the general characterisation of female emancipation as one achieved through Western (coloniser) notions of 'modern' freedom (often received through representations such as Hollywood films). Such a depiction was also often favoured by women's movements across the region, which tended to ally themselves with nationalist trends. The central figures in films such as *Suriyothai* and *Behind the Painting* certainly exemplify the nationalist sacrificial narrative and form a key part of the New Thai industry and its corpus of Heritage productions. The extreme depiction of the pacification of Nak and the character's corresponding sacrifice in *Nang Nak* is also a strong case in point and should be added to this list.

Within the moral sacrifice of *Nang Nak* lies a regressive nationalist ideology, itself in service to wider economic interests. Removing any responsibility from Thai elites for the difficult wider context, the film instead implies that this status quo is both desirable and should be achieved and maintained through great personal cost and suffering from the individual. This can be interpreted as an allegory of the forces that engulfed the defenceless Thai citizen in the late 1990s after the economic crash encroached upon and destroyed the affluent progression they had been promised. As with the impoverished victims of the economic crisis Nak's treatment is extremely unfair, and her refusal to bow to the many laws that dictate she must move on from her husband is impressive. Yet for all the sympathy invoked towards Nak's unfair position, the film clearly advocates the pacification of her impressive fighting spirit and the acceptance of the outside forces that she as an individual cannot control. This order is the natural circle of life and death, one enforced by the Buddhist monks who first try to uphold it by destroying Nak, eventually succeeding through logical persuasion.

Instead of championing Nak's personal quest for unity with her family, the film instead concentrates upon her final submission to this 'natural' order, ending with her eventual acceptance of her new situation when she is made to relinquish her own desire for Mak and her baby by the high monk. This is portrayed very effectively in the drawn-out final scene, in which a submissive and sobbing Nak sits low in her grave, accepting that she cannot continue to exist in the situation she desires. As Nak sits crying the message is clear: her idyllic previous life with its rural paradise and true love is now over, and despite the mourning involved this transition must be accepted and not challenged. The contrast between this huddled and isolated figure framed in a high-angle shot, and the previous omnipotent supernatural all-powerful figure earlier destroying and towering above the group of village men who tried to remove her by burning her house, could not be starker. While Nak's desire to preserve her family unit may be an extremely sympathetic one, this merely exemplifies the degree of personal sacrifice required by the masses of Thailand in such despairing and unfair circumstances. If it is possible to read her situation as allegorical and articulating the plight of late 1990s Thai people, then this is one that promotes conformity to the elite status quo and discourages personal expression.

The Connection Between the Female and the Supernatural

Similar to previous decades of horror films, the major themes and the storyline of this Heritage horror production also continue to associate the supernatural with independent and mobile women. Hierarchical divisions of class and gender continue to imbue modern Thailand: the feminine is a rural, chaotic, backward and monstrous animist spirit realm, one that is diametrically opposed to the organised, urban, patriarchal Buddhist order. In *Nang Nak*, Nak's opposition to the ruling patriarchal Buddhist order is emphasised by her position deep in the untamed forest. The monk who eventually pacifies her angry spirit must travel from the town to her grave located deep in the jungle. Likewise, when Mak finally discovers the truth about his wife, he deserts his jungle home and runs to the safety of the village and its temple.

The supernatural still operates as the means by which the marginalised feminine can exercise power or influence in society, indicating the patriarchal structures that continue to permeate gender roles and constructions in Thailand. *Nang Nak* demonises independent women by connecting Nak's agency and autonomy to the supernatural and her dangerous mobilisation of such techniques to achieve her goals. Similar to the abused and vengeful lower-class women of the 16mm era and the B-grade productions, Nak's monstrous, unnatural and undesirable status begins when she exhibits independent mobility, agency, desire and a position outside of the family. This includes the ghostly Nak travelling to kill both an old woman who stole from her and then a friend who tried to warn her husband Mak. Nak's monstrous arrival at their homes is heralded by a terrifying thunderstorm, in which the characters scream and cry and doors and windows flap open and shut. This is also depicted in Nak's pursuit of Mak when he flees from her after discovering the truth. Nak hangs upside down from the temple ceiling above Mak, calling out his name while the collection of all-male monks try to protect him below, a frightening display of female power that absolutely must be defeated in order to maintain the status quo. This ability contrasts with the terrified Mak and the all-male Buddhist order huddled below. Likewise when a shaman later attempts an exorcism spell, Nak commandeers his hand and forces him to bash in his own skull with a rock. During this sequence Nak's disembodied laughter echoes throughout, illustrating her immense power over her environment.

This Othering of the demonic feminine indicates how Thai horror continues to function as an avenue for the 'return of the repressed', and how this repression is still concerned with characteristics that are considered deviant and forbidden in women. Such a depiction again links back to the 16mm era productions that also promote such reactionary control over women as a response to wider social instability and upheaval. Yet rather than a means to negotiate traumatic upheaval and changes to society (as in previous decades), Heritage films such as *Nang Nak* instead deploy such a depiction to place blame upon female agency for the unstable present and so promote a return to reductive constructions of the past.

Inherent in the nostalgia of Heritage culture is, of course, a retrograde gender ideology that places emphasis upon the idealisation of traditional gender roles and a return to this status. In the contemporary context, such blame is rendered distinctly unfair given the contribution made by exploited female rural migrant workers during the 1980s, one which led to the extraordinary economic growth enjoyed by Thailand. As I have already argued, the economic boom had destabilised traditional conceptions of male and female, as women had now moved away from the static home and exercised independent mobility in their migration to cities in search of work and prospects. These provincial female migrants were both exploited during and suffered the most after the economic downturn. Yet the final ending of *Nang Nak*, in which the spirit Nak must go to serve the Buddhist order as penance for her refusal to accept her fate, suggests that blame lies with women for refusing to accept their true place in society. Functioning as a conservative reaffirmation of patriarchal discourses, films such as *Nang Nak* advocate the controlling of independent femininity as a means to preserve a mythical idealised status quo and a still-patriarchal present. In the end, patriarchy must conquer this archaic, lower-class female and exercise control in order for equilibrium to be restored.

The Presence of Previous Thai Film Stylistics

The political categorisation of New Thai film in its heritage incarnation therefore seems to be a somewhat reactionary response to the wider crisis-influenced context. The seminal horror film *Nang Nak* offers a portrayal of Thailand and rural provincial life that sought to pacify rather than negotiate such trauma, adhering to a localist discourse that came from outside of this suffering community.

It is therefore significant that despite being so removed from the 16mm era and its viewers, this film (along with other heritage productions) still displays many of the stylistic characteristics identified in Chapter 1 and associated with the post-war audience and context. Developed from the culturally diverse, communal society and collective viewing scenario Thai film had previously catered almost exclusively for, such a presence indicates how while New Thai Heritage film (and the model of horror represented in *Nang Nak*) may be ideologically elitist in the message conveyed, this film form remains a hybrid product representative of a culturally and socially complex nation even into the contemporary context.

Such a film style represents both the cultural diversity and inequality of Thailand, one that bleeds into New Thai films as a traumatic presence, so operating as a stylistic undermining of the politically reactionary discourses which infuse these productions. Such an influence remains to 'haunt' New Thai productions, surfacing to influence cultural texts and simultaneously betray the origins of contemporary Thai film as a lower-class mass entertainment form made by and for the people that Localism was now attempting to control ideologically. Building upon Blake (2008) and Lowenstein's (2005) interpretation of horror films functioning as an outlet for traumatic expression, the form of New Thai film overcomes the pacification of Localism to become a representation of repressed communities and an expression of the trauma endured by so many Thais at this time.

Rather than merely thematic, this traumatic expression is stylistic, and becomes most evident through the reception of Thai film upon the international scene. Indeed, the deviation of *Nang Nak* from the stylistics generally associated with horror as a genre and its 'high-brow' forms causes problems for non-Thai viewers who (perhaps inevitably, given the continuing Orientalised depictions of Thailand internationally) interpret such stylistics as inferior and unsophisticated. The disdainful attitudes that were earlier directed towards lower-class Thai films by Thai elites are now apparent in derogatory comments from viewers outside of Thailand. Responses interpret the attributes designed for Thai audiences as a flawed and inferior imitation of the globally standardised horror genre, rather than a culturally specific film form. Thai film and the Thai spectator are depicted as deviating from a filmic 'standard', one that begins to explain both the incomprehensible nature of Thai film to non-Thai audiences and the unfavourable non-Thai reviews and interpretations of productions that are otherwise successful within Thailand.

For example, in keeping with the conventional post-war film style, *Nang Nak* still blends different genre traits within a single production. Such blending becomes very difficult to understand for a viewer expecting a stylistic and thematic demarcation of the 'horror' and 'romance' genres. As one American reviewer states:

> Why turn a film about an immortal love story into a film about a ghost that whips up harsh rainstorms and breaks people's necks? It just doesn't make sense, and the film would have been better if it had stayed true to its roots – that is, Nak's neverending love for Mak, and her desire to live happily ever after. (Beyond Hollywood, 2002)

Such a response illustrates how it is the conventions honed in an earlier Thai film style and specific to a particular set of cultural logics (and which were the product of a very specific cultural and historical context) that cause non-Thai viewers to interpret Thai film as a flawed imitation of horror. For this 2002 non-Thai viewer, visceral horror numbers and overly emotional romance numbers cannot occur concurrently within the same production. The reviewer wants to separate Nak and Mak's love from Nak's horrific actions. Including such emotions and actions as attributes of the same character prevents this viewer from having empathy for Nak and her situation.

The blending of such attributes and emotions within both a single character and a single film also indicates how the many 'flavours' that Sukawong noted as such significant characteristics of Thai film are still a prominent feature of the New Thai industry. Indeed, as a text *Nang Nak* is not concerned with eliciting merely the fear and disgust associated with the horror genre but instead includes romance, history, a possible nature documentary and even comedy. As a result *Nang Nak* could be equally labelled a historical or romantic film as well as a ghost or horror film (though it is always marketed as a 'ghost' or 'horror' film). We do see plenty of horrific moments in *Nang Nak*, including the depiction of Nak's agonising labour and her later demonic terrorising of the villagers and monks. There is also a short scene in which an old woman who stole the wedding ring from Nak's corpse is killed and the body then eaten by lizards. However, these examples sit alongside historical drama and romance numbers, much of which are drawn out histrionic spectacles that inspire nostalgia for a time now passed.

Such examples make up a series of 'numbers', indicating *Nang Nak*'s status as a cultural product descended from a tradition of visceral entertainment which places emphasis upon a visual and emotional rather than narrative and cognitive appeal. Indeed the corpus of Heritage films in the New Thai industry display an obsession with the presentation of visual signifiers to construct the idyllic fantasy world of historical (and often rural) Thailand. Such an emphasis is evident in the elaborate aristocratic *mise-en-scène* of *Suriyothai* (such as the lavish royal palace, props and costumes) and the traditional rural tools, haircuts, clothes and even animals of *Bang Rajan*. These 'displays' of history construct nostalgia for a previous historical era within a narrative that is often little more than a nationalistic portrayal of a series of simplistic good vs evil conflicts. The aesthetic of attraction is deployed as a primary means to mobilise discourses of nostalgia and nationalism, a technique that Ingawanij recognises in both the heritage productions and the earlier teen productions, both of which possess a textual mode distinguished by pastiche and a strong degree of visual excess (Ingawanij, 2006: 147).

Ingawanij's 'pastiche' and 'visual excess' is also present in the earlier post-war era, further identifying a common stylistic linkage between these very different periods of filmmaking. Earlier post-war depictions of Nak's story such as *Mae Nak Prakanong* similarly extol numbers rather than narrative integration and rely upon these moments of heightened horror, tragedy and even comedy to elicit emotional effects from the audience. Yet the display in this Heritage version of *Nang Nak* is very different to any previous incarnation. *Nang Nak* offers a display of historical lower-class rural Thailand that operates to support dominant ideologies of national identity and interpellates its audience accordingly. The film deliberately cultivates discourses of nostalgia and authenticity through constructing an idyllic and pre-modern 'display' of lower-class rural Thailand that is very different to earlier productions. The film goes back to a previous era long before the introduction of Western-style Capitalism and locates this deep within the jungle. These visual splendours of rural pre-modern Thailand and the 'unique' aspects of Thai village life immerse the viewer in the constructed mythical purity of this pre-modern world through the aesthetic of attraction.

For instance this recreation of 'Old Thailand' in all its rural splendour involves extended scenes that highlight the rural environment and traditional way of life, continuing what Ingawanij calls the positioning of 'old Thai things' (2006) as connotations of a past idyllic, unspoilt and completely Thai existence. These consist of long shots displaying saturated sunsets across the landscape of rice-paddies and close-ups of rice plants with small animals slithering between them. This is all underscored by dramatic music from traditional Thai instruments and ensembles. The rural historical Thai scenery (in its rivers, rice paddies and jungles) provides an exoticised spectacle of Thailand and Thainess that evokes nostalgia for a previous simplistic and distinctly Thai era.

Together with the emphasis upon pure and idyllic scenery, the costume and make-up have also been changed in keeping with such a display. Most strikingly, Nak's appearance has changed from the beautiful long-haired light-skinned woman (who conforms to international conceptions of femininity) in productions such as *Mae Nak Prakanong*, to a dark-skinned peasant wearing old-fashioned Thai clothes with a cropped helmet hairstyle and blackened teeth. This adheres to the dress of pre-modern Thailand before the introduction of the 1940s Cultural Mandates.[4] Such mandates were designed to 'civilise' the country and bring it up to Western 'standards' and involved, among other aspects, the rejecting of loose clothing and short hair in favour of trousers, shirts, skirts and long hair on women (all of which are notably uncomfortable to wear within a hot and humid climate). The appearance of the dark-skinned peasant Nak, with her blackened teeth stained by chewing betel-nut and her old-fashioned hairstyle, is such a diversion from previous long-haired conventionally beautiful incarnations that she becomes an icon of old Thailand.

This environment forms a series of numbers that dramatically display the raw beauty of rural Thailand against which the tragic relationship of Nak and Mak is performed. Even the film's final ending sequence of Nak's submission to the Buddhist order becomes an emotional number that foregrounds the *mise-en-scène* rather than a narrative episode. Instead of providing an answer to questions regarding Nak's fate, the scene functions to emphasise the spectacle of rural Thailand and Nak's emotional performance within it. Little occurs other than extensive crying and there is very little dialogue. There is no moral ambiguity and, crucially, no questions posed or answered to create suspense in a scene that could easily function within such a structure. The couple's ending separation becomes a number that depicts images of rural Thailand and Nak's idyllic past life along with her absolute despair at having to part from Mak and their life together. Long shots display the two lovers swimming in the river together outside their isolated wooden home in the forest, and sitting upon a tree branch looking out over a landscape of paddy fields while a buffalo grazes gently beneath them.

In keeping with this emphasis upon visual numbers, the narrative of *Nang Nak* adheres to the causal structure we saw prioritised in earlier eras of Thai film and which is suited to a communal aware audience and a collective society that favours affective empathy over that of cognitive empathy. *Nang Nak* does not adhere to the question-and-answer suspense structure that Carroll (1990) associates so strongly with the horror genre. Scenes are not structured to create curiosity through posing or answering questions and there are very few moments when narrative effects are delayed and questions are posed in order to create curiosity and suspense; instead the film depends largely upon viewers' prior-knowledge of this old story and its characters. The film is so dependent upon prior-knowledge that (largely non-Thai) viewers who are not familiar with this story even express confusion as to the status of Nak herself and her transition between the living and the dead (which is not explicitly stated or confirmed until much later in the film).

For example, the love and devotion between Mak and Nak (around which the story is constructed and the means through which a substantial amount of the emotional 'numbers' are produced) is not developed as a characteristic, but simply exists. Rather than devoting narrative time to constructing this romance and marriage, the film instead relies upon the prior-knowledge of the Thai citizen who is already familiar with this story element. This is reminiscent of the instant devotion between the *Nang Ek* and *Phra Ek* figures from indigenous Thai entertainment and the 16mm era, illustrating how characteristics from traditional forms of entertainment still imbue this contemporary text.

There are also no questions raised regarding the status of Nak, her eventual fate and the process of discovery Mak must undergo to find out about his wife. Although *Nang Nak* does give an answer as to the final fate of Nak, the film does not pose or raise questions around her changing status. Instead it simply presents Nak's transition from the living to the dead, Mak's horror when he finds out the truth, Nak's later tormenting of those who stand against her and then her final pacification. Nak's predicament is known by the viewer long before Mak discovers the truth and so Mak's journey of discovery is not one that inspires curiosity, mystery or suspense, even though this would seem to ideally fit such structures.

Nang Nak even further relies upon the prior-knowledge of character types by depicting the famous figure Somdej Toh[5] as the final stoic authoritative monk who is able to convince the ghost Nak to leave the world of the living and progress to the dead. This recognisable real-life religious figure negates the need for an introduction or even a lengthy speech; indeed the dialogue in the scene in which he pacifies the angry Nak by talking to and teaching her of the need for her sacrifice is not even audible.

As such a well-known horror story and cultural text that has been remade countless times throughout Thai film history, this reliance upon prior-knowledge is perhaps understandable. However a prior-known story does not discount using erotetic structures, the many screen adaptations of stories such as Dracula being an example. Instead, the reliance upon prior-knowledge becomes another means to further address and position viewers as distinctly Thai, so cultivating the conservative nationalism of the Heritage productions through positing this story as traditionally Thai. Beforehand, the prior-known causal narrative was a means of cultivating shared pleasure for a lower-class audience and functioning within a rowdy lower-class cinema. Alongside the visual signifiers of Thai-ness, the narrative's appeal to prior-knowledge now functions as a means to inspire a distinct nationalistic Thai identity that becomes profoundly reactionary given the context of localist discourses and the economic crisis.

In the film's display of rural Thailand, the film style of *Nang Nak* also deploys the objective cinematography and editing recognised in earlier Thai films, techniques suited to prioritising numbers and the aesthetic of attraction. Such a film style indicates how despite the movement to darkened urban cinemas, there is still little evidence of 'immersion' into a diegesis and the 'phenomenological proximity' that Hanich noted as so important to the film viewing experience (Hanich, 2010). Instead, the film is still a display, an objective spectacle, rather than that designed to absorb the viewer into an individual character's psychological point-of-view and experience.

While *Nang Nak* certainly displays expert deployment of the continuity editing system and includes many point-of-view shots and shot-reverse-shot structures, many of the nostalgic numbers depicting Nak and rural Thailand do not employ the voyeuristic, subjective and point-of-view orientated shots associated with the suspense narrative that generally follows a character's personal subjective experience. Instead, the film style of *Nang Nak* favours the objective 'independent automate shots' of post-war Thai cinema, placing strong emphasis upon long shots and takes. These transform scenes into objective displays of both rural historical Thailand and graphic horror numbers rather than subjective narrative episodes. Indeed, such shots are particularly evident in the many numbers that are solely concerned with displaying the natural *mise-en-scène* of rural Thailand. These shots operate as almost complete breaks from the narrative, which pauses numerous times from the story to scenes of rural Thai nature in long shots and takes. These include forest scenes, sunsets and rice-paddies and primarily serve to display rural Thai scenery.

However, this style is also evident in scenes depicting characters and events. This includes the ending of *Nang Nak*: a drawn-out histrionic number in which Nak rises up out of her grave to be pacified by a monk and finally agrees to leave Mak and pass over to the world of the dead. A final goodbye then follows between the two lovers before Nak sinks back into her grave and withers into a corpse. The cinematography in this scene does include a brief shot-reverse-shot structure between Mak and Nak themselves, but more prominent than this is the repeated return to long shots that encompass the entire scene, including the watching villagers. Positioning the camera behind the watching villagers also suggests that the scene is being performed to this communal audience, linking back to the presentational mode and aware audience of the 16mm era productions. The scene is also inter-cut with a montage of flashback shots depicting Mak and Nak's life together within rural Thailand, all of which are again long shots of the two lovers together within the rural scenery. This includes the couple playing in the river together and sitting on a tree branch overlooking a buffalo calmly nosing through a rice-paddy. Mak and Nak's relationship therefore becomes a display of rural Thailand in the same way as the objective rural nature shots that permeate the film, and the cinematography assists in creating this display; again evoking nostalgia for both the beauty of the idyllic rural scenario and the tragedy of Nak's being forced to leave.

Such characteristics reflect how, despite modernisation in the form of increased urbanisation and industrialisation throughout the nation, Thai society remains strongly collective. Despite the movement to modernisation over the 1980s and 1990s, together with the corresponding radical social changes that came with it, Thailand remains a strongly collective society, with close social bonds and an interdependent self-construal (Hofstede, 2017). Echoing this collective dimension to society, *Nang Nak* and the New Thai heritage productions deploy the formal characteristics associated with entertainment products from collective societies; characteristics that alter this film's relationship to horror as a genre. This significantly affects the form of Thai film and the horror genre in particular.

The objective 'display', the emphasis upon 'numbers', the causal narrative and the blending of genres are all indicative of the prevalence for affective empathy over that of cognitive empathy, a characteristic associated with the cultural products of collective societies. Yet this emphasis upon emotional rather than cognitive affect not only highlights the continuing collective nature of Thai society at this time but also indicates how film could also provide an important means to negotiate the traumatic and changing wider context.

Collective emotional expression is understandably attractive during a time of social upheaval and economic devastation, and the outlet provided by film viewing is appealing given the tendency of collective societies to encourage the suppression of individual emotional expression in order to cultivate group harmony. The act of cinema-going involves an assertion of collectivity, one formulated through the communal emotional attunement that comes from viewing films together (Grodal and Kramer, 2010). In Chapter 1 I argued that viewing films during the post-war period as part of a community undergoing the varying impacts of modernity functioned to reaffirm the social and behavioural norms of an increasingly fragmented society. This was not only through thematic issues such as the reinforcement of traditional gender roles. Film viewing in post-war Thailand also offered relief from the general suppression of emotional response that is a feature of such collective societies, particularly during a traumatic period of social upheaval. Cinema-going was not a transgressive act in the same way as the viewing experience could be in more individualistic-orientated contexts, but a comforting (and conservative) affirmation of social norms that were otherwise changing rapidly.

Such analysis seems even more relevant to Thailand at the cusp of the millennium, given the much more substantial and traumatic impact from modernity. Certainly, as a larger and more modern, urban social group, Thailand on the cusp of the millennium would have weaker social bonds than those of the collective provincial Thai audiences of decades past. The self-construal and the defining of the self would be less dependent upon others, coupled with a general growth in individual freedom and less of a need to adhere to social hierarchies. The cinema, and horror in particular, therefore became a way for urban Thai audiences to retain the reassuring sense of collectivity that was diminished by urban immigration and rapid industrialisation of the economic boom throughout the 1980s and 1990s. In this way, cinema and the horror film now seem much more amenable to Hanich's assessment, functioning as a cultural product that can alleviate loneliness and isolation amidst the isolating experience of modernity. It would appear that in Thailand, after such rapid urbanisation and economic crisis, the strengthening of communal identity and bonds was greatly needed.

Natural Law

Adding to such stylistic scrutiny, close analysis of *Nang Nak* also highlights how the supernatural remains an integral part of modern Thai society. As in the 16mm era productions, we see the supernatural and fantastical elements bleeding into the diegetic world without an obvious violation of social norms. The story and events of *Nang Nak*, based around a woman whose husband does not realise she is dead, indicates that even in the contemporary New Thai industry the supernatural can still interject into the diegetic world without becoming a violation of 'Natural Law'. While emphasising the monstrousness of the supernatural, the film does not treat this as an unnatural or even surprising occurrence. Instead the supernatural still operates as an important form of social organisation in the contemporary context, reinforcing conformist discourses of Localism. Indeed, a frightening and horrific violation would actually distract from the nostalgic conservative message of sacrifice and conformity.

In the contemporary context, such an attribute is still a part of entertainment products, despite the substantial changes of this industry, and can be attributed to developments in wider society. Throughout the 1990s in Thailand, there was an increase in supernatural beliefs and organisations, both official and unofficial. Paradoxically, this existed alongside urbanisation, industrialisation and the increased standardisation of state-identified Theravada Buddhism. This resurgence is somewhat counter to the assumed impact of modernity, in which modern technology replaces magic and the supernatural as a part of a new age of 'reason' (Tamborini and Weaver 1996). Such beliefs were even harnessed by state actors, with many feeding into discourses and constructions of monarchical divinity.

Rather than a persistence of pre-modern forms of superstition that should be displaced by the wonders of modernity, Jackson sees the resurgence of supernatural beliefs and spirit cults in Thailand from the 1990s onwards (many of which concern themselves with economic prosperity) as a culturally specific refraction of modern capitalist beliefs (Jackson 2014, 13–14). In particular, both modern global Capitalism and new technology operate as uncanny and inexplicable powers, lending themselves well to discourses of magic and enchantment, and thereby defying the supposed logic, empiricism and rationality which supposedly characterises the modern world. In this way, beliefs in magic, religion and the supernatural are a direct (by)product of twenty-first-century modernity, rather than existing 'despite' such developments.

The modern resurgence in and salience of such beliefs can explain why the supernatural continues to inexorably exist as part of the diegesis in New Thai film and can so easily sit alongside other genre traits. Due to the integral connection between magic and modernity, a film about 'a ghost that whips up harsh rainstorms and breaks people's necks' can also be 'an immortal love story', albeit not to a Hollywood reviewer, but instead to a viewer from within the Thai context. In *Nang Nak*, Nak herself does not violate natural law; Nak is not horrific because she is a ghost, she is horrific due to her refusal to accept her situation and let go of Mak.

Indeed, Nak's existence as a ghost is concrete and absolute. She is not a frightening flimsy spectre or a violation of 'normality' but instead cooks meals, has sex and takes care of her baby. When Mak returns from his army service Nak appears, both to him and the viewer, exactly as expected with her baby.

Even when a visiting local monk observes Nak and Mak's house in a ghostly state of decay (so explicitly emphasising that Mak is being deceived), the monk does not express shock or fear at the situation, indicating that despite its need for correction (Nak must be banished to the world of the dead) it is still an accepted part of the diegetic world, not a violation.

Nak's transition to the supernatural – her death and then ghostly incarnation – is also an accepted series of events that needs few extraordinary special effects. The final ending separation number in which Nak submits to the 'natural' order is an elongated tragic goodbye sequence between the two lovers while the villagers sit quietly and traditional music plays. The two lovers are able to caress and hold hands while they tearfully bid goodbye; behaviour that it is difficult to associate with an unnatural violation. Emphasis is upon the nostalgic longing for an idyllic past, cultivating nostalgia in a way that would not be possible in a spectacular number that terrifies both the audience and characters in its violation of normality. While Nak's existence is not permitted, it is still a part of nature and exists within this. Rather than destroying Nak, the ending merely forces her to comply with the natural order she must obey – the separate worlds of the living and the dead – reinforcing the monk's statement that 'ghosts must be with ghosts'.

Perhaps the film's most extraordinary scene is that in which Mak and (the now dead) Nak first have sex after his return from war. This illustrates the very physical status of Nak that she is able to both deceive and conduct such relations with her husband without him realising that she has died. This sex scene is also disturbingly inter-cut with earlier scenes depicting Nak's death in childbirth, while in both scenes a thunderstorm echoes outside. The two scenes appear to be associated by their mutual status as traumatic occurrences, as they both depict a negative event that should not be occurring. However, despite such an implication, the film does not suggest that either event is wholly unnatural. Death within childbirth is a natural, if traumatic incident and sex with a ghost after such a deception is also therefore implied to be an equally frightening, yet also an entirely natural, occurrence.

Conclusion

This chapter has conducted an in-depth analysis of *Nang Nak* as a horrific representation of the New Thai industry. While this film holds a different ideological position to Thai horror films of decades past, it is still stylistically representative of the various audiences and social forces across this divided nation. Likewise, *Nang Nak* still operates as an important means of traumatic expression during a time of social and economic upheaval, albeit one which follows the Heritage and localist solutions of regressive nostalgia for a mythical previous pre-modern scenario. The film demonstrates how Thai society remains collective and how its cultural products reflect the nuances associated with this form of social organisation, despite the movement to an urban modern context.

The next chapter will move on from the analysis of the Heritage films to address another thematic phenomenon found in horror of the New Thai industry. Building upon the ideological and stylistic characteristics of *Nang Nak*, the chapter will indicate how horror films at this time not only construct a homogenised nation through an imagined past, but also through constructing a monstrous 'Other'.

Notes

1. Both Chaiworaporn (2002) and Seveon (2006) formulate an ideological connection between the 1997 economic crisis and a search for the authentic Thai-ness contained in the discourses of the New Thai movement. Ingawanij (2006) conducts this on a very concrete empirical level.
2. It apparently cost 400 million Thai Baht, the equivalent of £6.1 million (BBC News, 2001). The Bangkok Post also continues to position it as the highest grossing film even as late as 2009 (Rithdee, 2009).
3. These include four awards at the 1999 Asia Pacific Film Festival, one award at the 1999 Bangkok Film Festival, one award at the 2000 Rotterdam International Film Festival and seven awards at the Thailand National Film Association Awards in 2000.
4. As stated earlier, these were introduced during the rule of Prime Minister Pibun at the stage when Thai authorities were attempting to cultivate a strong sense of nationalism both within the country and from abroad and wanted to model the country as civilised and Westernised (Van Esterik, 2000).
5. Somdej Toh was born in the eighteenth century and was a famous Buddhist monk.

4. THAI HORROR AND THE 'OTHER'
Zee Oui *and* Ghost Game[1]

With analysis now firmly situated in the New Thai industry, Chapter 4 continues to illustrate how these contemporary films remain a hybrid form that retains characteristics associated with the earlier provincial 16mm era. The chapter progresses such an argument by examining two significant New Thai horror films in depth: *Zee Oui* (Nida Sudasna and Buranee Ratchaiboon, 2004) and *Laa Thaa Phii/Ghost Game* (Sarawut Wichiensarn, 2006)

Similar to *Nang Nak* (Nonzee Nimibutr, 1999), the thematic depictions in and subject matter of these films uphold elite discourses and reject the lower-class Thai perspective articulated by Thai films (and specifically Thai horror films) in previous eras. Demonstrating a similar will to the Heritage films, *Zee Oui* and *Ghost Game* attempt to unify a nation stratified by class, region and culture in order to promote adherence to the state in this era of continuing social instability. However, rather than through a nostalgic retreat into the past, these films propagate such an ideology through a motif that is both a familiar and common characteristic in the horror genre. This involves constructing a homogenised national identity through portraying a monstrous alien Other. Such a construction attempts to inspire conformity to the status quo through reinforcing the superior qualities of Thai-ness and simultaneously demonising the vulnerable foreign Other who exists both within and outside national borders.

In such a depiction these films attempt to erase and silence the lower-class perspective that previous eras of Thai cinema were concerned with negotiating and articulating. However, further analysis indicates that characteristics from the 16mm era can still be detected within such productions. These characteristics cannot be entirely erased and continue to imbue productions as a representation of lower-class Thailand. What is more, the films begin to problematise the creation of a viable ethnic Other and the elitist ideology it upholds. The lower-class perspective therefore begins to possibly undercut the unfair hierarchy of Thailand in the contemporary age.

Horror and the Other

The construction of a threatening and frightening Other is a staple and prevalent discourse in the horror genre. By far the most dominant and influential study of the Other in the horror film is that of Robin Wood's (2004) now infamous 'horror as the return of surplus repression' concept. This refers to the shaping of existence under patriarchal Capitalism and the means by which those outside such a conception of 'normality' are subjugated to it. This very negative representation of difference is deeply reactionary, functioning to uphold and preserve the 'normality' of the status quo. Indeed, surplus repression (Ibid.: 111) is the force by which people become 'monogamous, heterosexual, bourgeois, patriarchal capitalists' (Ibid.: 108) and hence conform to a version of 'normality' that adheres to the ideology favoured by dominant social groups and their corresponding social norms.

The monstrous Other in the horror film becomes a representation of desires and behaviours repressed under such a system, constituting 'that which society cannot recognize or accept but must deal with' (Ibid.: 111). These undesirable and repressed elements are 'dealt with' by being projected onto a threatening monstrous figure to be rejected and/or destroyed. Horror responds to and engages with such a practice in a very blatant way, whereby 'the true subject of the horror genre is the struggle for recognition of all that our civilisation represses or oppresses' (Ibid.: 113).

Academic analysis of horror texts identifies multiple incarnations of this motif. For instance, Othering homosexuality and any alternative sexual behaviour becomes a means to uphold the dominant heterosexual nature of 'normality' (Benshoff 1997, Hutchings 2004). Otherness is coded as queer and horror is produced through a 'disruption' and destabilisation of the normality associated with 'the heterosexual status quo' (Benshoff 1997: 6). Such a notion can also be extended to and recognised in other genres such as the construction of Native Americans in the Western, which function to uphold the superiority of civilised White America (Wood, 2004). In all these cases, the Other must be defeated in order to uphold 'normality'.

In New Thai cinema we see similar dynamics in Heritage productions such as *Suriyothai* (Chatrichalerm Yukol, 2001) and *Bang Rajan* (Thanit Jitnukul, 2000). These films depict conflicts and invasions from previous centuries in order to reinforce both national identity and the need for state security. In both films the Burmese are a cruel and devious Other opposed to the positive qualities and 'normality' of Thai-ness. Burmese soldiers massacre defenseless Thai civilians for their own pleasure and greed, including the beautiful Thai princess Suriyothai, who bravely rides out on her elephant to fight them.

Along with Myanmar, Laos has also been portrayed as an Other, but as an inept and bumbling inferior rather than a murderous invader. The film *Mak Tae/Lucky Loser* (Adisorn Tresirikasem. 2006) tells the story of the (fictional) Laotian football team that manages to qualify for the World Cup with the help of a Thai coach. The team members are comically ignorant of the ways of civilised life and express dissatisfaction with their own nationality, instead trying to emulate Western footballers by doing hilarious things such as dying their hair (and even their underarm hair) blonde. The film was considered so offensive and racist that it was eventually withdrawn and re-edited to make the team's originating country fictional instead. This was in response to Laotian officials, the Laotian Ambassador and the Thai foreign minister, who all warned that the racist portrayal and belittling of Laotian people by a Thai film would damage and jeopardise the diplomatic relationship between Thailand and Laos (The Nation, 2006).

Surplus repression and the monstrous Other becomes a particularly appropriate means through which to explore New Thai horror. Such a construction is prevalent in horror internationally; indeed the genre has 'persistently endowed the primal forces it unleashes, and so often relishes, with racial undertones' (Gelder, 2000: 225). Horror texts represent threatening 'foreign influences' that a nation must expel (Gelder 2000), often depicting the foreign ethnic Other as backward and savage (Rony, 2000) and attaching an incarnation of the Other to a particular race, as well as 'other cultures' and 'ethnic groups within a culture' (Wood, 2004: 112).

In Thailand, the racialised Other of New Thai cinema functions to promote the superior qualities of Thai-ness, constructing a homogenised and unified Thai nation. The suppression of internal difference was (and continues to be) very important to Thai authorities. The period of social upheaval and economic instability in the late 1990s (as explored in the previous chapter) required authorities to unify and pacify the population in order to rule. Yet the repression of ethnic difference is also related to the racial hierarchy practiced within Thailand, as well as the corresponding social anxiety caused by such dynamics (Young, 2000). In the diverse Thai nation, ethnic and racial diversity was historically repressed in order to create a mono-cultural mono-ethnic nation of authentic Thai-ness. The many different citizens in this diverse nation, with their various traditions and identities, were subsumed into a nation state in which everyone was described as Thai, a process of 'forced inclusion'. Correspondingly, to be a Thai citizen was to be of the Thai race, yet this ideal was represented most completely by light-skinned central Bangkokian Thai-ness (Streckfuss 2012, p. 307). In promoting the qualities of Thai-ness, the various ethnic identities of the different social groups within Thailand were erased (with citizens now referred to purely as Thai) as a means to consolidate power over this diverse population.

This created a strong historical association between Thai nationalism and race, and such a construction is deeply problematic in terms of its racist implications to the aspirations of darker-skinned provincial Thais. This internal racial hierarchy is reminiscent of (and indeed, inspired by) older European-originating colonial discourses, whereby darker and poorer provincial Thais are at the bottom and Bangkokian light-skinned elites at the top (Streckfuss 2012; Keyes 2002). Many citizens were therefore simultaneously pushed to conform to a racial ideal they could not obtain, while also being constructed as an ethnic 'Other within', a proxy against which to construct authentic Thai-ness.

In New Thai horror, the monstrous Other functions to uphold these racist values and the dominance of a particular ethnic group. New Thai horror productions which deploy this prevalent and reactionary horror motif of a foreign and/or ethnic 'Other' seem to promote and uphold Thai-ness and Thai values through their difference to a monstrous foreign-ness. Subordinate groups and behaviours are attached to desires and behaviours that are rendered as inferior, threatening and monstrous and so must be repressed.

In a similar manner to the conformity promoted in *Nang Nak* therefore, New Thai horror films function in service of the top-down model of ideological manipulation seen in Althusser's Ideological State Apparatuses. As in *Nang Nak*, this depiction again upholds a dominant order and system of inequality that is responsible for lower-class suffering, so erasing the lower-class perspective that Thai cinema had previously articulated in favour of a nationalistic model of conformity to the status quo. This can be seen in the horror productions *Zee Oui* and *Ghost Game*. These key films continue the Heritage discourses of representing and promoting conformity to a true and pure Thai-ness, one that erases any potential dissatisfaction in favour of a top-down model of conformity. Rather than the historical depiction of *Nang Nak*, however, these productions construct Thai-ness as desirable and superior by its opposition to a monstrous and undesirable foreign 'Other', and one that threatens Thailand and its borders.

ZEE OUI AND THE RESURRECTION OF ANTI-CHINESE-NESS

Zee Oui tells the story of a Chinese man in Thailand in the 1950s who murdered and ate up to eight Thai children. As in *Nang Nak*, this is a remake of a well-known story that has been adapted for the screen before. It is based upon the true story of the Chinese serial killer Li Hui, who entered Thailand in 1946 and was executed in 1959 for killing and eating up to eight Thai children. The 2004 film follows the main protagonist (played by the Chinese actor Long Duan) from his arrival off a ship in a bustling port in Bangkok, his work as a servant for a local Thai-Chinese family and his later movement around the country looking for work. It is during this time that Zee Oui begins to kill and then eat the various children, before he is finally apprehended and caught by a local female journalist and the police.

Similar to *Nang Nak*, the film promotes the mythical qualities of Localism. The construction of Thailand is again one of idyllic paddy fields and smiling children far away from the dangerous outsider influences perceived as responsible for economic devastation in the late twentieth century. However, rather than the excessive displays of historical and rural *mise-en-scène* seen in *Nang Nak*, the positive qualities of this nationalistic image are reinforced through its difference to the barbaric exploits of the Chinese-ness of the killer Zee Oui. This monstrous Chinese protagonist threatens Thailand and Thai people, becoming a damaging Other that must be defeated. Dominant Thai identity becomes desirable through demonising a minority ethnic group, reinforcing the definite and positive characteristic of Thai-ness (*Kwam ben Thai*) through its difference to monstrous Chinese-ness (*Kwam ben jiin*).

As per Wood, Thai-ness becomes 'normality', and one that is reinforced by demonising those who fall outside such a definition. This depiction stokes paranoia and xenophobic anxiety to protect the superior Thai-ness from the introduction of a damaging Other. Thai national identity is both inherently superior and under threat, so encouraging both conformity to and defence of this nationalist identity during an era of instability. Rather than challenging the rulers who were responsible for the economic situation of Thailand after 1997, the film removes blame from Thai elites and projects this onto a vulnerable foreign Other within the country.

This dynamic is evident in a scene halfway through the film that depicts Zee Oui preying upon village children at a local temple fair. The temple fair is a community event that consists of a large travelling fair, often with fairground rides, a make-shift cinema screen, a boxing ring, a beauty contest, stalls selling food and sweets and a stage with a dancing and/or musical performance. The activity occurs outdoors, often at night, around the village temple, an institution that often functions as the centre of communal activities and is particularly significant in small rural villages, becoming a major social event. A temple fair either allows a community to come together and celebrate (most likely) a Buddhist holiday or a funeral/remembrance service, or is simply a travelling commercial fair. Attending the fair upon a significant religious occasion and spending money can also be seen as a way to make merit and curry favour with the Buddha.

Thai films, novels and situational comedies often deploy the temple fair as a device to begin developments in the narrative. Events occur that can only come about through this situation, as the protagonist can come into contact with people and situations to which he or she would not normally have access. There is also a large amount of stimulation such as flashing lights, music and fast-moving objects. There is a degree of autonomy allowed, as women and young children are able to stray from their family. In earlier 16mm era productions such as *Mae Nak Prakanong* (Rangsir Tasanapayak, 1959), the temple fair is used as a means of introducing future lovers and rivals. This narrative device also continues in New Thai productions. In *Monrak Transistor/Transistor Love Story* (Pen-Ek Ratanaruang, 2001), the temple fair is where the hero and heroine are first able to meet and dance together, away from disapproving parents and rival suitors, so beginning the tragic love story. In *Beautiful Boxer* (Ekachai Uekrongtham, 2003), it is at a temple fair that the future boxing champion Nong Toom first views the sport of Muay Thai boxing, and also discovers his enthusiasm for cross-dressing when he steals the lipstick of a dancer.

In such a scene, Zee Oui's monstrous Chinese-ness contrasts with and reinforces the innocent and idyllic carefree image of rural Thailand. The occasion becomes a means by which the monstrous foreign Other can intrude to cause havoc and disruption. The sequence even suggests that somehow this outsider may already be within Thailand and that society has already been penetrated by this dangerous and threatening stranger who targets the most vulnerable situation (the temple fair) and people (Thai children). The film depicts the murderer arriving into the village and sneaking around during the temple fair, tempting stray children with sweets and balloons before he seizes them, runs away with them and then murders them horribly. This safe and enjoyable part of provincial life, and one that was formerly used as a light-hearted situation for plot development, is now turned into the most horrific opportunity for a serial killer to invade a community and snatch children.

Despite such horrific exploits, it is therefore surprising that *Zee Oui* initially begins by deliberately portraying the character in a surprisingly sympathetic light. The film depicts the anti-Chinese racism Zee Oui encounters within Thailand and the poverty-stricken conditions he is forced to live in by cruel exploitative employers. In the opening scenes of his arrival in Thailand on a huge Chinese ship, Zee Oui is surrounded by hundreds of dirty and impoverished Chinese immigrants and is hurried through a chaotic immigration system. He cannot communicate with Thai officials and his treatment by the Thai immigration authorities upon arrival in Bangkok is particularly brutal. Alone, isolated and unable to communicate with those around him, his head is forcibly shaved, he is thrown in detention and his name is entered incorrectly. The incorrect pronunciation of the character's name is a recurring theme throughout the film, with Thai people constantly denying him subjectivity by refusing to give him his correct Chinese name 'Li Hui' and addressing him with the corrupted Thai version of 'Zee Oui'. Notably he is labelled with the racist term *Jek baa* (a 'crazy chink') by callous Thai immigration officials, and during this opening ordeal high-angle shots position him as isolated and vulnerable. Zee Oui's first job in Bangkok is particularly brutal: he must slaughter chickens for a cruel Thai-Chinese family whose children taunt him and he is forced to sleep in the slaughterhouse surrounded by blood.

Such background exploration of Zee Oui's terrible abusive treatment in Thailand initially appears to be the source of his monstrousness, and could act as a progressive character study of the relationship between abuse, trauma and violent behaviour. Yet very quickly, this initially sympathetic opening is forgotten and Zee Oui's monstrous nature is strongly connected to his ethnicity. Right from the beginning Zee Oui is constructed as an ethnic Other who is different to Thai people. He is sickly, is constantly coughing and is not as strong as the other Thai workers in the mill where he works, implying that somehow his Chinese body is weaker and inferior to those of the Thais. Then, through a variety of flashback scenes in China, the character's cannibalism becomes more and more connected to his Chinese-ness. For instance, one scene flashes back to his time in the Chinese army. While his fellow soldiers are raping and murdering victims around him, the terrified Zee Oui is forced to engage in cannibalism of the Japanese enemy. Publicity and reviews surrounding the film in Thailand also encouraged this ethnic-identified monstrousness, referring to the protagonist's behaviour as his 'instinct', to which he eventually reverts after being unable to succeed in Thai society.[2]

Finally, the film ends with a flashback scene set in China depicting Zee Oui's peasant mother cutting out the heart of an executed criminal and feeding it to a young and sickly Zee Oui in an attempt at curing him from his illness. His cannibalism, his cutting out and boiling of the children's organs, is revealed as an attempt to make a Chinese soup, which his culture taught him will cure his illness and sickly disposition. This horrific practice is firmly situated as a Chinese custom, one that the surrounding sickly Chinese peasants take part in as a frantic massacre upon the body while his mother screams out 'the heart is mine!', so demonstrating the collective monstrousness of Chinese people and their culture.

Such scenes serve to excuse Thai abusers and undermine the idea of any sympathy for the corresponding trauma associated with such treatment. By the end of the film Zee Oui's abusive treatment takes second place to his Chinese-ness as an explanation for his behaviour. Rather than a complex bullied victim, Zee Oui becomes monstrous due to his Chinese-ness, and instead the film seems to warn against blaming Thais for actions that are instead an implicit part of Chinese nature. The monstrous Other is depicted as distinctly Chinese, becoming not only a dangerous individual but also a dangerous ethnic and foreign Other, so upholding the dominant discourse of superior Thai nationalism.

Publicity for the film also suggests that filmmakers very consciously attempted to connect with viewers through anti-Chinese discourses. The film was the directorial debut for Thai sisters and cinematographers Nida Sudasna and Buranee Ratchaiboon, and was also the first feature film release for the newly formed Matching Motion Pictures Co. Ltd. This company was one of many subsidiary companies of the largest advertising production company in Thailand, 'Matching Studio', which was keen to branch into filmmaking. For their opening production, Matching Studio deliberately chose this story. Executive Somchai Cheewasuthon, remarked in *The Nation* newspaper on 31 March 2003 that the Zee Oui story presented 'the best way to expand our company'. This is because the tale was already present in popular consciousness and was specifically remembered through the ethnicity of its monstrous figure. Viewers had grown up as children with the frightening tale of the Chinese foreigner who ate Thai children and remembered their parents' warnings 'not to wander out after dark or the Chinese would come for them' (Rithdee 2004a). This deliberate selection of a story associated with such a racist discourse as being the 'best way to expand' for this company suggests that filmmakers recognised the propensity of reactionary constructions and racist discourses in the wider context at this time.

Comments and actions from the Thai filmmakers also demonstrate a direct desire to construct an Other that is distinctly Chinese. Filmmakers notably took the unusual step of choosing a genuine Chinese actor from China to play the part of Zee Oui. This was an unusual move in Thai cinema, as there was no shortage of Thai and Thai-Chinese actors who could have filled this part, and who previously did (in an earlier TV adaptation in the mid-1980s). This casting choice was publicised widely in early pre-production press conferences. Buranee is quoted in *The Nation* stating 'A Chinese See Oui [Zee Oui] makes the character more realistic. The gestures are Chinese in nature as are the emotional expressions. Those elements would be lost if we used Thai actors' (Pajee, 2003). This choice demonstrates a similar aspiration for authenticity that was previously evident in the careful recreation of 'old Thailand' by New Thai heritage productions such as *Suriyothai*, *Nang Nak* and *Bang Rajan*. However, in *Zee Oui* this authenticity is a means to more concretely construct Chinese Otherness and enable it to more believably threaten superior good Thai-ness.

This depiction is also particularly disturbing in its attempt to disrupt social relations that appear otherwise quite content. The film resurrects anti-Chinese racism that, while it has never entirely disappeared, is not noted as a prominent part of Thai society in anthropological studies of the Sino-Thai Chinese community and ethnicity in Thailand since the Cold War. Scholars actually indicate a lack of social problems associated with this ethnic group in Thailand. For instance Bernard Formoso states that 'the social integration of the Overseas Chinese in Thailand is commonly presented as a model of success in the

Southeast Asian context' (Formoso, 1996: 218). Even the prominent position of this social group in the economic hierarchy of Thailand 'does not seem to create the interethnic tensions and resentment observed in other countries of Southeast Asia' (Ibid.: 218).

Likewise in a study of the Chinese population of Ayutthaya in 1977, Tobias indicates the lack of friction between, and common cooperation between Thai and Chinese households: 'Thai usually invite Chinese neighbours, without a thought of ethnic difference; and Chinese usually invite Thai similarly – to Thai style occasions' (1977: 310). While acknowledging that stereotypes do exist, these do not appear to play a significant part in relations between two communities. Indeed, the communities are not separated and inter-marriage occurs frequently. This integration is so prominent that people appear to perceive no conflict in identifying themselves as both Thai and Chinese: with university students 'disproportionately immigrants children (*luukciiin*), yet passionately Thai' (Ibid.: 305), with some expressing a 'commitment to be Thai *Chinese*' (Ibid.: 310).

The extent to which this social group is considered a part of Thailand is evident through an example given by William Callahan, who illustrates how even during the tumultuous post-97 period of the economic crisis, politicians could not use Sino-Thai ethnicity as a target for blame:

> Prime Minister Gen. Chaovalit Yongchaiyut tried to blame Sino-Thai capitalists for the 1997 economic meltdown, calling them 'the nation's problem.' Though this was a very successful diversionary measure in other countries – the state encouraged anti-Chinese riots in Indonesia to save Suharto – it did not work in Thailand. After a public outcry, Chaovalit apologized and complained that he had been misunderstood. (Callahan, 2003: 495)

Instead, the kind of anti-Chinese-ness that is propagated in *Zee Oui* appears to have been most prominent in the 1930s. During this decade the Thai government tried to force the cultural assimilation of the Chinese in Thailand, and so increase political control over this economically powerful minority group that controlled around 90 per cent of the country's rice mills (the biggest industry in the country at this time). This Thai hostility towards the Chinese is recognised as the result of a 'growing separatism' between the two social groups that was fostered by anti-Chinese rhetoric and unfair policies from the Thai government designed to control this powerful economic class (Coughlin, 1955: 313). Various oppressive anti-Chinese measures were introduced by Thai authorities to both restrict the growth of the Chinese community in Thailand and encourage its assimilation into the Thai majority. This involved limiting Chinese immigration into Thailand, levying higher taxes onto Chinese businesses and prohibiting education in the Chinese language (Leonard Unger, 1944: 206–207). Lin Yu talks of 'anti-Chinese feeling' in this period (1936: 197), and the ease of targeting this 'foreign' group at this point in time:

> The Chinese form about a quarter of the population of the country. They have not been assimilated; on the contrary, they are tenacious of their own language and culture. They dominate the industry and trade of the country, including the processing and marketing of its basic food supplies. Under the autocratic royal rule of Siam, up to 1932, the rise of nationalism was belated; but when the royal power was broken and national feeling given free play, the powerful Chinese minority, which could easily be represented as a community exploiting the Siamese, made an easy target. (Ibid.: 107)

Zee Oui appears to be yet again attempting to select this community as a target, yet one that is now an assimilated and integral part of Thailand.

The reactionary nature of this depiction is also heightened by its notable rejection of not only the social cohesion of this minority within Thailand, but also the erasing of previous progressive Thai cinematic depictions of Chinese ethnicity. In her analysis of the earlier 1980s teen cycle and its transformation to the New Thai industry, Ingawanij notes the loss of progressive representations that actually 'might represent popular cultural heritage of the kind as yet invisible among heritage films of the officially endorsed quality' (2006: 166). Ingawanij mentions the 'naturalization' of Chinese ethnicity which 'can be situated as part of a cultural break that occurred in the late 1980s, during which it became possible, and desirable, to out oneself as *luukjiin*' in a small number of the teen films where 'Chinese-ness dictates the look of a home, situating some of the characters as *luukjiin*, rather than connoting through character stereotype capitalist modernisations exploitation of the (ethnic Thai) people' (Ingawanij, 2006: 116, footnote 36). What Ingawanij identifies as a possible 'popular cultural heritage' now appears completely lost when faced with the monstrousness of Zee Oui and his Chinese-identified cannibalism, and is ironically erased in the pursuit of Localism, heritage and 'authentic' Thai-ness. *Zee Oui*'s disturbing depiction of 'otherness' in the form of monstrous Chinese-ness signals a departure from depictions that recognised an ethnically diverse modern Thailand, and instead constitutes a retreat back to earlier forms of anti-Chinese racism.

Ghost Game and the Cambodian Other

As in *Zee Oui*, the horror film *Ghost Game* can also be understood through Wood's framework. However, instead of Chinese-ness, this film depicts Khmer culture as a deviant, undesirable and demonic ethnic Other that threatens contemporary Thai society. Yet again, this is a directly racist and xenophobic means to promote the superior qualities of Thai-ness as well as adherence to the Thai state, largely by warning against the dangers of the non-Thai Other. The film tells the story of eleven contestants in a game show who attempt to win a five-million-baht prize by spending a number of nights in a former Cambodian Khmer-Rouge prison camp, in which people were tortured and killed during the genocide that was committed by this regime from 1975 to 1979. The contestant who can last the longest will win the cash prize. After journeying from Thailand through the Cambodian jungle (which also helps construct the savagery of the Khmer Other) the contestants enter the camp and are each haunted and tormented by the various angry ghosts who inhabit the ruins. Many of them leave screaming and eventually everyone is killed by the demonic spirit of the former camp commander. During their stay the contestants must also complete a series of macabre trials, some of which involve being strapped into the original torture devices and spending the night in coffins filled with skulls.

The narrative of *Ghost Game* constructs its characters as contestants in a game show. This familiar textual motif is often used as a narrative device to question society and provoke social scrutiny and critique, as seen in films such as *Running Man* (Paul Michael Glaser, 1987) and *The Hunger Games* (Lawrence and Ross, 2012). Horror films such as the American production *Series 7: The Contenders* (Daniel Minahan, 2001) and the well-known Japanese *Battle Royale* (Kinji Fukasaku, 2000) use the game show motif to challenge and critique a dominant order that produces entertainment out of encouraging (often violent) competition in the pursuit of capitalist gain. These films explore the relationship between violence, gun culture and entertainment within society.

However, the use of this narrative device in *Ghost Game* is very different to such internal reflexivity. *Ghost Game* does not present a critical examination of Thai society but instead draws upon an already existing reactionary racist discourse that was solidified in the colonialist era and promoted by elites throughout the twentieth century. As Thailand was never formally colonised during the period of European colonial expansion, nationalism as a concept developed differently to that of other Southeast Asian nations. Laos and Cambodia were occupied by French colonialist powers, while Burma, on the other side of Thailand, was colonised by the British and Malaysia passed between varying forms of Portuguese, Dutch and British rule. Thailand became a neutral space, a buffer zone for the colonial powers and so avoided formal colonisation. As part of ensuring such home rule, Thai elites were faced with the task of consolidating power over an area of land and a population that was both fragmented and diverse, having been historically divided up into various kingdoms with centres of power rather than solid borders.

Such consolidation was achieved through the construction of and corresponding conformity to a nationalistic Thai identity. The elusive superior qualities of this identity were largely defined against the construction of an inferior Other, one realised mostly through superiority to neighbouring countries. Cambodia, Laos, Burma and Vietnam were all constructed as inferior nations, in part due to their occupation by foreign powers. This Othering of neighbouring Southeast Asian nations was a crucial factor in maintaining political dominance by the Thai state in the twentieth century, to the extent that 'the state and its security apparatus survive[d] because of the enemy' (Winnichakul, 1994, 167). This enemy, therefore, always had to be 'presented, produced, or implicated, and then discursively sustained. It is always projected – if not overtly *desired*' (Ibid.: 167).

Cambodia and Khmer culture have been subject to a particularly interesting depiction by Thai nationalism. The racist construction of this nation and its citizens attaches mystical and black magic qualities to Khmer culture in order to other this country as barbaric. Pasuk Phongpaichit and Chris Baker indicate that 'In the Thai imagination, Cambodia is a source of great spiritual power, and Khmers have access to powerful techniques' (2008: 4). They give the example of Newin Chidchob (who in 2005 and 2006 was a close advisor to the then-prime minister Thaksin Shinawatra) to indicate that this discourse exists on a state level as well as a popular one. For Thaksin, Newin was notable not only for his vote-buying skills but also because he was Khmer. Although he had never made any claim of spiritual power, Phongpaichit and Baker state that 'the image clings to him because he is Khmer' (Ibid.), illustrating the strong association between Cambodia and the supernatural in Thai imagination. Prime Minister Thaksin enlisted Newin's spiritual expertise, travelling to various temples around the country and performing spells and ceremonies (including having an elephant walk under him) designed to draw spiritual power from ancient monuments (including Khmer ones). The extraordinary treatment of Newin after Thaksin's removal in the bloodless 2006 military coup indicates how this belief is not limited to one man, but is widespread and continues to exist on a state level:

> when he was arrested after the 2006 coup, he claimed his captors had stripped him down to his underwear before releasing him near his home. The army did not deny this accusation, but explained they were looking for his amulets. They had been told by a senior officer to take away his amulets in order to destroy his power. (Ibid.: 4)

New Thai horror draws upon this construction. *Long Khong/Art of the Devil 2* (Kongkiat Khomsiri, 2005) depicts Cambodia as a place of savagery, one identified as such through its portrayal of Cambodian shamans and black magic

Khmer-language spells. These encroach upon Thai citizens and cause chaos and horror that again specifically stems from this ethnically-identified Otherness. The opening sequence in this film is of a Thai fisherman screaming in pain with a number of fishhooks emerging from places on his body. An old woman hurriedly called to diagnose his condition immediately states in no uncertain terms, 'it's a Cambodian curse', underlining the severity of this particular affliction. The source of this curse is later revealed to be a Cambodian shaman to whom many of the protagonists went to cast black magic spells designed to harm their enemies. Later in the film, when the psychotic and abused teacher Miss Panor enacts her vengeance, she chants Khmer-language spells and carves Khmer characters upon her body. This black magic, which the film warns will never leave you and will eventually consume you, leads her to burn and skin her students alive before drilling into their skulls with a power drill.

Ghost Game also deploys this reactionary and xenophobic construction of the Khmer Other, whereby Cambodia and Khmer culture is directly associated with the demonic supernatural. In particular, *Ghost Game* serves to contrast demonic, disordered and dangerous Khmer culture with the civilised order of Thai-ness. From the very first moment that the characters arrive in the fictional camp, a dirty Cambodian shaman performs a ritual for the spirits of the dead in front of the skull-filled memorial, one designed to pacify the spirits. This is notably completely adverse to the ordered saffron-robed chanting Buddhist monks depicted in Thailand earlier in the film. It involves screaming and dancing while the performer himself wears few clothes and slaughters an animal, rubbing its blood on to the memorial as a sacrifice. There is no lengthy explanation for this ritual or indication as to how it will work: it is simply accepted as a necessary part of staying in the camp. Interestingly, this depiction is somewhat reminiscent of the northern female spirit cults, a lower-class minority culture that, I have previously indicated, has been similarly Othered within Thailand, so associating this discourse with the provincial minorities and lower-classes. Significantly, the Cambodian ritual fails and the Shaman is overtaken by the angry spirits and has to be removed, indicating even the lack of a rudimentary order in this barbaric land.

The difference between these two nations is also underlined by the emphasis placed upon clearly defining the physical boundary between 'safe' Thailand and 'savage' Cambodia. The film suggests that physical barriers against this dangerous, devious and harmful 'Other' must be maintained, promoting a nationalist vigilance to protect Thailand's borders. Such a practice has historical precedence: in order to promote the perception that Thailand is constantly under threat by barbaric others, Thai elites extend maps of Thailand deep into Laos and Cambodia and locate the country at the very maximum of its physical boundaries as they have been drawn at different historical periods. In particular this includes the northern parts of Cambodia and even (at times) the magnificent Angkor Wat complex, centre of the twelfth century Khmer empire that stretched across Southeast Asia. The claim for this area as Thai is still repeated by Thai nationalists and is well-known in Cambodia. The 2003 Phnom Penh riots were a result of a false rumour that a Thai actress had stated that Angkor Wat was actually Thai and had been stolen by the Cambodians. The Thai embassy was burned and the border crossing between the two countries immediately closed. That this fictional remark could spark such extreme actions indicates the extent of the animosity between the two nations.

The many border squabbles between Thailand and Cambodia also contribute towards this construction of an ancient enemy encroaching upon and damaging Thai-ness. An age-old border dispute between the countries concerns the Khmer temple complex of Preah Vihear, which sits directly on the boundary between Thailand and Cambodia. While the temple was designated by the International Court of Justice as being within Cambodian territory and belonging to Cambodia, it is only accessible through Thailand. The issue enrages Thai nationalists who claim that the temple is Thai. It has been used as a political tool by Thai nationalists attempting to portray the government as unpatriotic and 'selling out' to inferior Cambodian thieves. In 2008 Cambodian authorities attempted to register the temple as a world heritage site, an action that enraged Thailand and led to a stand-off in which several soldiers from both sides were killed.

Ghost Game places strong emphasis upon constructing this important physical boundary between Thailand and the Other. The scene depicting the contestants' journey into Cambodia strongly juxtaposes the savagery of the rural Cambodian *mise-en-scène* with that of the civilised urban Thai situation. Opening scenes in Thailand depict the contestants preparing for their trip into what they see and construct as a barbaric land. Saffron-robed Thai monks chant prayers for their wellbeing and the gentle sepia-toned temples and modern skyscrapers set against the Bangkok sunset are peaceful signs of a civilised and developed land. However, when the contestants physically cross the boundary into the Cambodian camp, the *mise-en-scène* immediately becomes threatening. The journey to the camp involves travelling deep into the jungle via a river boat; along the way there is no civilisation in the form of people, cities or infrastructure of any kind, again suggesting the backwardness and undeveloped nature of Cambodia. Trees overhang the boat and the contestants are warned not to dip their toes into the river, as though immediately after crossing the Thai border the environment has suddenly become dangerously savage and menacing. Much emphasis is placed upon the contestants physically entering the camp, with close-up shots of the rusty turnstile that admits them and long shots of them all staring up at the decrepit, aging camp entrance. The space immediately upon entering the camp is full of thick cobwebs and overgrown foliage that hangs menacingly. A memorial filled with skulls similar to the stupa that exists at the Choeung Ek killing fields greets the contestants; however, rather than a means of contemplation or respectful remembrance to the millions who were murdered (as in the real museum), this looming grotesque monument is a suggestion of the utter barbarity of Cambodia. Likewise the ending of the film features a desperate dash to reach the Thai border by the remaining contestant, implying that the evil of the camp can only be escaped by leaving Cambodia altogether.

Overall, the film demonstrates a shocking level of cultural insensitivity to Cambodian history. Genocide becomes a tool to construct the superiority of Thai-ness, a callous portrayal that is perhaps best illustrated by the Cambodian reaction to the film. This trivialisation of the Khmer Rouge genocide (a major national trauma that is still very much in living memory and was yet to really be acknowledged or negotiated on a personal or state level) was denounced by Cambodian authorities and the film signalled a new 'low' in Cambodia-Thai relations. The Cambodian culture minister Kong Kendara called the film disrespectful to the victims of the Khmer Rouge genocide, stating 'They want people to be scared, but the deaths (of hundreds of thousands of people) are not a game' (Bangkok Post, 2006). The interior ministry and the police even acted to hunt down and destroy any copies of the film found in Cambodia, with the reason given by Kendra that:

> The movie makes the dead out to be bad, but they are innocents. Our national tragedy is not a game. This movie looks like the Thais are not respecting the Khmer (Ibid).

The Bangkok Post reported that the film

> has united all factions of Khmer politics in indignation, with some saying they fear renewed friction between the two nations due to the Thai production's allegedly crass treatment of a highly sensitive and still painful period of Cambodian history. (Ibid.)

My Meak, the deputy governor of Pailin, a district in the Northwest of the country that was formerly a Khmer-rouge stronghold, also stated 'This is not a tool to make business. The killing has stopped. We do not forget our past, but it should never be repeated in any form, and especially not in this way' (Ibid.). The furore was so severe that the producers of the film sent a letter of apology to the Cambodian ambassador in Bangkok, and co-producers Tifa production house even issued a public apology to all Cambodians. The Thai filmmakers largely ignored such concerns however, as the film was still released in its entirety, indicating how marginalised Cambodian voices are within Thailand even on an official level.

Certainly, the film attempts to align its depiction as close as possible to the experiences of Cambodia under the Khmer Rouge, reinforcing this racist depiction through a supposed 'authenticity' similar to the Heritage films of New Thai cinema. Inside, the fictional camp has uncomfortable similarities to the original Tuol Sleng Khmer Rouge security prison. Protagonists are even told that the site is a former museum that was closed after mysterious deaths occurred and has now been neglected and abandoned. This again suggests the barbarity and lack of organisation or authority in Cambodia, conveniently ignoring the restoration of the actual prison as a well-kept educational museum in the heart of Phnom Penh capital city. The skulls and bones that litter the camp are also reminiscent of the piles of discarded bones in the Choeung Ek killing fields; however these have not been arranged into the memorials that now exist as part of this site. The torture devices that were found in each room of Tuol Sleng are also present in the camp, as well as full mock-up water torture boxes in which the prisoners were shackled and which the contestants now climb into as part of the 'trials'. The DVD case advertising the film even depicts a staring ghost-like corpse strapped to one of the iron bed frames used as torture devices in Tuol Sleng. Such devices became infamous due to photographs taken by the Vietnamese of the tortured corpses they found in this position in each room, pictures now on display in Tuol Sleng museum today. The walls of the fictional 'S-11' camp are also covered with the familiar black and white identification photographs of the Khmer Rouge victims, and both the Thai contestants and the Cambodian ghosts all wear the same prisoner-style regulation uniforms worn under the Khmer Rouge.

Hybrid Films

Again, similar to *Nang Nak*, these New Thai horror productions are politically reactionary. The films function as bourgeois tools of ideological manipulation during a period of economic trauma, promoting conformity to the Thai state and dissuading any questioning of authorities. However, Thai society remains both hybrid and divided; a status that is reflected in the film style of these ideologically conservative cultural products. Despite the reactionary nature of these films and their cultivation of discourses that uphold this elitist position, both *Zee Oui* and *Ghost Game* are still imbued by characteristics that can be traced to older forms of provincial Thai entertainment and the communal audience of the post-World War Two 16mm era, a segment of society that is otherwise excluded and/or pacified in elitist discourses.

For instance, while *Zee Oui* has been deliberately altered to move away from the narrative structure associated with these older forms of entertainment, the film still carries stylistic evidence of this transformation. The film therefore becomes a particularly interesting textual case study as to how this familiar story has been altered to adhere to Carroll's erotetic suspense narrative, a structure that (as I explained in Chapter 1) tends to be associated with more 'high-brow' forms of horror. The film constructs a story that seeks to pose and then answer questions as to why a real individual would commit such terrible crimes, with publicity stating: 'The intention of the directors, Nida Sudasna and Buranee Ratchaiboon, is to represent questions about the story of Zee Oui on what were the causes of Zee Oui's cruelty' (Quoted on the *Zee Oui* film website, 2004). As such, the erotetic structure slowly reveals the reasons behind the character's monstrous nature, all of which is part of the filmmakers' attempts to make Zee Oui a complex individual: 'our See Oui [Zee Oui] is a human being with severe psychological troubles' (Ibid.).

By altering the narrative structure accordingly, filmmakers sort to distinguish their contemporary depiction of this well-known figure from previous incarnations, stating 'In the way we discuss Zee Oui again here, we do not consider him in the old way' (Quoted on the *Zee Oui* film website, 2004). Such 'old ways', as Parinyaporn Pajee remarks, 'presented the murderer as a one-dimensional nutcase with an insane personality' (Pajee, 2003). This description is reminiscent of the emphasis upon spectacle, character types and stock narratives seen in the 16mm era productions, which (as I explored in Chapter 1) did not prioritise explaining actions and events through a cause-and-effect chain. Again, this 'old way' is associated with the communal audience and the cultivation of affective empathy common to collectivist societies.

Interestingly, the rejection of older communal stylistics then becomes quite a reactionary move. While posing and answering questions as to why this character may be driven to commit such terrible crimes is certainly worthwhile as an engagement, as I have indicted the film problematically roots the answers to such questions in Zee Oui's ethnicity. The adoption of the erotetic narrative is therefore a significant means through which to construct Zee Oui's monstrous Chinese-ness, upholding a racist and nationalist ideology. Shifting the film to a stylistic form associated with globally dominant forms of horror and moving away from the cultural logics of marginalised provincial culture also works in favour of upholding current ideological state discourse in the form of racist nationalism.

However, this attempt to erase such lower-class characteristics and incorporate the erotetic structure to construct an ethnic Other is ultimately unsuccessful. The film cannot successfully meld the erotetic structure and the reliance upon spectacle and numbers as a source of stimulation. The erotetic structure attempts to make Zee Oui's actions seem more comprehensible and logical, constructing a rounded study as a means to attribute the character's monstrous nature to his ethnicity. Yet the film eventually forgets this in order to resort to monstrous graphic display and a two-dimensional character type. Indeed, the text oscillates between the attempt to construct its main character as monstrous due to his Chinese history (in accordance with the erotetic structure) and the graphic 'numbers' and two-dimensional character types of the older 16mm era film style (in accordance with the aesthetic of attraction). In this way, Zee-Oui seems pulled between catering for a collectivist and individualist audience and adhering to a need for emotional affect over that of cognitive empathy.

This conflicting hybrid nature and corresponding lack of a coherent ideological message is evident in confused reviews of the film. Comments from *Bangkok Post* critic Kong Rithdee indicate how the film is pulled between these different styles of filmmaking. Rithdee describes *Zee Oui* as 'a film that's torn between its self-imposed dilemma of being both a psycho-slasher and a character study at the same time' (Rithdee, 2004b). The effort to 'psychoanalyze' the Zee Oui figure seems to have backfired, with Rithdee terming it an 'audacious attempt' that 'disintegrates into a tenuous drama and sub-par Gothic slasher' (Rithdee, 2004c).

Such older characteristics ultimately undercut the nationalist racism the erotetic structure aims to create, disrupting the creation of a convincing Other out of cultural alterity. It appears that the descent of the character into a two-dimensional monstrous 'type' prevents the production from adhering to an 'authentic' psychological study and constructing a viable erotetic narrative structure, potentially contributing towards the box office failure of the film. This background study that specifically constructs the character as a monstrous Chinese killer is not viable. The harrowing scenes at the temple fair render the complexity of Zee Oui unfeasible, and so likewise cannot convincingly construct him as an Other created as such due to his Chinese-ness. The stylistic characteristics associated with provincial Thailand therefore begin to undermine the elitist ideology propagated by this film. In this way, the marginalised perspective of provincial Thailand not only refuses to be erased but can also undercut the reactionary ideological agenda of social elites in the post-crisis era.

The attempt to construct Zee Oui as a monstrous Chinese Other is also undermined by the apparent need to connect and attribute the monstrous actions of this central character to the supernatural. This is very explicitly suggested by the DVD case for the film, which carries the question 'Man or Ghost' (*Phii ru Khon*) on the cover. The film's ending directly questions whether the protagonist's deeds are the work of a man or a supernatural force. Mingled with the end credits are a few closing depictions of Zee Oui's trial. In prison he is approached by a police officer who informs him that if he 'confesses' to the murder of all eight children, he will be allowed to return to China (a goal that he has spent the second half of the film pursuing). In a scene immediately following his confession, the heroine journalist, who played a big part in capturing him, then confides to her colleague that there is no possible means for Zee Oui to have been in all the many places where the murdered children were found, so he cannot be responsible for all the deaths.

The filmmakers note this complication very deliberately, illustrating their desire to insert a supernatural motivation into the film: 'Sometimes two murders occurred in consecutive nights or even the same night, while the locations were quite far apart. At that time, the media posted a question whether this is the act of a human or a ghost' (Quoted on the *Zee Oui* film website 2004). The promotional website for the film also carried a suggestion that the cannibalism could be attributed to 'demons' and 'possession':

> even after his death, the killings of children with their internal organs consumed continue even up to the present time. That might mean that the demons that possessed Zee Oui are still here, moving from person to person as long as the society is still materialistic and forgets about the frailty of human soul [sic]. (Quoted on the *Zee Oui* film website, 2004)

The suggestion that Zee Oui may in some way be supernatural is somewhat unexpected given the film's efforts to 'psychoanalyse' this character and attribute his cannibalistic actions to his (racist but entirely non-supernatural) Chinese background. Again this follows the characteristics of the earlier 16mm era, in which, as I have indicated, the supernatural acted as a legitimate means of social organisation in the provincial context. Similar to the conflict in narrative structure, such a characteristic begins to problematise the film's construction of the character as a distinctly Chinese Other. Rather than attribute Zee Oui's actions purely to psychological and cultural factors, the film appears to need to attach it to a fantastical source. The ending therefore also undermines the construction of Zee Oui as a disturbed and monstrous Chinese man who has been created as such by his Chinese background. Instead, it begins to attribute what is initially portrayed as the cultural practices of a disturbed individual to the supernatural, an element that is not actually connected to any specific ethnic or cultural Other.

This conflict between these different film styles is also evident within the hybridity of *Ghost Game*. Again the emphasis upon numbers and the aesthetic of attraction problematises the attempt to create a viable erotetic narrative that upholds the construction of civilised and superior Thai-ness through its opposition to a monstrous Cambodian Other. In this case, while the aesthetic of attraction does function to create the monstrous Cambodian Other, the simultaneous lack of character development inherent in the concentration upon graphic display rather than narrative integration prevents the production from constructing the Thai characters as rounded individuals who can reinforce the superiority of Thai-ness.

THAI HORROR AND THE 'OTHER'

For instance, throughout the film there is little introduction to any of the Thai contestants or any time devoted to exploring and/or defining their personalities. The characters are introduced only as a group and are rarely distinguished as individuals. As a result, there is little attachment to each when they are killed. Rather than upholding national superiority as Thai victims of a demonic ethnic Other, the frightened contestants and their eventual demise instead functions merely as a series of graphic 'numbers'. They cannot be constructed as viable superior beings over that of the Cambodian savages nor elicit the sympathy required to sustain such a depiction when under threat from this monstrous Other. Instead, the contestants' pain and suffering becomes merely another part of the graphic display, rather than a means to uphold an ideology.

Such difficulties are particularly evident in the ending number of *Ghost Game*, in which the ghost of the camp commander chases and finally kills the last remaining contestant. This female character could function as what Carol Clover (1993) recognises as the 'Final Girl'. This character is the final survivor of films such as *Halloween* (John Carpenter, 1978), *The Texas Chain Saw Massacre* (Tobe Hooper, 1974) and *Friday the 13th* (Sean S. Cunningham, 1980), and is an integral part of the horror genre. Clover describes the character of the Final Girl as being 'watchful to the point of paranoia' and 'intelligent and resourceful in a pinch' (1993: 39). She is boyish, and it is the adoption of characteristics that are typically considered masculine traits that sets her apart from other characters (especially other female characters) and ultimately allows her to survive by escaping from or even defeating the killer. The character is notably developed throughout the narrative of such horror films, to the extent that she is 'presented from the outset as the main character' (Ibid.). Therefore 'The practiced viewer distinguishes her from her friends minutes into the film' (Ibid.).

Yut from *Ghost Game* could easily be identified as a Thai incarnation of this characteristic. Yut is the last contestant left alive and the only one who attempts a viable escape. She could easily function to demonstrate the superiority of Thai-ness through her daring escape from the demonic ghost of the Cambodian camp commander and certainly appears designed to do this. However, due to the emphasis placed upon the numbers and the aesthetic of attraction over that of erotetic narrative integration, the character development that Clover notes as being integral to the construction of the Final Girl is absent in *Ghost Game*.

Indeed, *Ghost Game*'s residual emphasis upon the visceral numbers of the 16mm era means that there is no viable erotetic structure through which to construct this characteristic. The Final Girl should be an intelligent and resourceful figure who is distinguished from other characters from the very beginning. She eventually outwits, defeats and in some way escapes from the killer in a structure reminiscent of answering questions/scenarios posed by the killer. In *Ghost Game* however, Yut is not singled out from the group at the beginning of the film and does not display any particularly incisive abilities. As with the rest of the characters, she therefore does not embody a particularly positive or superior construction of Thai-ness. Her final escape from the camp inspires little reaction when, rather than reaching the safety of Thailand, the contestant fails and is killed suddenly by the commander. Indeed, this resolution instead serves as a graphic number and to emphasise the lack of emotional attachment to and investment in the character, rather than her superiority to Cambodian savagery.

Conclusion

An analysis of these two films that embody and deploy the staple horror motif of a demonic ethnic Other illustrates the reactionary nature of New Thai horror. Similar to *Nang Nak* and the Heritage productions, both *Zee Oui* and *Ghost Game* are concerned with upholding and promoting the inherent superiority of Thai-ness. In order to do so, the films engage in Surplus Repression, demonising different ethnic and cultural groups within and outside the nation. The New Thai film industry now draws upon this elitist reactionary discourse, constructing this enemy not only through Othering the Chinese citizen *within* the country, but also the Southeast Asian border nations *without*.

The demonic 'Othering' of Cambodia and its tragic recent history in *Ghost Game* indicates how New Thai horror cinema functions as a bourgeois means to exercise control over the Thai nation in the post-crisis era. This agenda will even stoop so low as to alienate Thailand's immediate neighbours and hijack their traumatic history for the purposes of promoting Thai nationalism and superiority. Likewise, *Zee Oui* departs from previous valid explorations of ethnicity in Thailand and resurrects an anti-Chinese discourse from the 1930s as a means to create a Chinese Other that can also uphold the superiority of Thai-ness yet has the potential to disturb relations with this social group.

However, yet again, previous eras of Thai cinema resurface in the formal parameters of such productions, which become hybrid texts encompassing the different elements of film style designed to cater for the different communities of Thailand. This is realised in conflicts between aspects such as the depiction of the supernatural and the alteration of narrative structure, both of which are pulled between catering for the communal audiences of provincial Thailand and the later urban viewers of contemporary Thailand. Most significantly, such hybridity and conflict disrupts the attempt to both create a viable ethnic-identified other and emphasise the superiority of Thai-ness. In the New Thai industry therefore, provincial Thailand and its viewers not only refuse to be erased from this contemporary industry but also return to stylistically disrupt such bourgeois ideology in this increasingly elitist age.

After two chapters outlining how contemporary horror in the New Thai industry takes a conservative ideological stance, Chapter 5 will explore a different ideological perspective. Rather than the conservative discourses of Heritage in *Nang Nak* and the monstrous other of *Zee Oui* and *Ghost Game*, the next chapter examines films that can both highlight and critique the abuse of lower-class Thais during and after the economic crisis. Focusing upon the abuse of women in particular, the chapter indicates how such films can offer an alternative thematic and stylistic engagement with this wider social context.

Notes

1. Parts of this chapter have been previously published as Ainslie, M. (2009) 'The Monstrous Chinese "Other" in the Thai Horror Movie *Zee-Oui*', in R. Cheung and D. H. Fleming (eds) *Cinemas, Identities and Beyond* (Newcastle: Cambridge Scholars Publishing), pp. 97–113 and Ainslie, M. and Blake, L. (2015) 'Digital Witnessing and Trauma Testimony in *Ghost Game*: Cambodian Genocide, Digital Horror and the Nationalism of New Thai Cinema', in L. Blake and X. Reyes (eds), *Digital Nightmares: Wired Ghosts, CCTV Horror and the Found Footage Phenomenon* (London: I. B. Tauris), pp. 69–79.
2. Pajee, Parinyaporn. 2003. 'What Made Him Tick?', *The Nation*, 31 March.

5. THE MONSTROUS THAI FEMININE

Shutter *and the 'Vengeful Ghosts'*

As my analysis has so far demonstrated, many key horror films of the New Thai industry uphold elitist ideology in the post-crisis era, particularly through reactionary constructions of heritage. However, Chapter 5 now begins to explore an alternative body of films with a very different relationship to wider Thai society. This body of films I call the vengeful ghost films, and, similar to the supernatural in earlier eras, the subject matter of these texts tends to embed itself within social attitudes and constructions of gender. Films insert a traumatised lower-class female ghost into the narrative, who proceeds to take revenge upon and disrupt the bourgeois equilibrium of her male abusers. In Chapter 5, I argue that this 'vengeful ghost' motif lays bare the abuse and inequality upon which the nationalist ideology of Localism is based, particularly that directed towards and experienced by lower-class women. These films therefore begin to offer an alternative response to the wider social context, one very different to that represented in the Heritage productions.

The chapter conducts a close analysis and case study of *Shutter* (Pisanthanakun and Wongpoom, 2004). This film remains the most internationally successful example of such patriarchal critique in the crucial New Thai cinematic development of the 2000s and came to represent Thailand within the wider corpus of Asian horror films at the time. The chapter indicates how while *Shutter* is a clear example of this vengeful female ghost motif, the film also removes the stylistic characteristics associated with Thailand's lower-class collective audiences. While this subject matter may therefore seek to expose discrimination and abuse, the removal of this film style erases evidence of the inequality that was responsible for this different stylistic model of entertainment. This constitutes an essential loss of a form of lower-class Thai subjectivity and signals an erasing and conservative marginalising of such a perspective, particular on the international stage.

The New Thai 'Vengeful Ghost' Films

Thai culture's ongoing strong association between women and the supernatural is specifically reincarnated in the modern context and retains a strong presence in the New Thai industry. As explored earlier in analysis of *Nang Nak*, many New Thai horror films depict the spirits of ghostly young women returning from the dead. Films such as *Shutter, Body ... Sop 19/Body* (Paween Purijitpanya, 2007), *Buppha Ratri* (Yuthlert Sippapak, 2003), *Faed/Alone* (Banjong Pisanthanakun and Parkpoom Wongpoom, 2007), *Art of the Devil 2/ Long Khong* (Kongkiat Khomsiri, 2005), *Krasue Valentine/Ghost of Valentine* (Yuthlert Sippapak, 2006), *Phii Chong Air/The Sisters* (Tiwa Moeithaisong, 2004), *The Unseeable* (Wisit Sasanatieng, 2006) and *Coming Soon/Program Na Winyan Akat* (Sopon Sukdapisit, 2008) all display this connection and take demonic and/or ghostly women as their grisly subject matter. This construction of women as a monstrous Other is a discourse common to both Thai cinema and horror internationally. Depicted as unclean, monstrous and archaic, the female must be defeated and/or pacified as seen in heritage films such as *Nang Nak* (Nonzee Nimibutr, 1999). The desirable 'normality' of patriarchal Thailand is upheld, so reinforcing patriarchal order.

This demonic female abject is evident throughout Thai film history and bespeaks the continuing patriarchal nature of Thai society. Patriarchy underpins contemporary Thailand and the post-1997 New Thai industry, recognised in Localism, a construction that (I have indicated) idealises the rural scenario and feeds into reactionary discourses of nationalism and chauvinism. In glossing over the social inequality that led to economic devastation, Localism promotes conformity to a dominant patriarchal order and deflects criticism of this hierarchical exploitation (Hewison 1999). Heritage productions such as *Suriyothai* (Chatrichalerm Yukol, 2001), *Bang Rajan* (Thanit Jitnukul, 2000) and *Nang Nak* all depict women and the marginalised lower-classes as willingly sacrificing themselves to uphold this dominant order. *Nang Nak*, as I have indicated, continues the association between women and the supernatural, which operated as a vehicle through which to uphold the nationalist construction of Localism, largely through a narrative of self-sacrifice and a lavish display of heritage *mise-en-scène*.

In contrast to the reactionary depictions of New Thai horror productions such as *Nang Nak*, *Zee Oui* (Nida Sudasna and Buranee Ratchaiboon, 2004) and *Laa Thaa Phii/Ghost Game* (Sarawut Wichiensarn, 2006) however, the women of the Vengeful Ghost films represent a potentially progressive ideological position. An integral part of the New Thai industry, the vengeful ghost films generally follow a lower-class woman who died under tragic circumstances now returning from the grave to enact vengeance upon her male abusers. Rather than upholding the dominant order through the sacrificial conformity of women in conservative films such as *Suriyothai* and *Nang Nak*, this narrative motif depicts these mistreated young women using supernatural powers to take revenge upon their abusers.

Such a depiction functions as a critique of both patriarchy and the treatment of the rural lower-classes, becoming a traumatic response to the continuing abusive and unaccountable surrounding context of Thai social inequality after the crisis of 1997. Indeed, Thai women and the lower-classes suffered the most throughout Thailand's economic boom and bust, being exploited in the economic push of the 1980s. The abuse of lower-class women in particular, as I indicated in Chapter 2, was a significant source of cheap labour in the postwar decades and created the economic boom that, as Peter Bell indicated, was built 'on the backs of women' (1997: 55).

When the economic boom collapsed in 1997, the abuse of the poor continued. Thai workers remained extremely vulnerable to and were not adequately protected from wider economic difficulties (Akkarakul et al., 2009). Workers also continued to enjoy very little employment security due to the lack of labour rights in Thailand and the continued (at times, violent) suppression of the trade union movement. An inherent part of such exploitation was the continuing mistreatment of women. Female workers are still much more likely to experience aggravated working conditions and receive unjust treatment from employers than male employees. Such exploitive practices include not being paid salaries or other money they are owed, being ignored by employers and even scolded, while female workers are also the first to be terminated in any difficulty. Such unfair treatment is also particularly significant given the extremely high rate of female labour force participation in Thailand, whereby women workers make a significant contribution to the Thai economy. Women also shoulder increased financial responsibilities, traditionally carrying the main responsibility for financially supporting their extended family, most likely their elderly parents (Akkarakul et al., 2009).

While Thailand is portrayed as an exoticised idyllic land worthy of preservation through personal sacrifice in the New Thai Heritage productions, this image is sabotaged and exposed by the vengeful ghost films. The women horrifically subvert the glossy, highly-refined state-promoted hypocritical image of 'Amazing' Thailand and its 'flowers of the nation' (Van Esterik, 2000: 105) by exposing both the grim reality of patriarchal abuse and its consequences: female suffering that is later followed by anger and vengeance. If modern horror 'inhabits the very fabric of ordinary life, daily picking away at the limits of reason and the aspirations underpinning "moral improvement"' (Gelder, 2000: 2), then these tales of female-abuse and vengeance can be interpreted as a critique of the repressed anxieties 'picking away' at the hypocritical 'moral improvement' embedded in the Localist ideology of Capitalist and patriarchal late twentieth-century Thailand that has resulted in such an unjust society. The abused and angry lower-class female *Phii* expose the hidden exploitation upon which this elitist patriarchal fantasy is based. They insert the exploited and marginalised lower-class and female perspective into depictions of Thai society, forcing it to re-accommodate that which was previously ignored by the elite-sponsored Heritage productions. This formerly invisible underbelly with its tales of mistreatment and exploitation now shatters the glossy nationalistic depictions of the Heritage productions.

Indeed, the vengeful ghost films' characters refuse to accept unfair treatment, becoming a recognition of the marginalised and exploited status of the rural and urban poor as well as a critique of the corresponding inequality this hierarchical system breeds. By rejecting the ideology of Localism promoted in the Heritage productions, the films force a confrontation with both the exploited angry feminine and the marginalised lower-classes, a perspective that is otherwise erased by the Heritage productions. Instead of championing idyllic nationalist scenarios by rejecting, changing or forcibly expelling this undesirable social abject, the films blast open such a facade to depict a traumatised and marginalised perspective that demands to be noticed. The nationalistic and patriarchal social order is forced to recognise this marginalised perspective that now terrorises and horrifies the status quo. The wronged women force society to accommodate their subjectivity by enacting their frustrations and vengeance upon those who have abused them, compelling their tormentors to not only recognise but also pay the ultimate price for previous unjust behaviour.

Films such as *Buppha Ratri*, *Body*, *Phii Chong Air*, *Art of the Devil 2* and *Shutter* all follow this structure of an abused woman and her righteous revenge. *Buppha Ratri* tells the story of the shy and solitary lower-class female student Buppha, who is seduced by the rich young narcissistic playboy Ek. Ek targets Buppha due to her solitary and diligent character, which seems to present a challenge to his seduction techniques. Ek's seduction of Buppha is actually part of a bet and he even secretly videotapes them having sex, showing it to his laughing friends afterwards. Adding to this cruel and humiliating treatment, Ek then abandons Buppha to go and study in England. Buppha later dies from a horrific botched abortion while waiting to be evicted from her tiny apartment in Bangkok. At first, Buppha's death appears to have little impact upon the immediate environment, an illustration of the elitist nature of Thai society. There is no particular concern or commotion when it is revealed that Buppha has died, and her landlady appears much more concerned with removing the body so she can rent out the room again. Rather than the story ending here, however, Buppha's tormented and angry ghost then stays in the apartment, making her presence and treatment known. Buppha resists all attempts at exorcism, and instead remains to terrify her landlady and neighbours. She later forces Ek to pay for his cruelty: when Ek returns, Buppha murders him horribly by sawing off his legs, and then attempts to kill his new girlfriend.

Body also tells a similar story of exploitation, this time via the ghost of Dararai, who is haunting her former lover, the doctor Sethee. The film reveals how, as a means to keep their affair quiet, Sethee murdered Dararai and flushed pieces of her body down the sewer in Bangkok. Dararai torments Sethee from beyond the grave by hypnotising him to believe he is a student investigating her murder. Sethee is constantly plagued by terrifying hallucinations and flashbacks, illustrating how Dararai's complete control and manipulation disrupts any sense of social order, forcing the killer to confront the true horror of the brutal murder. Sethee is eventually driven mad and arrested for the murder, but is impaled by metal pipes when trying to escape. Dararai's gnarled corpse is then revealed to have been watching this torment throughout, finally enacting her ultimate revenge by waking Sethee up screaming from his hypnotic state when he is in the midst of being operated on in hospital for his terrible injuries.

Art of the Devil 2 also depicts an abused woman, Miss Panor, who, similar to Buppha and Dararai, refuses to accept her fate and instead pursues her abusers in search of vengeance. The teacher had her reputation ruined by students, who sought to punish Miss Panor for her relationship with another male teacher, a crime of female sexual autonomy in a patriarchal world. The narrative then reveals that Miss Panor was also cursed by men who visited a black magic shaman seeking to cast a love spell on her. Having been driven insane by such magic, Miss Panor refuses to accept such treatment; instead, she lures the students to her house in the forest and kills them in various ways. Using newly acquired black magic skills, achieved through shamanism, occult worship and cannibalism, Miss Panor hunts down the students, enacting a shocking series of vengeful punishments. One student is put in a soup for her classmates to eat, another has lizards crawl out of his back, and another is fried on a hot plate after having gouged her own eyes out. Miss Panor's most gruesome feat is burning a student alive, stripping his skin off, pouring boiling water down his throat and then inserting a power drill in his forehead.

Shutter's ghost is that of the university student Natre, another solitary, diligent and shy dead female student, whose spirit is now haunting her former boyfriend Thun and his new girlfriend Jane. As with Ek's selection of Buppha in *Buppha Ratri*, the quiet Natre was singled out and seduced by Thun, who then later grew tired of her attention. Thun begins to prefer the group of thuggish male bullies who torment Natre and who are later seen boasting about their sexual exploits together. Eventually, the group of male friends brutally rape Natre while Thun photographs the assault in order to blackmail her into silence. Meant as a means to punish Natre for her continued pursuit of Thun after he had tired of her, Natre commits suicide soon after. As a vengeful spirit, the angry and abused ghost Natre pursues Thun, and, in a show of potential female solidarity, attempts to warn his new girlfriend Jane about her boyfriend's previous actions.

These films function as a critique of the unfair and unequal nature of patriarchal modern Thailand and Localist ideology. While the vengeful female protagonists may seem to be dangerously unstable, these characters are clearly driven to commit such acts by the treatment they endure from their male abusers. The actions of these women are terrifying, gruesome and excessive, yet are clearly motivated by their terrible treatment. Such grievances are genuine, and the ensuing revenge is righteous; the characters all led a previously normal and fairly content existence that was in some way disrupted by the cruel actions of a more privileged man. For instance Buppha and Natre were quiet and diligent students before Ek and Thun singled them out, Dararai was a university lecturer with a PhD before she was murdered horribly, while Miss Panor was a teacher at the local school before her reputation and sanity was ruined by the gang of students. None of these women exhibited any pretensions towards extreme violence or mental instability beforehand, so attributing their terrible actions to their unfair and appalling treatment. Such depictions suggest that the continued abuse of marginalised social groups and perspectives will have terrible social consequences, ultimately leading to instability, violent behaviour and chaos.

The films also extend this critique to the treatment of the lower-classes. Many of the abused female protagonists are distinctly lower-class when compared to their male abusers, so intensifying their critique by addressing this aspect of social inequality within Thailand. The terrible treatment and corresponding vengeance critiques exploitive and cruel urban upper-class Thailand. In *Buppha Ratri*, Buppha is of a significantly lower social status than Ek: her apartment is tiny and cramped and she is also isolated and alone. In contrast, her cruel abuser owns a flashy car while his elitist parents live in luxury in Bangkok, and with their immense riches are even able to send their spoiled son abroad to a rich country for his studies.

Art of the Devil 2 also engages very much with the disparity between the rural lower-class and urban upper-class, locating the abused and vengeful Miss Panor in a distinctively rural lower-class setting. Miss Panor lives in an isolated wooden forest house located on the banks of a river (one very similar to Nak's in *Nang Nak*) and the visiting students must travel away from the urban university via train and then river boat deep into the jungle to reach it; a journey that very clearly takes them away from the city and deep into rural village life. This transition to the countryside is deliberately included in the beginning of the film to indicate the shift between these very different environments, so illustrating how these modern urban students have mistreated and then spurned the lower-class rural female in their quest to better themselves. The rural Thai setting, ill-treated and then rejected by the city elites, becomes a suitable site in which Miss Panor's terrible revenge is played out.

Likewise, in *Shutter*, the two main characters are intricately associated with this wider arena of rural and urban inequality. The cruel abuser Thun is located within Bangkok and his world echoes this modern context. Thun's everyday life consists of fast cars, sexual freedom, skyscrapers in vast city-scapes, alcohol, stylish apartments and technology. When Thun and his girlfriend try to uncover Natre's fate, they journey upcountry to visit her home and her unhinged mother. This *mise-en-scène* encompasses rice-paddies, traditional wooden houses, jungle foliage and Buddhist monks. Natre's former existence is represented by old country houses, jars of dead preserved animals, ragged worn clothes, decaying country roads, leaking fluids and intense devotion. Such settings and props are indicative of a connection to an older, traditional, rural and lower-class context.

This critique of Thai inequality and Heritage ideology is further illustrated by the unresolved endings of the New Thai vengeful ghost films, in which stories are not satisfactorily concluded and the equilibrium is not restored. Rather than neatly concluding their narratives by pacifying the threat or restoring order, the vengeful ghost films instead end rather ambiguously. For many, this is a stalemate that does not restore the previous status quo or indicate the eventual fate of the characters. The lack of narrative closure further serves to disrupt dominant ideology, as the ghost is not pacified or destroyed for refusing to conform to the status quo. Instead, the films seem to indicate the presence of an ongoing anger and conflict within Thailand that needs to be addressed. The texts ultimately posit no outcome to the mess and horror that is internal Thai relations.

For instance, *Buppha Ratri* ends in a stalemate with the ghost of Buppha still un-exorcised and living in her apartment with the abusive boyfriend she has killed. The ghost of Ek now also lives in the apartment, permanently begging for a forgiveness that Buppha does not appear to grant. The building's other residents must now learn to accommodate their new ghostly neighbours and Buppha's landlady ceases trying to exorcise her ghostly tenant. *Body* ends with the trial and conviction of the main character Sethee for the murder of Dararai. Yet the film seems to suggest that such punishment is not a sufficient price to pay. Instead, Sethee is impaled through the chest by a number of steel pipes in a horrific road accident, with the ghost of Dararai finally waking him up screaming in agony in the midst of the operation to remove the pipes, his final fate unknown. *Art of the Devil 2* is similarly unsatisfactory in its ending: Miss Panor is shot by the authorities and one of the students is finally revealed to have been a ghost, terrifying the only survivor, who then throws herself out of her hospital window. The death of all characters involved suggests the inevitable meltdown of the contemporary social order and the absence of any available social model. *Shutter* likewise ends with an injured and silent Thun sitting in a mental hospital with the ghostly Natre still draped over his shoulders: the two socially-opposite former lovers now trapped together and immobilised in a disturbing and tragic stalemate. After having killed all members of the gang who mistreated her, Natre hangs forever perched on Thun's shoulders, refusing to leave. In all these films, it appears that each character is resigned to their fate of communal existence, yet possesses only incomprehensibility, fear and contempt for the other.

In depicting this stalemate of anger and incomprehensibility, these films articulate both the wider political and social upheaval caused by Thailand's ongoing starkly unequal social divisions as well as the general lack of any solution to this situation. The consequences of such inequality continue to encompass Thailand up to the present day (an impact that I continue to explore in later chapters). The country remains torn between competing factions and interests, all pushing in various opposing directions. One highly significant development was the Thai aristocracy's 2006 military coup, which ousted the democratically elected government and replaced it with a military regime that still continues today. Inevitable class conflict followed, resulting in a tumultuous stalemate of demonstrations, occupations and outright violence between the various factions in Thailand (the effects of which I address in more depth in later chapters). The inevitable chaos that was to follow was a result of the unfair and abusive nature of contemporary Thai society, which, despite the aristocracy's attempt to end any expression of dissatisfaction by staging a coup, continues. The ending of the vengeful ghost films reflects this stalemate. The sense of a future that cannot yet be born suggests that the abusive and hierarchical order cannot continue; it ultimately must be destroyed and society must in some way be built anew. Unlike in the Heritage films, the nation cannot go back to the previous state of being and society cannot go back to the original status quo. However, the films posit no clear way forward, and it is unclear what and where characters should progress towards.

The Vengeful Ghost Films and the 16mm Era Characteristics

While this progressive depiction of female agency may be very different to the reactionary position of the 16mm era narratives, the vengeful ghost films continue to display stylistic characteristics associated with this older era of Thai cinema. For example, the supernatural characters and occurrences of *Buppha Ratri*, *Art of the Devil 2*, *Body* and *Shutter*, while frightening, do not generally constitute a violation of natural law. Despite the solidly urban settings of many of these films, the supernatural fits comfortably (and righteously) within the diegesis. In *Buppha Ratri*, Buppha's very practical landlady employs a number of potential exorcisers to remove the ghost and enable her to rent out the apartment again, demonstrating how everyday urban life continues around the supernatural disruption. Likewise, the abusive students of *Art of the Devil 2* are revealed to have visited a shaman themselves and are deeply embedded within the supernatural, despite their preppy urban demeanours. Shock and devastation stems from Miss Panor's vengeful violence towards them, rather than her actual use of black magic.

Interestingly, in *Buppha Ratri*, *Body* and *Shutter*, incredulity towards the existence of these vengeful women is generally expressed by male abusers when they receive the first signals of their haunting. This contrast in male and female attitudes serves to emphasise the vast gulf between the male and female experience in Thailand at this time. As explored in previous chapters, as a 'natural' part of society in keeping with the anthropological studies cited earlier in this volume, the supernatural appears to remain a female-centric domain and one which male characters seem to generally have very little control over. Notably, for male characters, the supernatural is less of a shock than the power these abused women are now able to wield. In *Shutter*, for instance, we see Thun's girlfriend Jane visiting spirit mediums, temples and journalists as part of her investigative narrative to discover more about the spirit and educate herself about the supernatural. Jane's much calmer demeanour when confronted by the existence of Natre contrasts dramatically with Thun's terror (though his reaction, we learn later in the narrative, can be attributed to guilt rather than fear).

Close examination of *Buppha Ratri*, *Body* and *Art of the Devil 2* also indicates how these films are imbued with a film style and narrative format that adheres to the viewing preferences of collectivist lower-class Thailand. *Buppha Ratri* in particular becomes an excellent example as to how, despite the creation of a new and commercially viable industry through high-grossing blockbuster productions and an infrastructure of multiplexes to support them, the influence of this previous primary audience is still very evident. The film follows a causal narrative structure that blends visceral traits from many genres, privileging the aesthetic of attraction as a source of stimulation over that of narrative integration. While opening scenes set up the tragic narrative of Buppha's abuse and then death, the film shifts to become a series of graphic comedy, horror and action numbers that follow a very loosely discernible climactic plot. There is no attempt to construct a question-and-answer suspense and/or mystery structure. Although the ending provides a surprise revelation that the abusive Ek is actually a ghost and had been killed by Buppha as part of her revenge, this detail is only added within the last ten minutes of the film and does not impact the rest of the plot.

Art of the Devil 2 also exhibits such characteristics. The overcomplicated and unclear narrative again privileges the aesthetic of attraction. The main source of stimulation is a series of graphic numbers, the majority of which elicit extreme fear and/or disgust. For instance the film's opening scene is highly graphic: a fisherman in a rural village is taken to an old woman's house in terrible pain after being cursed by catching a catfish laced with fish hooks. As he screams in pain, a variety of extreme close-up shots reveal fish hooks emerging from various parts of his body. This sets the tone for the rest of the film, in which the aesthetic of attraction – in this case extremely graphic horror numbers – takes precedence as source of stimulation. The film also ends with an extraordinarily graphic torture scene, in which Miss Panor ritually burns, skins, extracts teeth from and drills into the live body of the student who tricked and abused her.

The presence of this lower-class collective film style is also evident in the confused and disdainful international responses to these films, which echo the attitudes expressed by Thai elites and non-Thais in previous decades. The vengeful ghost films were particularly successful both within Thailand and within the burgeoning international market. *Art of the Devil 2*, *Buppha Ratri*, *Nang Nak*, *Body* and *Shutter* were all shown at international film festivals and released on DVD internationally, with copies containing both Chinese and English subtitles. In this international reception, we begin to see a dissatisfaction with the film style of these productions: for critics and viewers the privileging of the aesthetic of attraction over that of plot adheres to 'lowbrow' horror: the overt and graphic low-budget incarnations that exist on the fringe of 'good taste' (Hunt, 2000: 326) and are regarded as inferior to a rounded erotic suspense/mystery structure. Responses focus upon the privileging of visceral numbers over that of a coherent suspense structure as well as the corresponding blending of genre traits.

For instance, while *Buppha Ratri* performed well in Thailand, non-Thai reviewers appear perplexed by the film's strange format. As one critic writes after viewing the film at the Toronto International Film Festival 2004:

> After a fairly promising start, *Rahtree: Flower of the Night* quickly transforms into an incredibly lame horror/comedy. It's actually quite remarkable how fast the film goes from semi-interesting to all-out disaster. (David Nusair, 2004)

While the mixing of these visceral genre traits is regarded as a 'disaster' by this non-Thai viewer, my close analysis has indicated that the characteristic of privileging the aesthetic of attraction and the blending of various genres into a single film were historically both integral parts of Thai film. These characteristics catered for a collective provincial audience and have continued to imbue productions in the contemporary era. Comments regarding *Art of the Devil 2* from the popular film reviewing website 'Twitch film' also illustrate a dissatisfaction with these stylistic traits. The reviewer states, 'It's less concerned with plot than with shocks' and 'as a narrative it sputters badly, but as a visceral experience it makes for powerful stuff' (Brown, 2006). Rather than crude and 'lowbrow' however, as I have already illustrated, this visceral aesthetic of attraction is a significant characteristic of Thai cinema due to its origins and development.

Evidently conscious of this negative international reception and keen to achieve global success and distribution, we begin to see a movement away from this older provincial film style by Thai filmmakers. Certainly, such a movement is evident in the international DVD case design of *Buppha Ratri*, which attempts to erase this evidence of lower-class Thai subjectivity in generating international appeal. There are radical differences between the marketing styles of the Thai DVD and the international DVD. The Thai version conforms to the comedic visceral excess of the 16mm era Thai film form in its presentational style. However, the international adheres to more global horror trends, suggesting subtlety and inviting questions about the protagonist rather than giving direct information.

A very deliberate change to film style then becomes particularly evident in close analysis of *Shutter*. As probably the most successful New Thai production to engage with the vengeful ghost motif, *Shutter* is a particularly significant example of this theme within the New Thai industry. Made by Phenomena Motion Pictures, an affiliate of the much larger Phenomena film productions, this small company (similar to Matching Motion Pictures who made *Zee Oui*) was set up to capitalise on the success of the New Thai industry. Of the forty-eight Thai films released in 2004 (eleven of which were horror films) *Shutter* was the highest grossing by far and was the fourth highest grossing film overall, beating the Hollywood historical epic *Troy* (Wolfgang Petersen, 2004) and the sci-fi blockbuster *I, Robot* (Alex Proyas, 2004). It achieved an astounding level of success for a domestic horror film, taking over two and a half million dollars, almost one million more than the second-highest grossing Thai film for 2004, *The Bodyguard* (Petchtai Wongkamlao, 2004). In the first week of release it grossed $1,406,196 million dollars. In the second week the film shot up to claim a further $2,182,160 million dollars.[1] Even many years later, a fascination with *Shutter* remains within Thailand, as well as a degree of 'pride' in the international success it achieved. Internet message boards still host discussions in which it is referred to as the 'best' Thai horror ever and the only genuinely frightening Thai film, and major film websites at the time devoted pages to its beginnings and the continuing antics of its directors.[2]

However, Shutter's significant success (both international and domestic) and corresponding milestone status in the New Thai industry appears to have been achieved through removing the subjectivity of lower-class Thailand. Firmly designed for an individualised viewer in an urban cinema far outside of the collectivist social norms of provincial Thailand, close analysis indicates that *Shutter* does not display the lower-class collective stylistic traits still evident in *Buppha Ratri* and *Art of the Devil 2*. Indeed, *Shutter*'s filmmakers deliberately constructed the film to privilege narrative integration as a source of stimulation. Recognising the significance of narrative structure in the global appeal of horror, they are quoted on a popular Thai film website stating that the source behind the (perceived) bad quality and lack of success of Thai films lay in problems with the plots.[3] In *Shutter* the vengeful ghost motif is therefore mapped onto a carefully constructed suspense narrative. Rather than a prior-known causal narrative structure and the privileging of the aesthetic of attraction as a source of stimulation, *Shutter*'s filmmakers have constructed a story in which the vengeful ghost Natre and her backstory of abuse is slowly and terrifyingly revealed to the viewer through questions posed that the characters must then solve.

For instance, many questions are created through earlier unexplained scenes, such as when Thun's friend Ton shows up terrified at Thun's apartment, repeatedly asking for some photographs and whispering 'it's that bitch'. These questions are then answered later in the film, when it is revealed that Ton was one of Natre's rapists and was asking for photographs Thun took of the assault. Questions are also raised regarding the overall significance that is attached to the camera and the university biology lab. These are again answered later when the biology lab is finally revealed to have been the site of Natre's rape and the camera as having been used to take the incriminating photos, a symbol of Thun's ultimate betrayal of Natre. In particular, the character of Thun's girlfriend Jane shares the viewer's lack of prior-knowledge about the characters and situation, with the character conducting her own investigation to answer the mystery. Through Jane's perspective and investigation, the audience slowly learns the truth about Natre, Thun and Thun's friends' past actions, as well as the reasons behind Natre's quest for vengeance.

Shutter therefore appears very different to the cinematic style and viewing traditions that have influenced Thai cinema and imbue this national form of popular culture. Instead the film appears much more in line with global 'high culture' conceptions of the horror genre. The film's deliberate altering of its narrative structure and *mise-en-scène* in particular evidently enabled *Shutter* to achieve a much wider popular distribution than any other Thai horror film at this time. Rather than the sporadic festival showings of *Buppha Ratri*, *Shutter* appeared on global high street DVD racks in the mid-2000s alongside East Asian horror films such as *Ringu* (Hideo Nakata, 1998) and *Ju-On* (Hideo Nakata, 2002). In a contradictory fashion however, the film alters the style of this thematically progressive film style to conform to the parameters of more globally desirable dominant horror conventions. This results in the potential marginalising of the lower-class provincial and collective Thai audiences whose abusive treatment the story purports to address. Such audiences and their preferences are not acknowledged or accommodated, but instead represented through a film style that is removed from their own subjective experience.

This erasing of the 16mm era characteristics within this film then corresponds to an erasing of Thai subjectivity on the global scene at this time. *Shutter* adopts the *mise-en-scène* of globally successful East Asian horror films and appears much more in-keeping with global conceptions of a 'high-brow' version of horror associated with East Asian countries such as Japan and South Korea. *Shutter*'s *mise-en-scène*, costumes and even performance are reminiscent of internationally renowned East Asian horror films such as *Ringu*, *Dark Water* (Takashi Shimizu, 2002), *A Tale of Two Sisters* (Kim Jee-woon, 2003) and *Ju-On*. Thai and non-Thai viewers alike both recognise this stylistic similarity.[4] For instance, the long black hair, white face, stilted crawling and staring eyes of Natre are reminiscent of the vengeful Japanese *onryou* in Japanese horror films such as *Ringu* and *Ju-On*. A scene in which Natre crawls slowly and stiffly up Thun's bed is similar to both Sadako emerging from the television in *Ringu* and Kayako crawling down the stairs in *Ju-On*. Likewise, Jane stays in her university uniform for a significant part of the story, echoing the prominence of Japanese school girl costumes in films such as *Battle Royale* (Kinji Fukasaku, 2000), *Suicide Circle* (Shion Sono, 2001) and *Ringu*. In manners and dress, Thun himself can easily be paralleled with Ruyuji, who assists the protagonist in *Ringu*.

Instead, this standardised and globally prominent cinematic conception of 'Asian horror' is very different to the Southeast Asian visceral Thai numbers with their traditional haunted forest houses, slapstick buffoons and gory scenes. Thun's dark enclosed apartment with its linear contours is comparable to apartments in the prior-mentioned Japanese ghost films, ones very different to the shoddy Thai apartments with their make-shift washing lines and hair salons in *Buppha Ratri*, and completely separate from the upcountry Thai village of *Nang Nak*. The pre-modern *mise-en-scène* of historical rural Thailand as depicted in *Nang Nak* is absent, as is the dark-skinned Nak sporting her traditional peasant hairstyle and blackened teeth. Similarly the slapstick comedy and teenage rockstars of *Buppha Ratri* are absent from *Shutter*, while the blood and vomit splattered hacksaw-wielding figure of Buppha is a world away from the more refined Natre. Indeed, for many international viewers unfamiliar with Thai language, it appears difficult to recognise and identify Thailand as the film's country of origin. Online discussion boards and reviews erroneously refer to the film as Japanese, with viewers also expressing surprise that the film is actually Thai and confusion at being unable to recognise any distinguishing features of these national origins.

The global marginalising of Thai subjectivity through the erasing of the 16mm era characteristics then perhaps becomes most evident in *Shutter*'s 2008

Hollywood remake (Masayuki Ochiai, 2008). Following in the footsteps of *Ringu* and *Ju-On*, *Shutter*'s adherence to such global aesthetic and narrative trends ensured Hollywood interest enough to purchase and re-make its tale of abuse. This ensured that any lingering connection to Thailand and the preferences of the Thai provincial audiences was finally erased when the film was instead located in Japan, employed a Japanese director and followed an American couple, Ben and Jane Shaw. The protagonists are now haunted by a genuine *onryou*, the abused young Japanese woman Megumi Tanaka. The central motif is now mapped upon a wider discourse of Western masculine abuse vs Eastern feminine revenge, with an American Jane now occupying the conflicting position of the affluent modern female who uncovers this hidden history of abuse.[5]

Conclusion

This chapter has indicated that in contrast to the Heritage productions, certain horror films within the New Thai industry do critique the unfair hierarchy of Thai society and the corresponding ideology of Localism. The vengeful ghost films offer a representation that highlights the abusive nature of Thai society and can be interpreted as a critique of the continuing abuse of the Thai lower classes and women in particular. The ambiguous endings of these films further suggest that such a system cannot continue and Thai society in its present form must be dismantled, potentially foreshadowing the military coup and social conflict that I will explore in the later chapters of this volume. However, analysis further indicated that the most successful of the vengeful ghost films, *Shutter*, actually erases the 16mm era characteristics and that this removal then signals a loss of the Thai-ness that has come to define these productions on the global scene. This is most especially evident in the American remake of *Shutter*, which erases all connections to the film's Thai origins in favour of a Japanese connection. Such an absence suggests that an authentic Thai cinematic identity can be found in the diverse stylistic practices which represent the wide and divided nature of Thai society.

The next chapter moves on to explore another phenomenon in Thai horror that is closely related to (and, indeed, at times thematically overlaps with) the vengeful ghost films. Building upon the progressive interrogation of Thai social inequalities through horror, Chapter 6 examines how the cinematic technology itself is used within this process. Again linking back to the audiences of the 16mm era, the chapter indicates how this engagement with cinematic technology and interaction with an aware viewer becomes a means to give voice to a subaltern perspective and continue the social critique evident in the vengeful ghost films.

Notes

Parts of this chapter have been previously published as Ainslie, M. (2011) 'Contemporary Thai Horror: The Horrific Incarnation of *Shutter*', *Asian Cinema*, 22(1), pp. 45–57. DOI: https://doi.org/10.1386/ac.22.1.45_1

1. Source: http://www.boxofficemojo.com/intl/thailand/?yr=2004&currency=us&p=.htm
2. This can be seen on websites such as www.siamzone.com, www.popcornfor2.com and www.thaifilmdirector.com
3. This is discussed in an article on leading Thai entertainment website Siam Zone, in which Phenomena Motion Pictures state that they acknowledged the trashy 'pure entertainment' element of Thai horror when planning *Shutter* and that the source behind this (perceived) bad quality and lack of success lay with problems in the plots. Retrieved from www.siamzone.com/movie/news/index.php?id=1999
4. An extensive article in Thai at www.popcornfor2.com/movies/archives/ft_061.html discusses *Shutter*'s relationship to Japanese ghost films and marks the movie as stylistically similar to both *Ju-On* and *Ringu*.
5. A notable difference between these two productions is the ending, in which Thun/Ben sits silent and unmoving in a mental hospital with the spirit of Natre/Megumi draped possessively over his shoulders. The American version depicts Jane abandoning Ben to his fate as forever entwined with the angry *onryou*. In her Thai incarnation however, Jane returns ready to engage with this stalemate and so suggests that in her duality she can possibly construct a solution to the chaotic consequences modern Thailand finds itself entwined within.

6. HORROR BEYOND THE SCREEN
Victim, The Screen at Kamchanod *and* Coming Soon

So far, this book has indicated how New Thai horror films thematically and formally engage with the trauma and anxieties of contemporary Thailand. Films address the problematic position of women, ethnic minorities and the lower-classes from both conservative and progressive ideological positions. Such films have a complex relationship to wider society, addressing very different audiences in this increasingly polarised and unequal nation, an engagement and a position that is not only thematic but also stylistic.

Chapter 6 takes such analysis further to indicate how the filmmaking and film viewing process is often interrogated in New Thai film, a process defined as (self-)reflexivity. The chapter indicates how this frequent phenomenon in the New Thai industry is very different to comparable reflexive devices in international forms of horror, and is much more akin to the 'Cinema Spiritualism' of early film. Arguing that such a phenomenon draws upon the historical development of film as part of a tradition of communal 'display' (as explored and outlined in Chapter 1), the chapter then demonstrates how these films are indicative of a particular relationship between modernity and the supernatural and the continuing significance of ghosts and spirits as a form of social organisation in contemporary Thailand. Examining two significant films as examples of this interrogation, the chapter outlines how the depiction of filmmaking and screening technology becomes a means for oppressed and marginalised perspectives to be heard. In a similar way to the vengeful ghost films and the presentational film style examined in the previous chapters, these films force contemporary Thailand to acknowledge such a perspective, accosting cinematic technology to hold society to account.

(Self-)Reflexivity in Thai Horror

Connected to the hybrid style of New Thai film, one particularly interesting feature of productions in the contemporary New Thai industry is the capacity for experimentation with and extrapolation upon the relationship between viewer and film. A significant number of films in the New Thai industry tend to break the fourth wall and acknowledge, or make reference to, the audience and the viewing process. Limoges refers to such practices in film as 'self-reflexivity' and 'reflexivity', the former being when 'the enunciative apparatus (or supposed apparatus) of the work is intentionally revealed' (Limoges, 2009: 396), while the latter is rather the revealing of 'a' device, such as a 'film within a film' (Ibid: 393).

Within the New Thai industry both practices, which I refer to collectively as (self-)reflexivity, are particularly evident in Thai horror. Contemporary Thai horror films consistently display this characteristic, exploring filmmaking and viewing as a concept by foregrounding (self-)reflexivity as well as revealing the artifice of the film itself. Prominent and successful horror films such as *Coming Soon/Program Na Winyan Akat* (Sophon Sakdaphisit, 2008), *The Screen at Kamchanod/Pee Chang Nang* (Songsak Mongkolthong, 2007), *The Victim/Phii Khon Pen* (Monthon Arayangkoon, 2006), *Sars Wars/Khunkrabiihiiroh* (Taweewat Wantha, 2004), *Ghost Game* (Sarawut Wichiensarn, 2006) and *Shutter* (Banjong Pisanthanakun and Parkpoom Wongpoom, 2004) all seek in various ways to interrogate the medium and its relationship with the viewer. These particular films play with the viewer and the boundaries of the diegesis quite significantly, often acknowledging viewers and demonstrating awareness of the viewing process. For instance, the film *The Victim* is actually a film-within-a-film: the text breaks down halfway through and destroys the diegesis that it has just spent forty-five minutes building without any warning or prior indication. Likewise, *The Screen at Kamchanod* also engages the audience in such a process, setting its story around a mysterious film screening and implying that the actual cinema screen becomes a gateway for spirits to pass through into another realm. In another highly (self-)reflexive story, *Coming Soon* depicts a haunted film in which a spirit sucks viewers into the film and mutilates them, with a similarly angry and abused female spirit to that depicted in *Shutter*. Finally, with its crude effects and slapstick comedy combined with graphic violence, *Sars Wars/Khunkrabiihiiroh* acknowledges the viewer multiple times, even stopping the film halfway through, during which characters mock the audience for continuing to sit through the outlandish antics.

The interrogative and (self-)reflexive practices of these films seem in keeping with the general increased experimentation we see emerging in horror cinema globally over the last two decades, much of which involves various degrees of this reflexivity and self-reflexivity. Highly reflexive subgenres such as 'found footage' are attributed to the innovation of digital technologies and their new relationship to the spectral. Often recognised to have begun in the modern era with *The Blair Witch Project* (Daniel Myrick and Eduardo Sánchez, 1999) and successful franchises such as the *REC* (Jaume Balagueró and Paco Plaza, 2007) and *Paranormal Activity* (Oren Peli, 2007) series, the turn towards deploying 'found footage' and digital technologies as a means to interrogate the horrific effects of modernity is now a recognised film style, particularly in the horror genre.

However, in contemporary Thai horror (self-)reflexivity is a very different cultural phenomenon, and one that must be viewed and understood separately to that of recent developments in digital-era horror. Instead of the growing pervasiveness of screens and technology, the tradition of (self-)reflexivity in Thai cinema is much more indicative of the earlier function of Thai film as a communal display. Indeed, the fourth wall concept has always been less cogent in the Thai context, being attributed to the conventions of realist and naturalist traditions in Euro-American theatre from the nineteenth century onwards. Such productions tended to hermetically seal productions and their diegesis from any acknowledgement of or interaction with the audience. Being, as I demonstrated in Chapter 1, descended from and embedded alongside a very different tradition of representation that favoured an aware, interactive and communal audience, Thai productions lend themselves more readily to the conventions of (self-)reflexivity, which interfere less with the aesthetic illusion of cinema in Thailand. In communal traditions of entertainment, the diegesis is not hermetically sealed in the same way as the realist traditions that influence more individualist immersive Hollywood films. As a result, breaking down the fourth wall is far less intrusive to the viewing experience. This allows for more experimentation in mainstream filmmaking due largely to a more relaxed attitude towards the conventions of film.

Certainly, (self-)reflexivity is evident throughout Thai film history, providing an origin for this phenomenon in the contemporary industry. Live dubbing (discussed in Chapter 1), a practice that continued up to the 1970s, certainly foregrounds the strong self-reflexive element of cinema in the Thai context which, combined with the histrionic acting, long shots and long takes, creates a conscious display that allows the text to function well within the socialised collective atmosphere of shared pleasure. Through such practices, the artifice of film is not 'revealed' to or hidden from the audience and Hanich's 'phenomenological proximity' and the individual absorption discussed in Chapter 1 are absent. This lack of any immersive tradition between the viewer and the screen certainly allows for a strong self-reflexive streak to develop in Thai filmmaking, one encouraged by the lack of disruption to viewing pleasure such artifice may otherwise present. The diegesis can be disrupted because the diegesis doesn't have to be convincingly 'real' in the first place, and can be recognised as artifice and, in the case of (self-) reflexive films, even blatantly presented as such.

The frequency of (self-)reflexivity in Thai filmmaking further demonstrates how such devices are not only not a recent development, but also are not even a very modern phenomenon. In global filmmaking, the experimentation associated with found footage and (self-)reflexivity was originally positioned 'outside' of mainstream filmmaking conventions before it became a recognised film style. As such, this became strongly associated with horror and thrillers as well as the avant-garde (Heller-Nicholas, 2014: 3). Such a position is certainly not true in Thai cinema; films employing such devices are mainstream and (self-)reflexivity can stretch across genres. In New Thai cinema we see (self-) reflexivity in many films that span a number of different styles and genres. For example, the socially critical retro-nostalgic *Monrak Transistor* (Pen-Ek Ratanaruang, 2001) begins with a Bangkok prison guard walking past cells holding prisoners while directly addressing the viewer with a monologue explaining the story that is about to be depicted. Further demonstrating the unsealed nature of this world, the guard then appears again later in the film and is able to interact with other characters in the diegesis while also addressing the audience. This dialogue is deeply self-reflexive, even including reference to the audience's viewing of the film and their going home afterwards.

Similarly, the alternative postmodern saturated aesthetics of Wisit Sasanatieng's high concept nostalgia-driven film style also points to such self-reflexivity, with no attempt to disguise film as artifice. Productions such as *Tears of the Black Tiger/Fa Thalai Chon* (Wisit Sasanatieng, 2000) depict a cartoonish fantasy of histrionic, stylised performances and make-shift painted artificial sets, all designed to reference the previous post-war 16mm era. The exaggerated and excessive *mise-en-scène* again underlines the artifice of film, an element that does not disrupt viewing pleasure and which has been particularly successful with international festival audiences, to which it can represent the exoticised display often associated with Thailand and Thai-ness (Ingawanij and Lowell, 2005; Van Esterik, 2000). In a doubly reflexive portrayal, the aforementioned *Monrak Transistor* even includes a dubbed communal viewing of *Tears of the Black Tiger*, in which a dubber offers up a hilarious and crude commentary in place of dialogue between the hero and heroine.

Further engaging with such aesthetics, the normalisation of self-reflexivity in Thai film has perhaps allowed for the strong growth and success of the avant-garde in Thailand, which is now very much 'mainstream' thanks to the global success of auteur Apichatpong Weerasetakul. This movement fully embraces and encompasses self-reflexivity, with the normalisation of such a phenomenon arguably making stylistic experimentation less of a focus, so leaving auteurs free to explore socially pressing issues such as censorship and the attitudes towards ethnic minorities. Indeed, spurred on by the international success and ever-growing profile of Apitchapong Weerasetakul, films such as *Tropical Malady/Sat Pralat* (Apichatpong Weerasethakul, 2004) and *Uncle Boonmee Who Can Recall His Past Lives/Loong Boonmee Raluek Chat* (Apichatpong Weerasethakul, 2009) blend deliberate artifice with experimentation, spirituality and sensuality. In productions such as *Syndromes and a Century/Saeng Satawat* (Apichatpong Weerasethakul, 2006), a series of long shots and takes meditate upon everyday rural and urban Thailand, with such cinematography and editing again reminiscent of the 16mm era Golden Age productions (Boehler, 2014).

Accommodating the Supernatural through Technology

This tradition of (self-)reflexivity means that the engagement with the boundary between screen and viewer in New Thai horror is very different in function to that of the modern digital phenomenon. In her study of contemporary Thai ghost films, Katarzyna Ancuta (in one of the very few analyses to pay attention to the form of contemporary Thai film) attributes the frequent use of (self-)reflexive devices to technological improvements in Thai filmmaking and increased levels of experimentation by filmmakers (both of which are significant aspects that enabled the formation of the big-budget New Thai industry). Ancuta then further insightfully points out that many of these texts frequently use the viewer/film relationship as a means to question the nature of ghosts and spirits as entities (Ancuta 2011: 141). Building upon Ancuta's analysis, I posit that (self-)reflexivity in contemporary Thai horror can also function as a means to assess and interrogate the relationship between society and the (still very real) supernatural in the contemporary urban context.

Rather than that of the digital era, the social interrogation represented in (self-)reflexive Thai films is much more akin to the treatment of the supernatural in early film. Braunlein (2016) draws a parallel between Southeast Asian ghost films and the spiritualist tradition to which early cinema is attached (though, in contrast with the Victorian obsession, the [self-]reflexivity of the contemporary Thai context is less concerned with assessing or 'proving' the existence of spirits and the supernatural). At this time, the supernatural was less a violation of 'natural law' in the European context, whereby modernisation and the supernatural were not contradictions but intricately combined. Film represented a potential new means of facilitating both an engagement with and a wider understanding of this very real facet of society. Leeder (2017) argues against an ahistorical epistemological connection between film and the spectral, rejecting parallels between the spectrality and fragmentary nature of internet and digital film and that of the obsession with the supernatural in early cinema. Instead Leeder attributes early cinema's affinity between cinema and the supernatural as due to late Victorian society's obsession with the supernatural and its association with visual trickery, illusions and the projection of light, a context out of which cinema emerged (Leeder, 2017: 45). Leeder argues that the supernatural affinity of early cinema is connected to this context, whereby 'the association of cinema with the supernatural is reflective of the cultural role played by the supernatural more broadly at the moment of cinema's emergence' (Leeder, 2017: 28–29).

Such a relationship must be understood as not only historically but also culturally specific. The (self-)reflexive nature of contemporary Thai horror must also be placed within a specific context, one in which (as demonstrated in Chapter 1) the supernatural continues to act as a significant means of social organisation. As previously stated, an attribute of the human condition under rapid modernity was the increased need to curb and/or empirically explain 'things that could not be observed' (Tamborini and Weaver, 1996: 6). Such a desire speaks of an increasing lack of control and a need to exert power over one's own environment, a move that is also understandable within 2000s Thailand. Modern technology is imbued with the desire to interpret and understand a rapidly changing environment, an engagement that Peter J. Braunlein calls 'Cinema Spiritualism' (2016) when referring to the Thai context.

As a cinematic device, (self-)reflexivity becomes indicative of both the continuing importance of the supernatural in Thai society and the need to (re)negotiate this relationship in the contemporary context. In this way, while it may be tempting to argue that the (self-)reflexive nature of Thai horror is indicative of a specific connection between cinema and the supernatural in the Thai context, 'Cinema Spiritualism' is more reflective of the supernatural as an important facet of everyday Thai life, within which the cinematic technology becomes a 'tool' of engagement. As argued in Chapter 1, the supernatural, while frightening, has never really been positioned as a violation of 'natural law' in Thailand. Instead, supernatural beliefs in ghosts and spirits continue to act as an important form of social organisation on both an official and unofficial level, even far into the contemporary age. Given the ever-present spirit world within Thai society, the (self-)reflexive nature of Cinema Spiritualism represents how such worlds are ever-entwined and not separate. My analysis so far has demonstrated how this is evident in New Thai productions, with spirits and ghosts able to interject into the diegesis fairly freely and so bleed across genres, while also thematically engaging with wider social anxieties connected to patriarchy, racism and the treatment of minorities and lower-classes. Likewise, as Ancuta understands, filmmakers even often attempt to authenticate their films through attachment to supernatural occurrences, depicting and articulating how stories and spirits pertain to real life events (Ancuta, 2016: 134).

The (self-)reflexivity of Cinema Spiritualism therefore reflects how beliefs in the supernatural and the spirit world remain highly significant in contemporary

Thailand, and remain increasingly relevant as a means to cope with and understand a rapidly changing and confusing context. As explored in Chapter 3, official and unofficial supernatural beliefs and organisations actually underwent a degree of (re)surgence in the 1990s push towards modernity (Jackson 2014). Theorists understand that the relationships between modernity and the supernatural require new forms of understanding in the non-Western context and should not be automatically opposed. Instead, reflecting the uncanny and inexplicable abilities of global Capitalism and new technology, the supernatural sits well alongside the modern world. The engagement of state and non-state actors with such beliefs, as well as the growth and monetisation of spirit cults and the general 'prosperity religion' that dominates contemporary Southeast Asia, represents the interweaving of supernatural belief and the modern economy (see Braunlein, 2018; Jackson, 2014; Ancuta, 2016). The condition of modernity in Thailand resulted in a melding of modern life and the supernatural; a relationship that is reflected in Thai horror. The (self-)reflexive nature of Cinema spiritualism should be understood as a comparable intertwining of supernatural belief and modern technology.

Contemporary (self-)reflexive Thai horror films use the cinema screen and apparatus to interrogate the changing boundary between the everyday and the supernatural, with the cinema screen functioning as (a very physical) representation of that boundary. In a similar manner to the spiritualist performance, cinematic technology and the viewing process can operate as a 'space' in which to assess and imagine the relationship between these 'worlds' during the post-2000s period of rapid social change.

The Anxieties of Thai (Self-)Reflexive Horror, Technology and the Supernatural

Given this strong relationship between spirits and technology, there are significant differences between how social fears and anxieties are addressed and articulated in (self-)reflexive Thai horror and that of global forms of horror in the digital age. Global digital horror and its subgenre of found footage tends to display an explicit preoccupation with social anxiety around technological advances, one manifested largely through concerns around surveillance and social alienation. Technologies impact upon the individual's life in an uncontrollable and profoundly intrusive manner, one brought about by the increasingly invasive nature of digital technology in the modern world.

Yet in Thai horror the (self-)reflexivity of Cinema Spiritualism does not generally fixate upon such concerns. Given the continuing presence of the supernatural (rather than 'intrusion') as an important part of wider society, the anxieties represented in Thai (self-)reflexive horror are largely concerned with how society accommodates the supernatural within the rapidly developing modern context and its (in many cases, cinematic) technology. The films are therefore informed less by concerns around the intrusiveness of technology in the digital age and more by the need to accommodate and, in doing so, respect, supernatural beliefs alongside and as a part of modern urban life.

Amidst the corpus of (self-)reflexive New Thai horror films, *Coming Soon* and *The Screen at Kamchanod* both stand out as significant spectral interrogations of the relationship between viewer and screen. Both films are heavily (self-)reflexive, containing many shots of cameras, cinema screens and audiences watching films. *Coming Soon* includes long takes and shots of the projectionist protagonists unpacking and loading reels of films, foregrounding this technology throughout. In addition to such technology, *Kamchanod* also makes much reference to film history, depicting its protagonists around rusty cans of film, faded posters and cardboard cut-outs covered in cobwebs. Both tell the story of a film-within-a-film, while also breaking the fourth wall at various points in the narrative. Both films also address the potential for the cinema screen and the viewing process to act as the source of infusion and permeation of the living world and the spirit world, enabling spirits to interact with the characters. In both these films therefore, rather than excluding or replacing the supernatural, the technological advances of the modern world easily lend themselves to the supernatural, in a similar way to the cinema spiritualism of early film.

Coming Soon follows Shane, a projectionist who has received and is pirating a new horror film 'Vengeful Spirit'. When a spirit associated with the film begins haunting and terrorising the cinema, Shane and his partner travel to rural Thailand to find out more about the protagonist of the film, a disturbed woman called Shomba, who kidnapped children and gouged out their eyes to make them stay forever in her home. The protagonist is even filmed burning the celluloid film at one point, trying to destroy the spirit. However, in a later twist, the destructive and angry spirit is revealed to be the film's actress rather than the character the film is based upon. A secret tape reveals the filmmaking crew to have pushed the actress Ingchan to the limits of her performance ability. The crew accidentally killed Ingchan when filming a hanging scene, yet later covered up the death and retained the on-screen footage for use in the actual film.

The Screen at Kamchanod tells the story of a projectionist and his group of friends and colleagues trying to locate and recreate a film and film screening from 1989. Allegedly taking place in rural Udon Thani with no audience, the screening supposedly then gained an audience halfway through, who promptly vanished at the end of the film. The film's marketing makes much of being based upon a true story, an urban legend reportedly connected to the Thai practice of screening films 'for the dead', in reality as part of elaborate entertainments for funerals and often involving crude comedy films. The film follows protagonists locating the original film, which thwarted any attempt to destroy it, and eventually viewing and then later screening the film in the jungle in an attempt to recreate the original event.

The film style of both films follows the presentational style of Thai film, so demonstrating the ongoing connection of contemporary Thai horror to this aesthetic tradition and influence. There is a predominance of long shots and takes and very few close-up shots, with canted angles and low and high angle shots used to create the sense of unease throughout. Again the erotic devices of suspense and mystery are generally absent from the narratives, and both films seem to favour visceral numbers as a source of stimulation. The lose narratives are woven around the various numbers, with confusing motivations and occurrences that function largely to fill time between scenes of spirits terrorising the protagonists. At times there is very little narrative explanation; characters are chased down corridors by the ghosts for no apparent reason and with no explanation. Again, characters are frightened but not surprised, recovering quickly afterwards. Such scenes become a 'display' to the extent that non-Thai reviews stress the need for explanation, and critique both films' lack of narrative-based expositional dialogue. Indeed, in both films there are very few wider-explored social implications and no clear moral ending.

Yet despite these confusing narratives, both *Coming Soon* and *Kamchanod* clearly articulate the potential danger of using modern technology without respecting and accommodating the supernatural order. In both narratives we see the consequences of not recognising (and not respecting) the importance of the supernatural as a crucial part of modernity and technology. In both films the filmmaker and projectionist protagonists appear ignorant of and somewhat arrogant towards the need to appease and accommodate the spirit world. In *Kamchanod*, the protagonists are determined to find the old film and recreate the conditions of the original jungle screening, with no regard as to the consequences of doing so. Even when warned by a local monk not to cross worlds, they do not heed such advice. Protagonists even seize a protectionist amulet from the aged previous projectionist, who clutches the object in fear of otherwise being overcome by the spirits that have 'invaded' the cinematic realm. In *Coming Soon*, it is revealed that the filmmakers actually killed their lead actress during the filming process and then used this footage as a means to supposedly improve their film, later hiding the truth and displaying no concern for viewers, who are later subject to the wrath of the angry spirit. In an extension of the exploitation of the lead actress and her horrific on-screen death, the film is also routinely pirated by the cinema staff for their own gain, who are also haunted and pursued by the destructive angry spirit.

The technology and the screening process in particular then become a means through which spirits can enact power and take vengeance when they are not afforded such respect in the contemporary world. In particular, these productions interrogate Thai society and, similar to the vengeful ghost films, can be interpreted as socially progressive given the perspectives they represent. Certainly, *Coming Soon* can be placed within the corpus of abused vengeful female ghosts of New Thai cinema (as explored in Chapter 5) and interpreted as a similar critique of patriarchal abuse. The actress Ingchan has been abused by the male filmmaker and her death is now exploited by the male projectionist for the paying public, both justifications for anger and, ultimately, revenge. The film also constructs a similar link between women and the supernatural, blurring the heroine and the ghost when the ghost disguises herself as the protagonist's partner.

Similarly, *Kamchanod* inserts the subjectivity of marginalised and historically oppressed Northeastern Thailand, a perspective often represented in the repressed memories of the poetic and lyrical socially critical avant-garde films of Apitchapong Weerasetakul (Boehler 2014). The story is based upon a supposed true event, a screening deep in the jungles of the Northeast, far away from the urban centre of Bangkok. The mysterious film-within-a-film contains images of forests, of corpses and of authorities digging in a field, all grainy images of rural Thailand in the past. The screening took place in a cursed forest out in Udon Thani, the place where the contemporary urban protagonists must now journey to recreate the event. Overcoming physical barriers to enter the deserted clearing, the protagonists arrogantly underestimate the fate that awaits them.

Rather than being displaced, technology (specifically, cinematic technology) is used by the supernatural to become powerful and frightening, so forcing the contemporary urban viewer to recognise the suffering of a marginalised perspective. The significance of *Coming Soon* and *Kamchanod* therefore lies in the way in which (self-)reflexivity and the engagement with the cinematic technology become a means for the subaltern to hold modern Thailand to account. In both films, the cinema screen becomes a link with the supernatural, a means through which people and spirits can cross between 'worlds', and is eventually completely accosted by the supernatural. Using such technology, the supernatural forces both viewers and characters to acknowledge marginalised status and/or poor treatment and, by extension, that of the subaltern of wider contemporary Thai society.

In *Coming Soon*, this involves the spirit transferring people who view her death into her own filmic diegesis on-screen, mutilating and killing them in the manner of the original murderer she is depicting. In *Kamchanod*, a particularly memorable scene involves the protagonists viewing the scratched and almost unintelligible filmstrip in an aged and creaky cinema. The screening seems to act as a signal for the supernatural to emerge, with protagonists slowly surrounded by spirits, with hands reaching around and foldable seats creaking under the weight of invisible occupants.

In the end of both films, the protagonists are eventually taken into the screen, becoming a part of the spirits' diegesis. After realising, too late, that it is the actress they are seeing, not the character, *Coming Soon* descends into a nightmarish sequence of images in which Shane runs through darkened cinemas and corridors, pursued by the spirit who appears on screens all around him. Shane then eventually appears on the big screen, having been sucked into the film as punishment for watching the actress's death. His partner stares helplessly at the cinema screen, collapsing distraught in the middle of the cinema, while the ghost gouges Shane's eyes out. In *Kamchanod*, this melding of screen and protagonists is a more gradual process, with all characters starting to experience the supernatural more and more after initially viewing the film. While spirits interfere more and more with their everyday world, the suggestion is that the screening blurred and intensified their relationship with the supernatural. The protagonists' lives slowly become infested by spirits, driving various people crazy; one character kills his partner and himself, screaming that they should not have crossed between worlds. As the film progresses, the characters remark how they are beginning to see fewer living people and more spirits, a symptom of their movement into the supernatural. Finally, characters remark that there are no ghosts in the cursed forest, leading to the 'twist': that the spirits supposedly viewing and then sucked into the screen are actually them.

The films then extend such critique to the viewing public: in the ending of both films, the actual cinema audience takes the place of the protagonist to become the actual real-life viewer. In doing so, the audience members are prevented from distancing themselves from such abuse and so are directly accused, as modern citizens, of failing to realise the damage they are a part of. As recreational viewers of lower-class rural and/or female suffering, contemporary urban Thai audiences are forced to recognise and endure punishment. In *Kamchanod*, the cinema screen of the grainy film-within-a-film that swallows up the protagonists eventually becomes the actual screen of the film. Diegetic sound suggests the reel runs out, and a single long take and shot depicts the projector rattling away eternally inside the forest, the people and the field having all disappeared. The audience is then fully implicated, with the film's final shot implying they are trapped forever in the supernatural world. Likewise, *Coming Soon* ends when 'Vengeful Spirit' is released to the general public. A sequence depicts audiences in Bangkok queuing up to view the fictional film, complete with displays of real-life viewers filing into their seats, casually unaware of the terror about to be unleashed upon them. The coda shows audiences watching the film on its nationwide release, with the unsuspecting viewers about to be swallowed up into the screen and tortured by the ghost. Close-up shots of audience members and their eyes are then intersected with shots of the furious ghost, with her anger at so many people watching her death for entertainment very evident. In the very final shot, the fourth wall is completely shattered and the various diegeses are all blurred. In a final shot of Ingchan hanging just at the bottom of the screen, the spirit then fully breaks the fourth wall and interrupts the credits to scream accusatorily at the actual audience 'you want to see me die yes?' The furious spirit 'calls out' the audience in the final shot, implying that viewers are just as guilty of abusing the Thai subaltern as the fictional film's protagonists, and will also be sucked into the screen and mutilated.

Conclusion

This chapter has indicated how the (self-)reflexive horror films of the New Thai industry are a testament to the importance of the supernatural as a continuing source of social organisation in contemporary Thailand. Such films come from a long tradition of aware and recognised audiences, a phenomenon that enables cinema to operate as a form of interrogation as to the social position of the supernatural, rather than an articulation of anxieties over technological surveillance. Ultimately, the anxiety represented is less concerned with the capabilities of this new technology but rather addresses the potential use of the technology in the wrong way: a way that, ultimately, is not conducive towards a respectful relationship with the ever-present supernatural world. Analysis indicated how key films critique this lack of respect, even operating as a potential means for subaltern spirits to reassert themselves and hold society to account.

In the next chapter, I take such reassertion further and examine horror films that target and appeal specifically to provincial and lower-class Thais. Such films fully deploy and embrace an updated version of the 16mm era characteristics, becoming symptomatic of the increased polarisation and growing political and social divisions in Thai society in the 2000s. Originally a lower-class entertainment form, Thai film now seems to be increasingly polarised at a time when society is also developing stark social divisions. As the next chapter will illustrate, this continued division and inequality comes with particular social consequences, such as the increased polarisation of politics within Thailand and the creation of extreme political factors that result from the country's continued elitist hierarchy and inequality.

7. VILLAGE HORROR
Continuing a Provincial Film Style

Chapter 7 remains within the New Thai industry in terms of its analysis. However, this chapter now moves beyond the stylistically hybrid films aimed at the urban Thai and global market to address a body of films that are very different to these globally prominent productions. After illustrating how New Thai films employ a hybrid film style representative of this divided nation, Chapter 7 now examines New Thai films that fully embrace the narrative, thematic and iconographic characteristics of the earlier post-war era and which remain highly popular among provincial and lower-class audiences. Such films are aimed at provincial audiences and the many urban migrants from rural Thailand. This is again most evident in visceral, slapstick horror films, in which the narrative and film style are suited to communal audiences similar to 16mm era films of the post-war era. The chapter further outlines how the prevalence and thematic characteristics of such productions act as a progressive affirmation of lower-class subjectivity in the contemporary era, connecting this significance to recent oppressive political events within the country and the resurgence of lower-class social movements. A social sphere which otherwise appears marginalised in Thai society therefore continues to exert an influence on popular culture and one that is evident, the chapter argues, through the varying films produced in the New Thai industry.

Marginalised Viewers

Films targeting culturally and/or economically marginalised groups, including the urban and rural poor, have always been a part of Thai cinema, evident in the 16mm era, the Social Problem films, the B-grade productions and even the later teen era. Such eras and their productions also seem to have occupied an informal and almost unofficial position, and one that authorities always viewed with a slight tinge of embarrassment, despite the (at times) impressive output and wide success. As I have argued, Thai elites have generally held a negative attitude towards the representation and recognition of the marginalised perspectives these bodies of films represent. Such exclusion is likewise evident in the lack of official support afforded to these industries, with authorities instead prioritising the needs and status of officially endorsed filmmakers and/or foreign interests. Indeed, terms such as 'B-grade productions' and 'B-grade works' (explored in Chapter 2) also indicate the inferior and marginalised status of and attitudes towards such mass entertainment (Chaiworaporn and Knee, 2006). With the advent of the big budget New Thai industry, it would appear that marginalised upcountry viewers are no longer a prominent audience addressed by Thai film, with this presence and preference recognised only through the hybrid style that, I have indicated, continues to imbue so many contemporary productions.

Yet the popular mass-produced entertainment products addressing lower-class Thailand did not disappear with the advent of the big-budget New Thai industry. Throughout the 1980s and 1990s, films made by 'amateur directors' and 'aimed directly for second-run theatres or provincial audiences' (Ibid.: 59) indicate how the B-grade productions of the 1980s continued despite wider industrial changes. Chaiworaporn and Knee refer to this as the 'direct-to-video' phenomenon that largely targeted the masses in Thailand. This was the pirate videocassette and videocassette rental market, which increased rapidly between 1985 and 1990. It became a hub for provincial and suburban viewers of Thai films who now (with a slightly higher disposable income and a decrease in the cost of home viewing equipment) were able to purchase cheap videocassette players and make use of the video rental businesses that had sprouted up across the country from entrepreneurial shopkeepers (Hamilton, 1993: 523).

In the late 1990s and up into the New Thai industry of the 2000s, such a market was catered for by VCDs and VCD players. This inexpensive format became increasingly popular throughout Thailand, operating as a continuation of the videocassette market of the 1980s and 1990s. Even into the New Thai industry, we see productions such as *Coming Soon/Program Na Winyan Akat* (Sopon Sakdaphisit, 2008) referencing this pirate market as part of the plot, with the projectionists being paid to tape films for the black market before the official cinematic release. Many New Thai productions were not even released in DVD format but actually in VCD, which became a means to target those who were either far away from the multiplexes or simply unable to afford such luxuries. Certainly, the amount of VCD stalls in local villages and provincial markets indicates the popularity of these cheap VCD productions and copies with these viewers. Such stores primarily stocked Thai productions (though also dubbed Hollywood productions), a move very much opposed to chain stores in urban shopping malls (such as the popular chain Maeng Pong), which largely sold foreign blockbuster DVDs.

The differences in the provincial and urban market for Thai cultural products is perhaps an inevitable consequence of the late-1990s economic crisis, which exacerbated the already stark economic inequalities between provincial and urban Thais. At this time, Thailand became increasingly polarised and politically unstable, resulting in a situation some referred to as constituting an all-out 'class war' (Ungpakorn, 2009: 83). While the economic and cultural gap between rural poor and urban elites was both high and increasingly evident, this period also culminated in a significant effort by Thai elites to dispossess and completely erase the political voice of lower-class Thailand. Such expunging is most starkly represented by the removal of the democratically elected Prime Minister Thaksin Shinawatra in a bloodless military coup in September 2006.

The immense popularity and success of Thaksin and his 'Thai Rak Thai' (TRT) party since their election in 2001 represented the significant hope and anger emanating from the disgruntled and ignored Thai lower-classes. This segment of society was suffering after the economic crisis, and Thaksin was, arguably, the first political figure to realise this potential vote and tap into the strong discontent from this large social group. Such discontent resulted from the increasingly evident enormous disparity in income growth between that of 'privileged urban groups' and the rest of the country (Glassman, 2010). Thai political academic Giles Ji Ungpakorn understands that 'for the first time in decades, a party gained mass support from the poor because it believed that the poor were not a burden' (2009: 77). Thaksin and TRT introduced policies that directly targeted the rural poor, and these relatively simple programs nevertheless represented one of the first government agendas to directly assist the poor and even acknowledge the poverty that had been created after the economic boom and bust. These included populist spending programs such as 'national health insurance, a debt moratorium for farmers, and small and medium enterprise promotion' (Glassman, 2010: 766).

As the first politician to recognise and incorporate lower-class provincial Thailand into the political landscape, Thaksin's removal represented a significant marginalising of this segment of society. A millionaire media mogul and entrepreneur, Thaksin had been a relatively new figure on the Thai political scene who was apart from the traditional aristocratic Thai elites. His political success resulted in a level of control over and access to Thailand's resources that threatened older royalist elites and the opposition Democrat Party. These formed and led the yellow-shirted, ironically-named 'People's Alliance for Democracy' (PAD), whose street demonstrations called for the forcible removal of Thaksin by the monarchy. After the military-staged coup in September 2006, Thai courts 'dissolved TRT and barred over 100 of its leaders from politics' (Glassman, 2010: 767). The new regime then immediately set about dismantling the stronghold that the poor had held in society, reduced Thaksin's populist spending programs and refused to recognise the result of new democratic elections held in 2007. The Democrat party formed a government in 2008 without winning any elections and completely ignoring the will of the masses (Glassman, 2010: 768). Elites treated voters with strong disdain and contempt, claiming that the poor did not deserve a vote as they simply did not understand democracy (Ungpakorn, 2009: 78–79).

The response to this obliteration of the voice of the provincial and urban poor within Thai society was the formation of the red-shirt movement, a direct opposition to the PAD yellow shirts. Formed from the rural and urban poor, the red-shirt movement was organised through and originated from Thaksin's popularity and represented an expression of anger towards the unfair treatment and elitist hierarchy of Thailand. The movement was largely made up of 'agrarian, proletarian, lumpen-proletarian, and postproletarian workers, many from outside Bangkok, but many from Bangkok's periurban periphery and even from specific groups of workers in the city e.g., taxi drivers' (Glassman 2010: 769). Ungpakorn calls the formation of the red shirts 'a process of self-empowerment of the poor' (2009: 97) that became a representation of 'the poor and the thirst for freedom and democracy' (Ibid.: 97).

Provincial-Orientated Films

This dramatic and increased polarisation of Thai society, represented in stark visual terms through the red and yellow shirts of each side, is also reflected in the radically different films of the New Thai industry that were made during this period. Provincial market stalls were often filled with a very specific type of film – productions very different to the model of filmmaking represented in high-budget internationally renowned films such as *Nang Nak* (Nonzee Nimibutr, 1999) and *Shutter* (Pisanthanakun and Wongpoom, 2004). Instead, films such as the slapstick comedies *Luang Phii Teng/Holy Man* (Note Chermyim, 2005) and *Jaew/M.A.I.D.* (Yongyuth Thongkongthun, 2004), the comedic instalment of the long-running *Boonchu* series *Boonchu 9* (Bundit Rittakol, 2008) and the comedy horror films *Baan Phii Pop 2008* (Bunharn Taitanabul, 2008) and *Wor Mah Ba Mahasanook* (Bunjong Sinthanamongkolkul, 2008) are New Thai productions that were very successful within Thailand, but especially so with viewers who originally hailed from the provinces.

While Heritage films such as *Suriyothai* (Chatrichalerm Yukol, 2001) and *Nang Nak* uphold elitist discourses of Localism, and films such as *Shutter* focus upon the trials of urban protagonists, these provincial-situated films embed themselves deeply within the issues and scenarios pertinent to lower-class provincial Thailand and its viewers. Chaiworaporn describes these successful films as being 'locally-orientated', in that they are particularly successful in 'rural areas' (Chaiworaporn, 2007: 73), explaining 'These kinds of movies are always welcomed by local viewers. The stars are well-known and the films can reach audiences across the country, especially in the rural areas' (Chaiworaporn, 2007: 73). Viewers are whole families and appeal is across a wide age range, with the majority of audiences based outside Bangkok in the suburbs. Many of these films also did not enjoy wide success outside of Thailand and most are not available with any form of English dubbing or subtitles, further indicating the targeting of an exclusively Thai audience far beyond the English-speaking elite circles of Bangkok. Indeed, the main star in the slapstick comedy *Jaew*, Pornchita Na Songkhla (the most popular television star in Thailand at the time), spent time perfecting the Northeastern Isaan dialect for her character to use to specifically increase the film's lower-class and provincial appeal (Chaiworaporn, 2006b: 114).

The existence and success of productions that are aimed at and popular among the lower-class masses constitutes an interjection of this subjectivity into mainstream society during a highly significant period. Such productions represent and reaffirm a perspective that, I have indicated, is erased from the ideological agenda of the Heritage productions and the film style of *Shutter*, doing so at a time when this particular perspective is also under threat in the wider political arena. Certainly, Thai elites made a continued attempt to erase the lower-class red-shirt movement, in a very explicit display of elitist and discriminatory attitudes towards the urban and rural poor. This included military violence towards red-shirt protestors and extreme forms of legislation such as the strict 'Internal Security Act', which banned red-shirt demonstrations, increased censorship of online and printing material and intensified *lese-majesty* laws (Glassman, 2010: 768). Such measures indicate the extent to which Thai elites are prepared to go to erase lower-class subjectivity, yet also the strength of the rural masses, who continued to travel from distant provinces to attend demonstrations and rallies throughout Thailand. Indeed, state opposition actually resulted in the growth of this movement, which eventually shifted to represent the wider interests of the poor rather than concentrating upon following Thaksin.

Films that continue to address this audience during a period of severe oppression therefore operate as a progressive voice (and recognition of this voice) within the wider social context of Thailand and the big-budget New Thai industry. The increasing popularity of these films and the high revenue they generate is testament to the formidable presence of this lower-class sphere, and the refusal of these people to be silenced. Ungpakorn's 'class war' is therefore played out in the varying forms of Thai popular culture; films such as *Shutter* and *Nang Nak* represent the attempt by Thai elites to erase and deny lower-class subjectivity, while the films examined in this chapter are the corresponding attempt to reinsert it. Living conditions for the poor in Thailand are still radically below that of urban elites despite Thailand's 'economic prosperity', a discrepancy that I have indicated has led to the class war of contemporary Thailand.

This reassertion is evident in close analysis of two New Thai horror productions – *Wor Mah Ba Mahasanook* and *Baan Phii Pop 2008*. Both of these films specifically target the lower-class audience; neither are available outside of Thailand, neither have been released with English subtitles and *Wor* only had a VCD rather than a DVD release. *Wor* tells the story of an upcountry village that is being terrorised by a mad dog. The dog kills numerous inhabitants and livestock and the story depicts the villagers going through all sorts of bizarre, hilarious and silly remedies in their attempt to stave off the perceived threat. The villagers mistakenly flee from an intelligent temple dog called Chok; however, the threat is eventually revealed to be an escaped mad dog from outside the village that is eventually recaptured. *Baan Phii Pop 2008* meanwhile also tells the story of a rural village and its many varied inhabitants. They are visited by a group of doctors setting up a free clinic for the poor. The doctors interfere with the local shaman and prevent him from completing a violent exorcism. The shaman then casts a spell upon his wife that possesses her with the entrail-eating Pop ghost. However, the shaman later loses control over his incantations when the Pop refuses to allow him to exorcise his wife and continues to terrorise the village.

The provincial appeal of these productions is evident through the issues and scenarios that are depicted and addressed – ones relevant and even uniquely specific to provincial village life. Such depictions indicate the continued stark differences in living conditions that exist within Thailand. Both *Wor* and *Baan Phii Pop 2008* take place almost exclusively within a rural village, similar to other provincially-orientated films such as *Holy Man, Boonchu 9, Noodle Boxer* (Rerkchai Paungpetch, 2006) and *See How They Run* (Jaturong Mokjok, 2006). The characters and scenarios are associated with this setting; indeed *Baan Phii Pop 2008* even depicts a village temple fair, complete with rides and stalls. Likewise one of the very first scenes of *Wor* depicts a village market in which women are selling vegetables outside wooden houses while the background is full of chickens, pigs and buffalos. Motorbikes, the primary form of transport in rural villages, also abound, with characters arriving into scenes on them and using them to travel along the rudimentary country roads. In both films the houses and shops are also traditional rural wooden and bamboo dwellings, with many built on stilts above the ground. The characters gather to discuss their predicament in large wooden communal rooms such as the temple or in the eating areas underneath houses. They wear typical provincial attire, with baggy clothes such as bright t-shirts, loose trousers, flip flops and sarongs. Characters bathe in the local river and the surrounding woods, jungles, fields, rivers and trees are also depicted, illustrating how far removed the village is from the urban situations that are foregrounded in New Thai films such as *Shutter*.

This recognition and reaffirmation of the lower-class point of view is not only apparent through these specific characteristics directly, but also through a self-referentiality and nostalgia towards earlier eras of Thai film. In their depiction of lower-class provincial life, *Wor* and *Pop* make direct reference to and even pay homage to the 16mm era and the B-grade productions that were enjoyed by the lower-classes in previous eras. Such references indicate how relevant these earlier film eras are to the provincial audience at this time, forming a significant part of their cultural life. For instance, *Baan Phii Pop 2008* is a direct homage to the B-grade era, being a contemporary remake of the earlier B-grade *Baan Phii Pop* series to the extent that it even stars the same lead actress. Likewise the director of *Wor* states that his intention was to make a film very similar to the *Baan Phii Pop* series by simply replacing the main ghost with a dog. *Baan Phii Pop 2008* also contains a number of scenes identical to the earlier 16mm era productions. The lead actress is seen bathing in a sarong in the river and the group of fools are again spying on her in a direct parody of the scene from both *Phii Saht Sen Haa* (Pan Kam, 1969) in the 16mm era and later productions of *Baan Phii Pop* in the B-grade era.

Such references recognise and so reinforce this viewing community as essentially Thai and, crucially, essentially *provincially* Thai. This form of identity through nostalgia is very different to the retrograde and reactionary nostalgia of *Nang Nak* and the Heritage productions. The references to these earlier eras of film in *Wor* and *Pop* constitute a playfully subversive tribute to provincial life, one that ultimately serves to question the Localist rendering of lower-class passivity, sacrifice and conformity. Indeed, neither *Wor* nor *Pop* promote an agenda that would uphold the dominant ideology of Localism. While the Heritage productions promote submission towards a bourgeois ideology and an elitist social order, films which directly target the lower-classes such as *Wor* and *Pop* do not seek to uphold a dominant order through submission or sacrifice.

Unlike the Heritage productions, such films do not attempt to romanticise and/or idealise the rural setting and its inhabitants. Instead the stories appear to concern a threat to the everyday life of the village. Defeating or surviving this threat involves the villagers coming together to discuss and then defeat the danger in a communal group, a positive depiction that attributes the strength of provincial Thailand and its small village communities to their strong communal bonds. This show of community is very different to the individual tales of sacrifice promoted by Heritage productions such as *Nang Nak* and *Suriyothai*. For instance, after the mad dog begins killing people and livestock in *Wor*, the villagers come together to figure out how to defeat and escape it. Although there is a central leader, the whole village is involved in discussing the threat and making decisions; a very positive depiction of a community that is almost entirely absent from the blockbuster New Thai productions.

The same is true in *Baan Phii Pop 2008*, when the whole village arrives communally to confront the shaman about his possessed wife. This communal depiction also continues into the various 'numbers' and plot events in which characters take part in large groups. In several extended sequences the villagers are chased around and around en masse by the Pop host, with under-cranking adding to the comedy. In a similar comedic scene in *Wor*, all of the characters jump into the river en masse to escape the dog and huddle together at the end when cornered by it. The ending of *Wor* in particular reinforces the importance of the village community when the mad dog is captured by the outsiders who lost it and the temple dog Chok is exonerated. At this conclusion the various diverse village inhabitants come back out of hiding; they smile broadly at finally being able to go on with their lives while the central group of characters watches and rejoices.

This reaffirmation of lower-class subjectivity also takes place stylistically, with such films fully embracing the communal film style of the 16mm era and its corresponding characteristics – ones that are again most evident through a close analysis of horror. Rather than the hybrid status of New Thai productions, these films directly embrace the 16mm era characteristics, demonstrating a strong adherence to earlier forms of Thai film that also targeted the lower-classes. In keeping with the 16mm era films, *Wor* and *Pop* employ a presentational performance style addressed to a largely static camera. Similar to a theatrical performance, this includes the frequent use of independent automated long shots in which performance is used to draw the viewer's attention rather than directing it through editing shots together.

Both films also blend traits from various genres into one production, and favour emotional effect through spectacle, employing a series of 'numbers' that privilege the aesthetic of attraction as a source of stimulation over that of narrative. All the productions mentioned so far contain instances of extremely visceral slapstick comedy. Characters fall over, are hit on the head, dance wildly and generally elicit hilarity with their strange costumes and outlandish behaviour. A funny sequence in *Wor* includes the shy hero and heroine closing their eyes and attempting to kiss, but accidentally kissing the dog from the local temple that has sat between them. In another hilarious instance a superstitious character begins to believe that water is the way to ward off the threat, and hangs bags of water around his neck instead of amulets. Another comedy number is created when a female character arrives into the village on the back of the motorbike, and becomes so covered in dirt and dust from her journey that she must shake it all off before anyone recognises her.

Wor and *Pop* also combine such numbers with instances of graphic horror, so melding two genres that both privilege the aesthetic of attraction. For instance, when the first victim is killed in *Wor*, there are lingering shots of the mangled corpse and the investigator roughly prodding the wounds while suggesting hilariously inappropriate and outlandish sizes for the killer. Likewise after another murder, a character seizes a motorbike to drive off while the intestine of its previous owner is accidentally attached, allowing it to unwind from the body as he takes off. In another scene a character viciously beats another character in bed when he believes that the mad dog lies under the blankets, resulting in the victim spitting blood and gasping in pain.

Baan Phii Pop 2008 also blends such visceral graphic horror and slapstick comedy together. One disgusting and horrific number involves the possessed host surrounded by dead chickens busily munching their raw entrails. A recurring comic motif involves characters hiding from the ghost in large empty water jars, creating humour through squeezing an impossible number of people into one jar. The fight with and escape from the Pop-possessed host also creates many comedy numbers. People are hit in the face by opening doors and frying pans, they goad the ghost with a red flag as though she were a bull and then flee terrified in over-cranked sequences. At the head of the fleeing crowd is an injured man with a crutch who is covered in bandages: he is apparently able to run faster than everyone else due to his supposed terror, adding to the amusement of the scene. Another number involves a group of fools trying to sneak into an attractive girl's mosquito net. Her father chases them off, but as they flee their ladder becomes stuck between the trees. Later, the same fool accidentally puts a love potion on the wrong woman and is chased around by a lusting old woman. The villagers then ask the local monk for advice on how to deal with the Pop ghost, but when the usually stoic figure sees the creature he is so scared that he runs through a wall and even over the surface of a lake.

Given the emphasis upon this visceral element, the narratives in both films also become little more than a causal transition from one number to the next. There is very little trace of the suspenseful erotetic structure associated with horror narratives, as there are simply no narrative questions posed throughout the films. Instead of raising questions that demand answers, the films progress causally from one outlandish and visceral incident to the next, creating 'numbers' rather than plot events. The entire last hour of *Baan Phii Pop 2008* for instance is taken up purely with a series of 'numbers' depicting the villagers' various escapades as they try to escape the Pop ghost. They run round and round the village as they are chased and attempt to hide, and such entertaining sequences have no real narrative implications. The characters are again types that conform to pre-determined roles, something that can be seen most evidently in the young lovers of *Wor*, whose story simply seems to involve them eventually kissing, an action that was always predetermined.

The blending of genres also serves to illustrate the status of the supernatural as a concrete part of society, rather than a violation of 'Natural Law'. Belief in the supernatural and the presence of spirits continues to contribute towards social organisation in contemporary Thailand and, notably, has informed both sides of the political debate. In March 2010, red-shirt protestors splashed several buckets and bottles of human blood (collected from their supporters) outside the walled mansion of the unelected Prime Minister Abhisit Vejjajiva. This was the latest in a string of protest attempts to force the government to call democratic elections after the earlier military coup that had deposed the populist prime minister Thaksin Shinawatra. Although interpreted by many as a dramatic symbolic gesture to highlight Abhisit and his government's treatment of the lower-classes and the death of democracy, it was also intended to place a curse upon the government.[1]

The opposing royalist protestors also engaged in similar practices. Sondhi Lim, one of the Leaders of the PAD at the time, got female activists to break the spells of 'evil wizards' who were attempting to damage Thailand and its monarchy by instructing them to place their used sanitary napkins at strategic points around Bangkok's holiest sites. The negative power of the menstrual blood was intended to block any black magic and spirits, and also gives an indication of the continued negative connotations of female sexuality and biology in the contemporary age (as well as enabling Thai women to play their unique part in protecting the monarchy).

Baan Phii Pop 2008 and *Wor* both liberally insert the supernatural into the equilibrium. In *Baan Phii Pop 2008* the village shaman is part of the social organisation of rural society, with characters visiting him to buy potions or have exorcisms performed. It is therefore also entirely plausible to the villagers that the shaman has been casting spells and incantations that have damaged the village and caused the Pop ghost to possess his wife. Likewise, while the Pop ghost certainly disturbs the equilibrium through her scary antics, the villagers are very quick to accept her existence and do not question it. *Wor* also demonstrates this concrete belief system. Although the dog menacing the village is not actually supernatural, many characters initially believe that it is. They also attempt to warn off the danger with spells and incantations; beliefs that are then turned into a source of comedy.

The cinematography and editing structures of such productions also indicates how these films are specifically designed to function within the communal viewing scenario of provincial, lower-class Thailand. While these New Thai films have dramatically improved their production values and quality of filmmaking and demonstrate seamless editing and sophisticated cinematography in keeping with the big-budget New Thai industry, close examination also indicates that they still very deliberately deploy 16mm era structures that can function within this informal communal scenario of shared pleasure. This is further indicative of how, even in the late 2000s, the rural viewing scenario has changed little in the thirty years since the 16mm era: these areas still enjoy Fouquet's outdoor travelling itinerant cinemas and consume cultural products collectively, with films continuing to engender the 'shared pleasure' so crucial to communal enjoyment. Again such radical differences highlight the stark social divisions of contemporary Thailand, and how the 'class war' the nation now finds itself in is played out in the differing style of cultural products.

Indeed, the large single-roomed communal homes of the rural village – now complete with televisions and VCD-players – also engender such a scenario. Traditional rural homes often house an extended family of several generations under one roof and consist of a single long central room in which the occupants gather after dark. The family members gather in the large communal room and sit on straw mats. They talk, wind silk and may eat sweet things or occasionally drink alcohol. Other relatives and neighbours often join them. The television is central to this ending part of the day and is constantly switched on, but rarely the centre of attention. It is an entertainment from which and to which the viewers can turn intermittently while also engaging with other activities, illustrating how the viewing situation of 16mm era Thai film continues in this situation.

Conclusion

This chapter has demonstrated how, despite the prominence of the elitist New Thai Heritage films and the erasure of the lower-class provincial film style in globally successful films such as *Shutter*, the marginalised 'voice' of lower-class Thailand continues to impact upon Thai cultural products. Films such as *Baan Phii Pop 2008* and *Wor* embrace wholeheartedly the film style and thematic characteristics associated with the culture and viewing scenario of provincial Thailand, directly targeting this disaffected audience. By giving full acknowledgement to and embracing such entertainment preferences, these films become a progressive reassertion of this marginalised subjectivity at a politically expedient time. While the New Thai industry may appear to be an elite-sponsored ideologically conservative entertainment form that seeks to remove traces of its humble beginnings, the success of productions such as *Baan Phii Pop 2008* and *Wor* highlight the strong and ongoing presence of this subjectivity in mainstream Thai society.

The ideological and stylistic differences between globally-savvy films such as *Shutter* and the collectivist 16mm era film style of *Wor* and *Baan Phii*

Pop 2008 are symptomatic of the extreme social divisions that exist within Thailand. Such stark divisions enabled the stylistic characteristics coined in the post-war era to continue. If *Shutter*'s success internationally is partly due to the embracing of global models of filmmaking, then the success of these lower-class Thai films is due to the opposite embracing of 'local' models. The 16mm era-derived film form is still alive and well in the contemporary age and has not vanished from Thai films, but actually remains prevalent. As Thailand becomes increasingly polarised in the contemporary era, so its entertainment products appear increasingly torn between the aesthetics of these diverse social groups.

However, moving into the 2010s Thailand began a process of rapid modernity much different to the mid-2000s. Chapter 8 will examine the changing engagement of horror in this context, outlining how films addressed such rapid modernity and the growing youth movements that became a result of the continuing political authoritarianism and inequality.

Note

1. The shocking and rather repulsive nature of this protest was then attributed to the backward upcountry ways of the protestors, most of whom came from impoverished rural provinces, so highlighting the continuing derogatory attitudes towards lower-class Thais.

8. MIDDLE-CLASS HORROR AND URBAN MODERNITY

The Promise

Building upon the social divisions explored in the previous chapter, Chapter 8 now moves further into the twenty-first century. The chapter examines the very different stylistic incarnation of and social representation in Thai horror films in the 2010s, a period in which Thailand is considered to have transitioned to an upper-income nation. The chapter first outlines this economic development since the 1990s, highlighting the position of the country's economic growth within the cultural industries of the wider East Asian region. The chapter examines how, similar to East Asian film industries, Thai films of the 2010s engage heavily with a modern urban context, addressing the concerns of a middle-class viewer situated within wider consumerist forces.

With a specific focus upon horror, the chapter then explores how Thai films of the 2010s offer a critique of such rapid modernity, one in keeping with a similar representation in wider East Asian horror. These films encapsulate the middle-class lifestyle and its concerns well, reflecting the shift from a low-income economy to that of a middle-income economy. The chapter will argue that such horrific representations function to expose the repressed underside of economic growth and the reliance upon a consumer-orientated identity, shattering the illusion of greater social equality for all as well as the notion of happiness through consumption. Focusing upon the 2017 film *The Promise* (Sophon Sakdaphisit, 2017) as a key filmic engagement with this specific economic context, the chapter then moves on to address how Thai horror's representation of the Thai context specifically differs from the more globally prominent East Asian horror films' engagement and incarnation. Such differences lie in the depiction of the next generation of middle-class urban Thai youth, who, the chapter argues, become a necessary casualty of their parents' callous consumerist existence and may yet hold the key to changing these wider attitudes.

The Middle-Class in Thailand and Middle-Class Consumer Culture

As a part of 'developing Asia' (Estrada et al., 2017), contemporary Thailand has been touted as an economic success story, with increased welfare, social security and the movement of millions out of poverty (The World Bank, 2022). The 1990s was a period of dramatic economic growth, coming after the significant expansion of the middle-class from the 1960s onwards. As a social demographic, scholars note how the middle-class in Southeast Asian nations is probably much larger than previously thought and is spread much wider in terms of income disparity (Van Klinken and Ward, 2014). It is also significantly more diverse and complex, comprising different racial groups, and is very much split across rural-urban lines.

Thailand's middle-class became a substantial social phenomenon largely after the economic boom of the 1990s, with film being one of many industries that targeted this newly increased consumer base. As explored in the previous chapter, New Thai cinema, with its consolidation in a studio oligopoly investing in big-budget productions, was a result of the significant wider social change and economic reorganisation at this time. The increased experience of Thai filmmakers and the decreasing price of film equipment enabled Thai filmmaking to become both better organised as an industry and more profitable as an enterprise (Ancuta, 2011). In the 2010s filmmakers worked within a well-organised streamlined oligopoly similar to a Classical Hollywood-style production system, and one that increasingly functioned as an international hub for filmmaking with facilities often hired by foreign, notably Chinese, companies due to lower cost. This is evident in the formation of the major Thai film studios (many of which are conglomerations of previous smaller companies), including GMM Tai Hub (GTH), Five Star Production, Phranakorn Film, Sahamongkol Film International and Kantana Group. Filmmakers, producers, performers and writers exist under the same roof within a company that is also involved in distribution.

Films themselves were also thematically and formally indicative of the varying lifestyles and corresponding entertainment preferences across a nation that was changing rapidly yet remained socially and culturally – and now even more economically – divided. The rural-based horror comedies explored in the previous chapter and that of the Heritage horror films, vengeful ghosts, and (self-)reflexive horror productions, all existed within the same national industry, yet catered for the fears and concerns of very different audiences. In the 2010s however, the slick depictions in contemporary Thai productions now reflect the combination of a more efficient business model, increasingly experienced filmmakers and the targeting of a modern urban consumer. Notably, the subject matter and *mise-en-scène* of Thai cinema is definitively urban and follows the environment and lifestyle of its new primary audience. Films represent and engage with the lives of urban professional characters, their lifestyles and their environment, who, through the network of urban multiplexes, are now the primary audience of Thai cinema. This change in audience represents the corresponding economic changes that Thailand and other East and Southeast Asian countries have experienced since the 1980s and early 1990s, including the movement of rural workers to the cities, the creation of suburban living and the rise of the Thai middle-classes who became the new urban elite (Siriyuvasak, 2000).

While rapid economic growth is often associated with the 1990s and the turmoil of the Asian economic crisis, 2000–2010 was also a highly significant period of transformation for developing Asia, with the region undergoing much faster and higher economic growth than the 1990s (Estrada et al., 2017). This culminated in a substantial shift in Thailand's global economic position: in 2011 the World Bank finally announced that Thailand had moved from a lower-middle income economy to that of an upper-income nation. Implied within this shift is also the reassuring and aspiration goal of achieving a high-income economy, and indeed the country aims to transition from a 'low-income economy' to a 'high-income economy' by 2037 (Jitsuchon, 2012; Estrada et al., 2017).

This timescale is significant when placed within wider global development. Mimicking the 'waves' of economic development across the region, Thailand experienced a regionalised and indirect version of Americanisation that can explain the specific characteristics of cultural incarnations such as film. Ancuta (2014: 237) places Thai film industrial development within the context of Shiraishi's 'Third wave' of modernisation. In this process, 'Developing Asia' (countries such as Thailand, Malaysia and the Philippines) followed a model of modernisation based upon an Americanised construction of consumerism, albeit one filtered through several regionalised processes such as that of Japan (the 'first wave') and the wider East Asia region (the 'second wave'). In this way, the regional incarnation and development of modernity and urbanised middle-class culture in Southeast Asian nations such as Malaysia, Thailand and the Philippines was very much connected to the influence of this phenomenon in East Asian nations. The 'second wave' countries of South Korea, Hong Kong, Taiwan and Singapore became 'regional middle-class trendsetters', and their cultural impact upon the developing countries of the Southeast Asian region is and was substantial.

In filmic terms, dominant East Asian film industries such as Japan, South Korea, Taiwan and Hong Kong provided a model that encouraged Thai studios to reorientate stylistically and thematically to address an urban, modern viewer. While the highly significant influence of East Asian film and culture within Southeast Asia has often been overlooked in favour of Americanisation and Hollywood (Ancuta, 2014), these East Asian cultural products, particularly those associated with the Korean Wave, have been popular across East and Southeast Asia since the mid-2000s (see Jung 2009; Song 2016; Louie 2012 and many more for discussions of this phenomenon). Products offer a depiction of urbanised consumerism that reflects these significant changes in wider society through a regionalised and Asianised lens, particularly those connected to social constructions of race, gender and urbanisation. The term that encapsulates this construction of success and globalism is 'cosmopolitanism', defined as 'a commodity whose value lies in its diffuse associations with worldliness, refinement, enlightened sophistication, and intercultural aptitude' (Matthews 2007: 49) and which now operates as a form of 'global merchandise'.

In Thai filmmaking, the genres that begin to encapsulate the change to this urban consumer-based cosmopolitan identity and can be best understood through a regionalised form of middle-class modernity are romantic comedy and horror. Both of these categories are notably urban-based and strongly address urban audiences and their concerns and experiences, becoming representative of wider thematic trends that this (now very modern) film industry turned to address in this newly designated 'upper income nation' of the 2010s. Romantic comedy films such as *Heart Attack/Freelance: Ham puay ... Ham phak ... Ham rak mor* (Nawapol Thamrongrattanarit, 2015), *I Fine... Thank You... Love You* (Mez Tharatorn. 2014), *30+ Single on Sale/30+ Soht On Sale* (Puttipong Pormsaka Na-Sakonnakorn, 2011), *Bangkok Traffic (Love) Story/ Rot Fai Fa Ma Ha Na Thoe* (Adisorn Tresirikasem, 2009), *Hello Stranger* (Banjong Pisanthanakun, 2010) and *ATM: Er Rak Error* (Mez Tharatorn, 2012) all embrace this model of an urbanised middle-class existence based upon consumerism and participation in a globalised economy. The protagonists and their environments are internationally savvy and engage with symbols and behaviours associated with such an existence, something that is increasingly part of defining oneself as successful in the current globalised context.

Addressing and depicting the urban professional was part of the successful incorporation of East Asian aesthetics into Thai cultural products. East Asian TV dramas and films had long targeted the middle-class Asian consumer and found success in Southeast Asia due to the growing economic proximity of the East and Southeast Asian nations. Many of such products are part of the much studied 'Korean Wave': the exporting of Korean TV dramas, films, pop music and stars throughout the region during the mid to late 2000s, which replaced the previously dominant Japanese cultural products. Although such products may be most well-known through historical dramas, such as the phenomenally successful *Dae Jung Geum/Jewel in the Palace* (Lee Byung-hoon, 2003–2004) series, these texts also place a very strong emphasis upon depicting metropolitan life, an urban *mise-en-scène* of coffee shops and offices as well as professional competitive characters and, most significantly perhaps, the depiction of a new metrosexualised Asian masculinity that has led to much analysis of changing masculine and feminine depictions across East and Southeast Asia (see Ngo, 2015 for more discussion of this). This has likewise impacted upon Thai cultural products, which have also changed to depict such subject matter in terms of plots and *mise-en-scène*.[1]

Similar to the original East Asian films and TV shows that poured into Thailand in the mid-2000s, many of these romantic comedies are primarily aimed at and are popular with urban female viewers. The narratives of these Thai films often focus upon professional urban unmarried women in their thirties who are 'looking for love' and place their characters within a *mise-en-scène* of coffee shops, offices, bars and shopping malls. The characters are now sexually active, go on many dates with men and struggle to make relationships work while searching for a partner who is faithful, considerate and compatible. Large parts of the dramas take place in the workplace, with the heroine struggling to hold down a full-time job and trying to succeed in a business world. Grappling with the continuing gender inequalities of urban Thailand, many female characters in such films are suffering personally for choosing this new modern path. Amidst struggling with the patriarchal nature of the workplace along with the pressure to be professionally and economically successful, they must now 'land' an economically-viable and morally upstanding partner and also base such coupling upon passionate romantic love (from both sides). The depiction of such relationships remains largely chaste and conservative; however for many female characters, this chaste relationship comes after they have experienced the negative consequences of unmarried sex. Lacking assistance from the community structures that previously assisted and/or initiated such matchmaking in more rural contexts, the eventual pairings are often attributed to more abstract forces such as Karma.

The depiction of masculinity is also correspondingly changed; a recognisable and significant influence reflective of what Jung (2009) calls 'pan-East Asian soft masculinity'. This metrosexual 'Soft Masculinity' is a progressive form of hybrid masculinity involving both increased recognition of female agency and a more flexible and inclusive model of masculinity in the otherwise very patriarchal East Asia (Louie 2012). As a regional East Asian phenomenon, this construction draws upon the hybrid roots of traditional Confucian-inflected conceptions of Masculinity prominent in East Asian cultures and the more modern Western-originated metrosexual influences associated with global cosmopolitan modernity.

Horror as Critiquing Cosmopolitanism and Consumer Culture

These romantic comedy films are a cultural phenomenon that offers highly significant engagement with and mediation of urbanised consumer culture in modern Thailand. However, the positive conventions of this genre mean that these films generally do not overtly criticise the negative aspects associated with such wider economic changes. Instead, narratives tend to celebrate characters unrealistically overcoming social barriers and 'having it all', a degree of professional and personal success that would, in reality, be difficult to attain. For a critique of this difficult and conflicted existence, we must look to horror as the genre that can best articulate the potential fears and consequences of rapid modernity and expose the repressed underbelly of glossy cosmopolitanism.

Together with romantic comedy, horror is a genre that became significantly representative of East Asian popular culture throughout the region's rapid economic development of the 2000s. In East Asian horror, films from 'second wave' countries such as Japan, South Korea and Hong Kong all engage with the underside of modernity and modernisation, depicting the 'horrors' that lie beneath rapid urbanisation and the adoption of a Western-identified style of middle-class suburban life. Indeed, from the early 2000s, critics and academics began to notice a thematic trend in these globally prominent East Asian horror films. This offered a critique of modernity and the effects of 'turbo-capitalism' by placing contemporary modern society as 'the origin of horror' (Lee, 2014: 107). Such depictions are often attached to fears of a 'moral decadence' stemming from Western-identified materialism (Lee and Hyangjun, 2014: 26), one attached to the 'turbo-capitalism' of 'second wave' nations such as South Korea (Cho, 2005, in Lee, 2014: 111).

This emphasis upon contemporary modernity as a source of horror is also very much evident in post-2010 Thai horror and its engagement with wider social changes. Again, there is much to critique: Southeast Asian economies also followed the 'turbo' development of larger East Asian countries such as South Korea. Yet in comparison to the previous 'second wave' global transitions, countries under the rubric of 'Developing Asia' made this economic change much more quickly that was expected, transitioning in almost half the projected time (Asian Development Bank, 2017). The newly monied Thai middle-classes, created as a result of this rapid economic growth, then sought to define themselves heavily through such consumerism and globality. Given the wider uncertainty around Thailand's fast economic growth and the uncontrollable and unaccountable global forces the country is now subject to, this identity also remains fragile and stressful. Certainly, becoming so enmeshed within the global economic system invites greater threats from global instability, with, for example, the Thai economy feeling the impact of the US-China trade tensions around 2018 (The World Bank, 2022). Thailand's ability to continue such economic development in the near future is also under question, and recent growth has slowed considerably, with concerns over the development of a 'middle-income trap'. In this situation, low-income growth strategies are no longer effective in an increasingly high-income environment and the economy can therefore stagnate (Bulman et al., 2017).

Similar to Thai romantic comedies and following the East Asian horror films, prominent Thai horror films into the 2010s move to depict urban middle-class protagonists and the wider social pressures attached to being a part of a modernised way of life. Such a depiction can be recognised in Thai horror films such as *The Swimmers/Fak wai nai gai thoe* (Sopon Sukdapisit, 2014), *4bia/Si Phraeng* (Youngyooth Thongkonthun, Banjong Pisanthanakun, Parkpoom Wongpoom, and Paween Purijitpanya, 2008), *O. T. The Movie/OT Phii Overtime* (Issara Nadee, 2014), *Rak Luang Lon/The Couple* (Talent 1 Team, 2014), *Kon Hen Pee/The Eyes Diary* (Chukiat Sakwirakun, 2014), *Chit Sam Phat/The Second Sight* (Pornchai Hongrattanaporn, 2013), *The Promise, Long Jamnam/Pawn Shop* (Pham Rangsee 2013) and *Laddaland* (Sophon Sakdaphisit, 2011). All of these productions engage with the difficulties of urban and middle-class protagonists in their depictions. The films all contain little reference to rural and/ or lower-class Thais, and largely remain within urban middle-class Thailand and its corresponding troubles. Characters are small business owners, office workers, graduate students, lawyers and real estate developers, all of whom are struggling (and very often failing) to keep up with the demands of rapid and intense consumerism and monetary commitments.

One director who can be heavily associated with this change is Sophon Sakdaphisit. As the screenwriter for key 2000s horror productions *Shutter* (Pisanthanakun and Wongpoom, 2004), *Alone* and *4bia* and director of later films from the 2010s such as *Laddaland*, *The Swimmers* and *The Promise*, Sophon's transition within the genre outlines these thematic changes. Certainly, while Sophon's earlier New Thai horror films such as *Shutter* seem to address the abuse of marginalised figures within the rapid development and discourses of modernity associated with the 2000s (as explored in Chapter 5), the filmmaker's later horror films focus more upon those who are part of this majority: the new middle-class and urban social elites. These contemporary productions reconfigure the formula of the Thai ghost story to incorporate and respond to the difficulties and contradictions of being part of the growing middle-class in contemporary Thailand. For these characters and their narratives, such an existence is no longer fulfilling and the promised happiness through consumerism has not materialised.

Ancuta (2014) particularly identifies the success of Sophon's 2011 film *Laddaland* as a major turning point in the construction of Thai horror and a significant example of the general change in both viewer preference and filmmaking style. In *Laddaland*, characters are trapped within 'the temporality of a dream of social mobility and economic success' as horror is brought much closer to home in its depiction of Thai suburbia and the middle-classes (Ancuta, 2014). Certainly the film indicates how the genre has now moved far away from the 'trashy' image and lower-class viewers of previous decades and was now almost exclusively addressing middle-class suburban viewers: there is little of the genre-blending and excessive visceral numbers of previous decades, though the film still contains an abundance of long shots and takes. Yet *Laddaland*'s major significance is its direct representation of and addressing of the Thai middle-classes, not only in terms of its 'coherent' script and suburban setting but also in its representation of a new figure of horror: 'the failed modern man unable to stay afloat in the globalized world' (Ancuta, 2014: 239). Indeed, Ancuta sees the consumer-inflected and stressed urban protagonists of *Laddaland*'s gated communities as leading a ghostly form of existence that is decidedly middle-class: 'Caught in the never-ending process of confirming their identity through the accumulation of material artefacts, they become living ghosts that are far more terrifying than the other more familiar monstrosities that continue to populate Thai films' (Ibid.: 245).

The Promise

While *Laddaland* is a significant text in beginning this change in horrific subject matter, it is in director Sophon's later 2017 production *The Promise* that we see a fully realised urban monied nightmare. While the struggle to stay afloat amidst a consumerist world is the source of fear and the eventual downfall of the protagonists of *Laddaland*, *The Promise* instead addresses the fallacy of social superiority and control that comes from defining oneself through consumerism, economic social status and transactional relationships. Characters are trapped in an isolated world of egocentricity and suffer from a fractured family unit, a lack of community, deep narcissism and a generally unhealthy obsession with wealth and material consumption as a form of fragile self-identity.

The film begins amidst the luxurious lifestyle of two teenage girls in late 1990s Bangkok, whose property-developing families have grown wealthy off of the 1980s economic boom. The two have evidently carved a deep friendship and connection amidst their condo-developing consumer-orientated families and lifestyles. Yet the coming of the economic crisis (represented by a montage of genuine newsreel footage from 1997 depicting the wider devastation and social destruction caused by this precarious existence) brings about a harsh environment of much-reduced living standards and an abusive family environment for both girls. Meeting in a now-derelict condo to carry out a suicide pact (the well-known Sathorn Unique Tower, a famous unfinished Bangkok skyscraper from the 1997 economic crisis), only one of the two girls, Ib, commits suicide, leaving the protagonist Boum staring in horror at her dead friend. The film then flashes forward by twenty years: an adult Boum has rebounded to become a hard-nosed property-developer living a fully realised morally-lacking and emotionally-detached luxury lifestyle, complete with her distanced teenage daughter Belle. When Boum moves to develop and gentrify the previously-abandoned condo complex where Ib committed suicide, Boum quickly loses control over her own environment as the angry spirit of Ib intrudes upon this luxury existence and specifically targets Belle. Similar to the exposure of Boum's parents' moral deficiency after the economic crisis, the dead Ib's intrusion results in an exposure of Boum's own cruel behaviour when faced with this loss of control.

As a post-2010 urban-set horror film, *The Promise* significantly divorces itself from the 'local' beliefs of previous decades. Indeed, Ancuta notes how, as part of this new middle-class depiction, contemporary Thai horror films often tend to distance themselves from the supernatural as an explanation for the violent occurrences (Ancuta 2014). While never entirely rejecting the spirits and superstition that (as Jackson 2014 points out) continue to imbue twenty-first-century Thailand, such films have come to be known in Thai vernacular as *Nang Sayong Kwan* (literally 'scary movies') and represent a movement beyond the ghosts and spirits of the more typical *nang phii* films explored in previous chapters. These films instead very much echo the visceral and presentational nature of Thai horror explored in the earlier chapters of this book. Many films single out mental illness, insanity and wider conspiratorial forces as a reason behind the social disruption their narratives represent. These include *Rab Nong Sayong Kwan/Scared* (Pakhpoom Wonjinda 2005), *Chuean/Slice* (Kongkiat Khomsiri, 2009), *Cheuuat Gaawn Chim/Meat Grinder* (Tiwa Moeithaisong 2008), *Khon Lok Chit/Distortion* (Nonzee Nimibutr, 2012) and *Phii Ha Ayotya/Black Death* (Chalermchatri Yukol, 2015). These films are more akin to 'thrillers', 'slashers' and 'torture porn', with diverse subject matters that bleed across the issues outlined in previous chapters, but all still tend to focus very much upon the negative trials introduced by an urban-based environment.

Despite its ghostly antagonist, *The Promise* also seems to follow this trend in its depiction and narrative. While the narrative of an angry ghost disrupting the protagonist's luxury urban life may seem to represent an embracing of the supernatural, the depiction of the ghost is never particularly explicit. In contrast to the very 'real' and socially present Nak in *Nang Nak*, Natre in *Shutter* and Buppha in *Buppha Ratri*, the ghost of Ib consists largely of shadowy silhouettes and occasional blurred figures within an abundance of long shots and deep space composition. Indeed, characters question the existence of the ghost for some time, and Boum herself remains in denial as to her predicament and her past for much longer than Thun in *Shutter*, Mak in *Nang Nak* and Buppha's landlady in *Buppha Ratri*. In a telling moment of filmic self-reflexivity, the protagonist's teenager daughter Belle and her friend even mock the long-haired ring-esque ghosts seen in earlier Thai films such as *Shutter*, implying a movement beyond the familiar yet tired conventions of this earlier genre incarnation.

Throughout *The Promise* there is also very little connection to any kind of traditional Thai belief system, ritual or superstition, and characters appear embedded in few social practices or traditions other than a hierarchy of wealth and privilege. Boum leads an existence that is detached from any 'traditional' emblems of Thai culture, and is instead fully immersed in luxury modernity as a form of identity. Later in the narrative, after realising her predicament and trying to save both her daughter and her luxury business, Boum turns to this belief system, attempting to burn candles and make offerings at the site of Ib's suicide. Such an attempt is of course futile, being a brazenly shallow attempt to deploy this emblem of traditional Thai culture to rid herself of her own past rather than engage with and fix her present exploitive behaviour. The spirit sends back the offerings of fruit, which become riddled with maggots, a rejection symbolising the immoral and 'rotten' nature of Boum's existence as well as her lack of control over a situation that cannot be fixed by economically-inflected threats and bribes.

In a similar depiction to the previously mentioned 'second wave' modernity represented in Korean horror films, close relationships and the home also become a significant locus of horror and the site upon which many of the violent encounters take place. High-profile East Asian/Korean horror films such as *Acacia* (Park Ki-hyung, 2003), *A Tale of Two Sisters* (Kim Jee-woon, 2003) and *Uninvited* (Lee Soo-yeon, 2003) all take as their subject matter the comfortable middle-class family domicile and the suburban professional protagonist (Chung, 2014: 87). Within this sphere, an 'Other' then intrudes to disrupt the supposed tranquillity of what appears to be an ideal home (Chung, 2014: 87). Such an intrusion serves to expose the repressed violence and trauma beneath 'the myth of Korean Economic Development' (Lee, 2014: 107), a development that is built upon suffering and exploitation. These films depict 'individuals living in seemingly comfortable, well-appointed, upper-middle-class domiciles which ultimately become settings for abjection, paranoia, terror and madness' (Chung, 2014: 87).

Thai middle-class urban-set horror films of the 2010s also depict close secure relationships and the family unit as a problematic entity that is a source of trauma and conflict. In contrast to the communities depicted in the earlier decades of Thai film and the 'local' films explored in Chapter 7, films such as *Laddaland, Chit Sam Phat/The Second Sight, Long Jamnam/Pawn Shop* and *The Swimmers* depict the family and close relationships as a source of stress and the site upon which (and from which) problems occur. There is an absence and/or breakdown of previously close family and/or community ties, which are instead replaced with competition, nihilism and even outright contempt towards others. Rather than the previous kinship ties that could be a source of strength and security, the community and the (now broken) family and its responsibilities become a burden and a source of stress with often violent consequences. Notably, the aforementioned romantic comedies also depict the family and communal environment as fractured and problematic in the modern context, with the single and aging protagonists facing a deluge of unfaithful partners and disappointed parents. Romantic comedy films solve the problems associated with this communal environment through reference to Karma, with romantic partnerships often occurring and resolving inexplicably through fate. Yet in horror such an absence is not resolved happily; instead characters suffer the consequences of an isolated and stressful consumerist-orientated existence.

Such family breakdown is evident in the beginning of *The Promise*. Boum and Ib's families fracture as the economy fractures, with the two girls then enduring and witnessing physical and verbal abuse from their stressed parents. After the 1997 crisis, main character Boum witnesses her father losing his mind in his inability to come to terms with his family's newly impoverished existence. Such trials occur while living in cramped and dirty apartments filled with the remnants of their previously luxurious lifestyle, a cluttered *mise-en-scène* of portraits, computers and big screen TVs. Both girls endure the realisation that their parents are not necessarily 'good' once the consumerist lifestyle that previously shielded them and governed their familial relationships has been removed. Transactions have replaced genuine human relationships and, once removed, the full morally deficient nature of such an existence is exposed.

When *The Promise* moves forward in time to 2017, we see that the adult Boum has clearly learned nothing from her experience, maintaining a detached veneer while engaging in the same kind of exploitation and empty consumerism that originally caused Ib to commit suicide. The character lives an isolated existence in her luxury condo and has a strained relationship with her teenage daughter. The family unit is fractured and incomplete, there is no husband/father (who is mentioned only in passing as having previously died) and no extended relatives. Boum seems to derive no significant pleasure from her existence and displays little emotional engagement with her surroundings other than anger directed at her subordinates. Consumerism takes the place of real human connections and relationships, with pills prescribed for Boum's daughter Belle's sleepwalking rather than any attempt to address the root emotional cause of such problems. Boum doesn't have any real social circle and is instead surrounded by employees and others who have an economic/working relationship with her. Her world consists of Maids, nurses, police, construction workers and a foreman as well as various businessmen, none of which she has any real emotional and/or personal connection with and whom, notably, are all subservient towards and/or intimidated by their employer.

The Horror of the Thai Middle-Classes

However, while the Thai and East Asian context have comparable similarities in both lived experience and filmic representations, the Thai experience of rapid modernity also diverges somewhat from that of East Asian 'second wave' countries such as South Korea. In film, this 'Third wave' (to use Ancuta's term) of globalisation is not only represented differently but also critiqued differently in the diverse nations of Southeast Asia and their complex media cultures. Indeed, together with the globally recognisable fears around rapid modernity and consumerism, the Thai middle-class has its own contextually specific anxieties around democracy and mass rule. Close examination of this situation suggests that there may even be much more to critique in the 'third wave' incarnation of 'Developing Asia'.

Such differences concern the extreme economic and political polarisation of the working- and middle-classes in Thailand. The increased speed in economic transition coupled with the lack of wider social progression means that there is little connection between the working-classes and the newly modernised consumerist middle-classes that these films now seek to address. Certainly, Thai inequalities in wealth and capital incomes remain significant, and, scholars suggest, are suspected to be much higher than actually stated (Janmana and Gethin, 2019). Studies conducted in the late 2010s suggest that Thailand remains one of the most unequal countries in the world in terms of economic inequality, which has even worsened since the 1990s. This fits with the general understanding of such rapid development: the strong emphasis upon economic growth increased as a priority with each 'wave' of global modernity, while the wider progressive social forces that should supposedly accompany such economic change actually decreased. Such rapid economic growth is also extremely fragile, and raises concerns around the possible exacerbation of social inequalities. Indeed, in the latter 2010s, Thai economic growth stalled and the percentage of the population living in poverty even increased slightly (The World Bank, 2022).

While the previous chapter addressed the problematic treatment and position of the provincial lower-classes, the situation of the Thai middle-class was also extremely concerning. After Thaksin's electoral success in 2001, the Thai middle-class began to feel excluded and alienated from the government organisation and democratic system that they had initially helped to bring about. The political orientation of this socio-economic group then gradually changed from that of a progressive force to one more associated with right-wing and anti-democratic forces (Lertchoosakul, 2021). This involved the complete abandonment of the democratic system, contempt for the rural lower-classes and even violent resistance against working-class movements.

This extreme reaction was connected to both the uncertainty and instability associated with the Thai democratic system as well as the lack of concrete benefits it specifically brought to middle-income people. This social class was not involved in or represented within the political system, which, under the Thaksin regime of the late 1990s, focused largely upon the welfare of the impoverished working-classes as a means to gain such votes. Alongside the organisation's dramatic increase in popularity amongst the rural masses, the regime also dismantled many of the social movements that had been supported by the middle-class. This social group was therefore left feeling particularly marginalised and powerless, being unable to establish its own interests within the democratic system that followed Thaksin's success and which, ironically, it had also played a significant part in establishing (Lertchoosakul, 2021). The lack of any political, social and cultural development alongside that of the turbo-economic development also meant that the new middle-classes clung to older hierarchical power structures and adopted this correspondingly right-wing position. The combination of such circumstances was enough to push this social group to support radically reactionary initiatives, such as martial law, restrictions to freedom of the press and the suppression of minorities and alternative political expression.

This situation and corresponding actions are indicative of a significant fear of the working-classes and democracy, a fear that is manifested as a very real practical political and social force in Thailand today. In a representation of such fear, along with the pressures of consumerism and the breakdown of previously stable family and community ties, post-2010 urban horror displays a need to both separate from and so control the working-classes. Such actions then create a cycle of suffering for protagonists, exacerbating the difficulties of social isolation and loss of humanity. This lack of humanity results in the stress, paranoia and loss of identity that characterises the horror encapsulated in these detached 'living ghosts' (Ancuta, 2014: 245).

Indeed, urban middle-class Thai horror films of the 2010s engage heavily with the stark social separation of working- and middle-class Thais. Such divisions form a very physical backdrop in films such as *Laddaland*, *The Promise*, *Chit Sam Phat/The Second Sight* and *Long Jamnam/Pawn Shop*, manifesting in a setting of walled-off condominiums, suburban estates and other forms of gated communities. Such complexes 'exacerbate already existing social fragmentation and inequality by way of surveillance, deluxe amenities, and extreme exclusivity' (Raisz, 2017: 2) and are designed to keep occupants far away from any breakdown of social hierarchies caused by economic growth, so evading the 'diversity and cultural integration' that would otherwise be associated with modern cities (Ibid.).

In *The Promise*, the setting of modern high-rise Bangkok functions almost as a character within the narrative, a physical representation of both social inequality and main character Boum's reliance upon this system to preserve her (upper)middle-class consumerist identity. In 2017, Boum herself lives in her own luxurious apartment, set against the backdrop of a now booming Bangkok skyline of multiple high-rise condos, safely isolated from the reality of life for working-class Thais. Boum's family's unfinished condominium towers over Bangkok and the Chaophraya river, a looming symbol of the stark inequality of the last two decades. The use of Sathorn Unique Tower, the most famous derelict skyscraper in Bangkok and an actual casualty of the 1997 economic crisis, as the premise and setting for Ib's suicide and Boum's condo development adds an uncomfortable layer of realism to this past tragedy and current inequality. Characters are dwarfed by buildings and framed by the vast derelict spaces of the now-abandoned condominium that Boum seeks to develop.

Further highlighting such inequality, the lower-classes and workers are largely removed from these post-2010 urban-set horror films. Unlike earlier films such as *Shutter*, *Art of the Devil 2/Long Khong* (Kongkiat Khomsiri, 2005) and *Coming Soon/Program Na Winyan Akat* (Sopon Sakdaphisit, 2008) in which class, gender and power relations are central to a narrative of abuse, this social division instead functions as a subaltern backdrop that serves to underscore the detached and isolated existence of protagonists. *Laddaland* and *The Promise* contain no corresponding upcountry journey to the impoverished outer provinces; instead the working class only exist in ever-present servitude amidst the wealthy protagonists with seemingly nothing in common. In this position workers are ignored and exist only to be chastised and used for personal convenience. Such people are often spoken 'at', but are never fully realised as a perspective. These characters appear only in the background and on the fringes of the consumerist world, as maids, construction workers and other manual workers, their fear of their employers evident through their minimal interactions and cowed demeanour. In *Laddaland*, the death of a Burmese maid could have become a similar vengeful tale to that of Shutter, yet becomes instead a footnote to demonstrate the callous nature of this environment. The erasure and insignificance of this perspective is ultimately part of the consumerist-orientated backdrop of stress and isolation that causes protagonist Thee's breakdown.

In *The Promise*, the exposed fear and trauma represented is not a result of the potential ability of the working-classes to wreak vengeance and destruction, but of mixing with these people and so exposing or even destroying the fragile consumerist-based superior identity that protagonists now rely upon. In *The Promise*, Boum expresses no interest in or empathy for the subservient workers around her, displaying a level of contempt towards the lower-classes and those working in servitude. She bullies and instructs such people, chastising nurses, her maid, construction workers and the terrified child of a worker who she forces to 'show' her the ghost he can supposedly see. In a particularly ruthless scene, Boum forces the terrified boy (Amon) and his mother to comply by threatening to dismiss the eight people from the boy's family who all work at the construction site of her condo development.

This scene also underlines the continued association between the lower-classes and the supernatural in New Thai horror. As illustrated in previous chapters, such a connection is evident in New Thai horror since the late 1990s, whereby those who are marginalised and ill-treated are able to accost this older traditional form of social influence associated with the rural and lower-classes and even deploy it against their abusers. Tellingly however, in these post-2010 films, such a perspective and ability is not connected to any degree of social power and is either ignored or abused. Rather than being fearful of the young boy's abilities, Boum drags the crying Amon to 'show' her the ghost, without any concern for his wellbeing or potential respect for his ability. Likewise, when Boum's maid is suspicious around the cause of Belle's 'illness', Boum dismisses such concerns in harsh tones.

However, *The Promise* becomes even more significant and interesting as a cultural text in its representation of the next generation of Thais. As previously stated at the beginning of this chapter, due to the diversity of factors such as income disparity, ethnicity and a rural or urban context, it is difficult to characterise the Southeast Asian middle-classes as a distinct social group with clear political attitudes and alignments (Van Klinken and Ward, 2014). Age also appears to play a significant part in problematising the social and political alignments of this group: while the middle-classes of Southeast Asia, and Thailand in particular, have clung to previous hierarchical power structures with particular vehemence, the political alignment of their children, who have now reached their late-teenage and university-age years, is far less clear. Many of this globally aware and internet-savvy generation appear to be rejecting the consumerist identity of their parents along with the associated anti-democratic and right-wing leanings that characterise middle-class Thailand. Social movements across Asia concerned with democracy, human rights and the end of authoritarianism overwhelmingly consist of young people, teenagers and university students, evident in the protest movements of Hong Kong, Thailand, Myanmar, Malaysia and many others. Such movements challenge social inequality and polarisation noted earlier, suggesting that this new generation recognises and rejects the problematic existence these divisions produce.

Notably, as part of rejecting the socio-political divisions of contemporary Thailand, these middle-class young people both immerse themselves in (often alternative) symbols of resistance from global pop culture (such as using the *Hunger Games* salute in their demonstrations and dancing to Korean pop music) and display a degree of interest in lower-class symbols of Thailand. The latter involves traditional foodstuffs, rural entertainment, artwork and activities such as silk-weaving. Accosting these alternative global and local symbols is connected not only to a form of resistance, but also to the general insecurity around the lack of personal authenticity provided by the consumerist urban middle-class existence. Such a lack comes from possessing a high level of social status attained through 'morally ambiguous' means, such as inheritance, rather than personal achievements (Hahl et al., 2017: 845). Individuals seek to consume alternative symbols as a means to achieve authenticity and lessen suspicions around their own moral character, simultaneously reaffirming this as an authentic and traditional representation of Thailand and Thai-ness.

In its depictions of Bangkok, *The Promise* alludes to the existence of such a group and its preferences. The long shots and takes of Boum's derelict condo foreground the colourful and illegally-drawn graffiti and street-art that covers every surface on the concrete walls and pillars. In contrast to Boum's stoic and detached consumerist persona, the artwork points to the lively Bangkok hipster scene, the alternative counterculture from the millennial next generation that is about to be evicted from the building. Sathorn Unique Tower itself has become a key site for urban explorers, free runners and graffiti artists, with videos posted on social media platforms, all of which continue to evade any clampdown from authorities who seek to prevent unauthorised access to the building. Notably, all of this artwork, and the building's very function as an artist's space, will vanish with Boum's plans to reconstruct and gentrify the building, indicating the cultural chasm that exists between these two generations within the same social class and environment.

In *The Promise*, Boum's daughter Belle also becomes indicative of the millennial generation in Thailand who are searching for an existence beyond the consumerist lifestyle of their parents and recognise the problems of contemporary Thailand. Belle is emotionally invested in her peers and stays distanced from her mother. She is first introduced as innocent, naïve and lacking the anxieties and worries that plague Boum. Boum attempts to shield and obscure Belle from the truth, so trying to 'save' her daughter from the suffering, lies and exploitation their success and luxury existence is built upon. When finally informing Belle about Ib's past suicide as a means to explain the current strange occurrences, Boum attempts to convince Belle that she is not in any personal danger because she is not connected to nor responsible for what happened in the past. However, Belle is not convinced, and appears to recognise her own complicity in the system of inequality and social division that her mother's company perpetuates. Likewise, the ghost does target Belle, taking her (through sleepwalking) back to Boum's old house in order to both 'show' Belle the truth and remind Boum of its continued relevance to the present.

Belle's realisation of her mother's empty existence and shameful past is indicative of the next generation's growing awareness and ultimately their corresponding rejection of inequality and consumerism. However, while Belle's awareness and rejection grows throughout the film, Boum does not display such an awakening, and is too firmly invested in her consumerist luxury identity to question this existence. The film therefore implies that it is only through the destruction of and violence meted out towards this increasingly aware next generation that middle-class Thais will begin to reject and assess the destructive nature of their social and political position. When Boum finally offers up her own suicide to placate Ib and save Belle from more torment, this offering is rejected, and instead Belle suffers an accident that puts her into a coma.

This ending mirrors the suffering of this next generation of young urban Thais, who endure draconian punishments from the state in their push for the social integration and democracy rejected by their parents. Politically aware Thai youth suffer heavy-handed police brutality while demonstrating peacefully and lengthy jail sentences for crimes as small as provocative social media posts. Ultimately, the film implies, the destruction of the next generation must incite middle-class urban Thais to both recognise and atone for their crimes of social inequality and authoritarianism, a necessary sacrifice that is deeply unfair and tragic. Ultimately, in *The Promise*, Boum's social responsibility and awareness is only roused by the destruction of Belle. By the end of the film, Boum has reorientated and reorganised her life around caring for her now-incapacitated daughter, reaching a state of sad tranquillity in her acceptance that consumerism doesn't automatically bring happiness. This ending is very different to the stalemate and continuing cycle of horror implied by the ending of earlier films such as *Shutter*, *Art of the Devil 2*, *Zee Oui* (Nida Sudasna and Buranee Ratchaiboon, 2004) and *Coming Soon*. Indeed, Boum is clearly a much warmer person by the end of the film: she has downgraded her luxury apartment, is friendlier to her maid, and is much closer to her (now comatose) daughter.

Conclusion

This chapter moved the analysis of Thai film firmly into the decade of the 2010s, exploring the distinctly urban incarnation of Thai horror in this now 'fully developed' nation. The chapter illustrated how the engagement with a cosmopolitan middle-class and urban-based consumer lifestyle became prominent in Thai horror films of the 2010s. These films are thematically comparable to horror from East Asian nations such as South Korea, offering a critical engagement with the effects of this 'turbo capitalism'. As part of the third wave of modernity in the Asia region, films address familiar issues associated with the trauma of rapid modernity, such as family breakdown, economic pressure and social isolation. However, in examining the wider context of the Thai middle-classes and their politically isolated consumerist existence, the chapter also indicated how these films are contextually specific, depicting the fear of and necessary separation from the working-classes as a key part of such an existence.

This trauma-inducing self-imposed cultural exile is played out in Sophon Sakdaphisit's significant film *The Promise*, close analysis of which highlighted the cultural chasm that now exists between the authenticity-seeking sacrificial next generation of Thais and that of their status-obsessed parents. This next generation, the chapter argued, is represented through Boum's innocent yet targeted daughter in *The Promise*. Such a depiction echoes the social movements across Thailand today, such as the urban teens campaigning for democracy on the streets of Bangkok. In a microcosm of horror, such teenagers pay the price for their parents' lifestyles and political decisions, yet may also offer a potential solution to breaking down the current stalemate of Thai social divisions.

However, such increased urbanism and economic development also means that Thailand, and by extension Thai film, is now part of a much larger global system of cultural exchange. Embracing modernity and middle-class Asian-ness opens film up to a much wider audience within the region, while Thailand's fast adoption of digital technology provides access to multiple online platforms. The next chapter will examine the wider distribution of Thai film internationally and around the Southeast Asian region as films become increasingly accessible through digital platforms. Again, horror plays a key role in such wide popularity, with Thailand now operating as a central horror hub within Southeast Asia, a construction that coincides with the wider promotion of ASEAN as a key and very new form of cultural identity.

Note

1. This impact can be a very direct one: the popular Thai films *Kuan Meun Ho/Hello Stranger* (Banjong Pisanthanakun, 2010) and *Love Sud Jin Fin Sugoi* (Thanwarin Sukhaphisit, 2014) both depict protagonists who are obsessed with East Asian pop culture, even travelling to South Korea and Japan respectively to indulge their fantasies. Such films illustrate how Southeast Asian producers actively respond to and incorporate such signifiers into their own products (see Liew Kai Khiun, 2015 for further discussion of these films).

9. REGIONAL AND INTERNATIONAL SUCCESS IN THE DIGITAL AGE
Folk Horror and a Southeast Asian Model

The previous chapter outlined how Thai film in the 2010s began to encapsulate the intercultural aptitude of Matthew's cosmopolitanism (Matthews, 2007: 49). It further demonstrated how this glossy modern depiction and sleek urbanised existence is best represented in Thai romantic comedy and horror. These genres engage heavily with the wider modern context, articulating changes and fears to notions of gender, race and inequality.

Building upon this previous analysis, the final chapter in this volume will move beyond the borders of Thailand and assess the growing international prominence of Thai film, within which horror becomes a necessary focus. The analysis will outline how these adept representations of modernity have contributed to the regional popularity of Thai horror within Southeast Asia. Yet it will also indicate how the international spread of Thai film in the digital era has resulted in a very different direction for the genre. Such depictions are much more akin to recent interest in folk horror and can potentially represent a resurgence of the social divisions evident in the immediate post-World War Two era of Thai film.

Thai Horror in Southeast Asia

Thai cinema is arguably the most globally visible of the Southeast Asian film industries, with both a Western and wider-Asian presence that eclipses the (nevertheless prolific) proximate industries of Indonesia, Malaysia, the Philippines and Vietnam. Within the region, Thailand has also been the only film industry to consistently export a substantial number of films into these neighbouring Southeast Asian countries throughout the 2000s, crossing borders that were not generally associated with such cultural exchange until much later in the 2010s. Indeed, despite the economic development of the region since the 1990s, awareness of cultural products and brands between the Southeast Asian nations remained relatively low until the late 2010s. Products from each country did not circulate widely across the region and did not feed into a distinct image of Southeast Asian-ness (JWT Asia Pacific and A. T. Kearney, 2013). Instead, scholars noted two dominant and distinct regional circuits of cultural products within Southeast Asia (with exceptions due to niche fan communities and those with their own familial connections across such borders). This includes a northern corridor largely dominated by Thai cultural products across Thailand, Laos, Cambodia (and to an extent Myanmar) and a southern circuit across the archipelagic region of Malaysia, Indonesia and Brunei dominated by Malay-language products (Chua, 2004, Jirattikorn, 2008).

The presence of Thai films in nations such as Malaysia, Indonesia, Vietnam and Singapore throughout the 2000s and 2010s is therefore an unusual phenomenon that bespeaks the significance of the Thai film industry in this wider region. What is more, close attention to popular culture in the region since the millennium indicates that it is Thai horror in particular that has carved a very successful regional market presence. This national genre dominated the cinema screens and DVD racks of Southeast Asia, potentially bypassing and breaking down the two circuits noted by scholars. Indeed, throughout the 2000s and early 2010s, Thai horror appeared to be the major (and sometimes only) representation of Thai popular culture throughout this region, and often the only representation of film from elsewhere in Southeast Asia.

For example, in Malaysia, six out of seven Thai releases in the top 200 highest grossing films for 2013 were horror films, and five out of six in 2014. Likewise, a substantial portion of the Thai DVDs available in Malaysian DVD stores such as 'Speedy Video' tended to be horror films, outnumbering romantic comedies and even the internationally renowned *Muay-Thai* boxing films. Similarly, when the famous Sentosa resorts in Singapore were designing their 'Spooktacular' Halloween event in 2013 (a horror film 'experience' concept based upon similar US-based events), organisers made a decision to specifically adapt Thai horror films for their initiative, choosing *Shutter* (Pisanthanakun and Wongpoom, 2004), *Pee Mak/Pee Mak Phra Khanong* (Banjong Pisanthanakun, 2013), *Body... Sop 19/Body* (Paween Purijitpanya, 2007), *Dek Hor/Dorm* (Songyos Sugmakanan, 2006) and *Coming Soon/Program Na Winyan Akat* (Sophon Sukdapisit 2008). Senior division director David Goh claimed that when organisers chose to seek an 'Asian' theme for the event, they immediately looked to Thailand because 'looking at the Asian horror film industry, Thai movies stand out' (Pajee, 2013). In Vietnam, the 2016 Thai Film Festival was held to 'deepen links between Thai and Vietnamese people' (Thai Film Festival 2016 in HCM City, 2016) and celebrate the fortieth anniversary of Vietnam and Thailand's diplomatic ties (Thai film festival kicks off in Ho Chi Minh City, 2016). Notably, horror was a significant part of the festival, with the screening of *Laddaland* (Sophon Sukdaphisit, 2011) used to promote the festival. Likewise in Indonesia, the country with a prolific legacy of domestic horror films similar to Thailand, one news site still claims 'Thai horror films are still the most popular films by the Indonesian people[sic]' (Leona, 2022).

This regional popularity has cultivated a clear image and reference point for both horror and Thai culture, and one that evidently began to be particularly recognisable to Southeast Asian consumers throughout the 2000s and 2010s. In Southeast Asian countries such as Vietnam, Malaysia, Singapore and Indonesia, Thai horror films were (and still are today) marketed clearly as Thai and connected to this wider body of films. Advertising displays in shopping malls clearly state the filmmaker and studio's connection to previous Thai horror films, evident in the international posters for films such as *4bia/Si Phraeng* (Youngyooth Thongkonthun, Banjong Pisanthanakun, Parkpoom Wongpoom, and Paween Purijitpanya, 2008) and *The Swimmers/Fak wai nai gai thoe* (Sopon Sukdapisit, 2014).

Online discussions also indicate that Thai horror of the post-97 New Thai industry is recognisable and highly regarded by Southeast Asian viewers. Again this runs contrary to the noted lack of awareness of other Southeast Asian cultural products and 'brands' within this region. For instance, the popular Malaysian forum Lowyat.net (said to be Malaysia's largest online forum) has many discussion threads that attest to the significant presence and popularity of Thai horror films among Malaysian viewers.[1] There is even a thread solely discussing recommended Thai Ghost Stories, with posters displaying an impressive amount of knowledge of Thai horror films, mentioning *Shutter*, *Long Khong/Art of the Devil 2* (Kongkiat Khomsiri, 2005) series, *Nang Nak* (Nonzee Nimibutr, 1999), *Coming Soon*, *Long Tor Tai/The Coffin* (Ekachai Uekrongtham, 2008),[2] *Faed/Alone* (Banjong Pisanthanakun and Parkpoom Wongpoom, 2007), *Dek Hen Pee/Colic* (Patchanon Thammajira, 2006), *Si 4bia/Si Phraeng*, *Buppha Ratri* (Yuthlert Sippapak, 2003) and even older and more obscure films such as *303 Klua Kla Akhat/303 Fear Faith Revenge* (Somching Srisupap, 1998).

Overwhelmingly, the film that stands out as an example of Thai horror's success and popularity in the region is *Pee Mak*, the 2013 blockbuster directed by horror-aficionado Banjong Pisanthanakun. The film is based upon the familiar (and countlessly remade) story of the pregnant woman who dies in childbirth and her husband Mak. This version differs from previous adaptations in that it largely tells the story from the perspective of Mak and his friends and is a tale of affectionate light-hearted comedy rather than tragedy.

At the time of its release in April 2013, *Pee Mak* became the second highest grossing local film at the Thai box office, taking almost $9 million (in USD) in the first two weeks (Noh, 2013) and eventually reaching around $35 million, whereby it 'redefined the scale of Thailand's movie market in 2013' (Brzeski, 2013). First released in the region in Indonesia to significant success, the film quickly spread across the cinemas of Southeast Asia. In Vietnam, ten days after its release, *Pee Mak* made almost VND 8 billion (US$380,300) with cinemas reportedly putting on extra screenings and many viewers going to see the film multiple times ('Thai Horror Movie Well-received in Vietnam', 2013). In Malaysia, *Pee Mak* was the fourth highest grossing film for 2013, and the only non-English language film in the top ten high-grossing films of that year. The success of *Pee Mak* within Thailand and across Southeast Asia was largely attributed to word of mouth online rather than marketing, with this surprise popularity also pointing to the importance of the future use of social media to promote films both domestically and internationally (Pornwasin, 2013). The film's success was widely reported in Thailand, with critics claiming that *Pee Mak* was the first Thai film to be released in all Southeast Asian countries. In an unusual move that is symptomatic of the wider significance of such success, even the British newspaper *The Guardian* reported upon this phenomenon: '*Pee Mak* could be too geared to Thai palates to travel all the way around the globe, but judging by a tight south-east Asian release schedule (Indonesia, 5 April; Hong Kong, 16 May; Cambodia, 23 May; Malaysia, 6 June; Singapore, 13 June; Taiwan, 6 August), it fancies its chance in the neighbourhood' (Hoad, 2013).

Cultural Proximity in Southeast Asian Horror

There are a number of factors that can explain the unusually wide popularity of Thai horror films such as *Pee Mak* across Southeast Asia. Exploring such popularity also offers a significant opportunity to culturally characterise this region and its specific incarnations of the horror film. Such factors begin to highlight a degree of 'cultural proximity' between the entertainment products of these various nations and potentially outlines Southeast Asian-ness as a cultural phenomenon. Such analysis also highlights the specificity of Southeast Asian horror, a regional incarnation of this genre that begins to be defined, and led, by Thai horror. 'Cultural proximity' is a complex and controversial concept that has often been used to explain the popularity of the Korean Wave across East Asia during the 2000s (see Shim, 2008; Korea Foundation, 2011). The term suggests that audiences prefer to consume media products that contain similarities to their own cultural background. In visual entertainment, such attractive commonalities can be found in any number of elements related to style, *mise-en-scène* and genre (Ksiazek and Webster, 2008 and Lu et al., 2019). Deploying 'cultural proximity' to explain the exchange of Southeast Asian products is complex, as the diversity of these countries and the previous lack of cultural exchange across the region meant that identifying Southeast Asian-ness as a cultural form was always difficult. Scholars note how in the mid-2010s such bilateral relations were still very underdeveloped (Khalid and Yacob, 2012). Even today when the region is much more conglomerated, it can still be difficult to concretely conceptualise a clear cultural identity from this geo-political label.

Close analysis suggests that cultural proximity is evident in both high preference for the genre itself as well as the style of the films. Similar to Thailand, proximate Southeast Asian nations such as Malaysia, Indonesia, Singapore, the Philippines and Vietnam also possess thriving and successful film industries that grew significantly in the twenty-first century (though enjoy less of the international prominence of Thai film). Within these industries, horror films are extremely popular. For instance, the 2007 horror production *Jangan Pandang Belakang* (Ahmad Idham, 2007) held the record for the highest-grossing Malaysian film for three years. In 2012, *Free Malaysia Today* news website stated 'Three of Malaysia's six top-grossing films are fright flicks made in the past two years, and the genre made up more than a third of domestic movies in 2011' (Zappei, 2012). Shariman notes how horror films are now a particularly important source of revenue in the Malaysian film industry, stating 'Even a poorly made horror movie can make lots of money if properly promoted. One good example was the recent low-budget *Momok The Movie*. It made RM2.1 million [approx. 600,000USD]' (Shariman, 2010). In Vietnam, *Vengeful Heart* (Qua Tim Mau, 2014) was reportedly the highest grossing domestic film in Vietnam at the time (Broxton, 2014), and recent horror film *The Ancestral* (Le-Van Kiet, 2021) stayed at the top of the Vietnam box office for two weeks, eventually grossing over 1.6 million USD (Wong, 2022). In Indonesia, horror is also particularly prolific, with many reports claiming that horror remains the most popular genre in the country with around 100 Indonesian horror films produced each year (see McKinney, 2022 and Tiwahyupriadi and Ayuningtyas, 2022).

As well as the popularity of the genre itself, close attention to horror films begins to suggest a possible common framework for Southeast Asian horror. Horror films from across this region certainly contain very similar depictions of the supernatural, ones in keeping with wider Southeast Asian belief systems. Beliefs in various animist spirits and their supernatural powers are common across Southeast Asia and these share many characteristics in terms of both the spirits themselves and their social effects (See Århem and Sprenger, 2015 for a full discussion of this). Such beliefs also exist alongside the dominant state religions, with spirits permeating the various Islamic, Christian and Buddhist beliefs in each country. In Malaysia and Indonesia, older animist discourses have always existed alongside Islam (which became the majority religion in both countries in around the sixteentth century). In Vietnam, dominant religions such as Catholicism, Taoism and Buddhism are heavily informed by Lên đồng, a ritual associated with local spirits and gods, and which involves mediums channelling spirits (see Nguyen, 2017 and Thi, 2007). Similar to Thailand, these ghosts and spirits, as well as the rituals, healers and mediums that accompany such entities, are all an important part of social life and the organisation of society. Such a phenomenon is also undergoing a revival of interest and relevance across the region as an important means of both understanding and negotiating with the fast-paced urbanisation of contemporary modernity.

As explored at the start of this book, such entities and their influence are often represented and become characters in Thai horror films, evident in the many incarnations of Mae Nak, Taman Krasue, Nang Tani and many more. Such deployment is also true in horror films from other Southeast Asian nations, and these depictions become representative of the wider cultural position and development of the supernatural in this region. Kong Rithdee even claims that 'Southeast Asian horror has always been folk horror' (Rithdee, 2021). In Malaysia, numerous horror films depict the well-known *Hantu* and *Pontianak* Malay spirits that are familiar and recognisable across the country, with one Aj-Jazeera report describing the 2021 film *Roh* (Emir Ezwan, 2021) as a 'mix of Islamic folklore and Malay black magic' (Ferrarese, 2021). In Vietnam, films such as 'Vietnamese Horror Story' involve characters approaching mediums for assistance, while in Indonesia, countless horror films depict the *pocong* and *kuntilanak* entities. As in Thai horror, these beliefs and entities often disrupt daily life and become representative of older beliefs and communities that must somehow be acknowledged and accommodated within the contemporary nation. Alongside such depictions, official religious figures and places of worship are often featured as trying to defend the characters (and, by extension, the nation) from these supernatural beings. For example, while Thai films such as *Shutter* and *Nang Nak* will use Buddhist monks and their chants to pacify spirits, Malaysian films such as *Jangan Pandang Belakang* and *Hantu Bonceng* (Ahmad Idham, 2011) use Islamic holy men for exorcisms and have protagonists chant verses from the Quran for protection.

Yet rather than seeking similarity through depictions of spirits, which can change radically over the decades and can often have very different functions in films, the most concrete example of cultural proximity seems rooted in the proliferation of films that can be described as 'horror-comedy', a subgenre that is very frequent in Southeast Asia. Indeed, horror-comedy is far less prominent in mainstream Euro-American and contemporary East Asian filmmaking. High-grossing Thai films such as *Buppha Ratri, Sars Wars/*

Khunkrabiihiiroh (Taweewat Wantha, 2004), *Mo 6/5 pak ma tha phi/Make Me Shudder* (PojArnon, 2013) and *Mathayompak ma tha Mae Nak* (Poj Arnon, 2014), all of which have been successful across Southeast Asia, can be described as horror-comedy. Even *Shutter*, a film which seems to leave 'local' characteristics behind in its decidedly East Asian *mise-en-scène*, still contains a very unexpected scene depicting a ladyboy joking about sex and defecation, indicating how comedy can be inserted very liberally within this genre.

Similar to Thai film, the insertion of comedy alongside horror is evident in films from across Southeast Asia. For example, Malaysian films such as *Hantu Bonceng*, *Ngangkung* and *Hantukaklimahbalikrumah/KakLimah's Ghost Has Gone Home* (Mamat Khalid, 2010) include many instances of very physical slapstick comedy and often mix these with graphic horror. The comedy horror *Jangan Pandang Belakang Congkak/Don't Look Back, Congkak* (Ahmad Idham, 2009) (a spoof of the earlier successful horror films *Jangan Pandang Belakang/Don't Look Behind* and *Congkak*) became the highest grossing Malaysian film ever up to 2009. In 2010 *Hantukaklimahbalikrumah*, a sequel to the smaller *Zombi kampong Pisang/Zombies from Banana Village* (Mamat Khalid, 2008), won several Malaysian awards and is included in lists of the top ten highest grossing Malaysian films. In Indonesia, horror-comedies are also numerous, evident in films such as *Kung Fu Pocong Perawan* (Yoyok Subagyo, 2012), *Ghost Writer* (Bene Dion 2019), *Ghibah* (Monty Tiwa, 2021), *Djoerig Salawe* (Sahrul Gibran, 2022) and *Pocong Minta Kawin* (Harry Dagoe, Suharyadi, Chiska Doppert, 2011), while even more serious horror films such as *Kuntilanak* (Rizal Mantovani, 2018) also contain comedy scenes. In Vietnam, successful horror films such *Tham Tu Hen Ry/Detective Hen Ry* (Tan Beo, 2015), *Benh Vien Ma/Ghost Hospital* (Vo Thanh Hoa, 2016) a *Phap Su Mu/Blind Shaman* (Minh Thang Ly, 2019) can all be described as horror-comedies. The latter is a strong example of Sukawong's blended narrative explored in Chapter 1 of this volume, including elements of fantasy, history and martial arts as well as horror-comedy. Vietnamese film commentator Nguyen Le even states that for horror 'The safest bet... is to include humor. At the most basic level, hahas are Vietnamese audience catnip and a revenue magnet in a country big on comedy' (Le, 2021).

This sub-genre begins to introduce the concept of 'genre proximity', a notion very evident in the horror-comedy films of Southeast Asia. An extension of cultural proximity, genre proximity refers to similar forms and conventions of storytelling that exist in certain societies and can be shared across cultures. Lu et al. (2019) argue that certain genres have 'similar structures, formulas, and archetypes that can reach past cultural differences and be accepted in different countries' while others are much more proximate to local viewers (Ibid.: 2). These scholars argue that horror is a middling case, whereby texts can be either wide-reaching and/or specific in cultural appeal. Such findings suggest that it may be very appropriate to characterise horror as a regional phenomenon in terms of form and subject matter. Texts are generally neither nationally-specific or internationally broad, but overlap both of such categories and are therefore best understood through regional preferences and conventions.

In Southeast Asia, the horror genre places strong emphasis upon visual stimulation and mixes elements from slapstick comedy, romance, action and other similarly visually-emotive genres into a single text. The very visceral slapstick, histrionic performance, gore and jump-scares of Sukawong's blended narrative (as explored in Chapter 1) create a genre proximity attributed to the diversity of the Southeast Asian region and its nations. As explored in Chapter 1, one major function of this blending of visceral genres is to bridge linguistic and cultural barriers and overcome divisions that may otherwise problematise wide appeal in diverse nations. Similar to Thailand, many of the Southeast Asian nations are divided by borders that were only established within the last century and the countries themselves consist of diverse ethnic groups, all of which possess their own distinct languages, cultures and religions. In their early development, cultural products across the region were faced with the problem of overcoming these internal differences and bridging cultural barriers in order to become financially viable. Visual entertainment therefore adapted to cater for the many diverse consumers within these nations and can be distinguished by such characteristics.

This emphasis problematises the existence of a horror genre in Southeast Asia as defined by both Euro-American and East Asian models of horror. Malaysian filmmaker Shuhaimi Baba recognises that there is something distinctive about horror in his country due to the horror-comedy sub-genre: 'Our local horror films are mainly comedy horrors anyway... Real horror films don't do well at the Malaysian box office' (quoted in Randhawa, 2011). While it may seem to have derogatory connotations, this distinction between Malaysian horror and what Baba calls 'real horror' nevertheless suggests that filmmakers see global horror as a different phenomenon to that which is produced locally. The notion is that the central emotions of fear and disgust (as outlined in Chapter 1) are what ultimately 'should' define horror as a genre, and the Southeast Asian emphasis upon eliciting humour moves this genre away from this dominant concept.

The incorporation of comedy has certainly enabled Thai horror to travel well across this region. When examining *Pee Mak*, journalists and commentators overwhelmingly point to how the film's comedy instances are well blended into the story and see this characteristic as the main source of attraction and reason behind the wide regional success. Film critic Kong Rithdee claimed in *The Nation* that 'the reason *Pee Mak* makes crazy money is because it's loose and funny' (Rithdee, 2013). Long time Thai film blogger Wise Kwai also claimed

'Distinguishing itself from most other Thai horror comedies, this one follows an actual script' (Wise Kwai, 2013) and goes on to note the inclusion of pop culture references and the buddy-comedy of Mak's four male friends as major factors in this wider success. The British Newspaper *The Guardian* also singled out the horror-comedy blend as part of the film's main appeal, describing the film as 'an irreverent take on tradition' that 'transformed from a lovelorn, nostalgic fable to a slick comedy that affectionately teases [its] source material' (Hoad, 2013). Likewise, the film's director Banjong Pisanthanakun also noted the wide appeal of this sub-genre, highlighting how horror-comedy allows the film to cross borders: 'since this film sticks mostly to the universal language of comedy, I found that more than 80 per cent of the gags get everyone laughing, no matter where they live. We never planned to "go inter", but this movie's pace and timing help it communicate with an international audience' (*The Nation*, 2013). Comments from Malaysia also focus upon lauding *Pee Mak* as both a comedy and a horror film. One blogger's review stresses the mix of comedy and horror as a major part of its appeal: 'it's quite impressive how they mesh the horror and romantic comedy genres in a movie. They use the story of *Nang Nak* (a Thai tale of horror) as the base of the horror part while the buffoonery of Nak's four best friends are the core of comedy. Every scene in the movie is so damn funny' (*NA*, 2013).

This regional model of horror is further supported by the strong disjunction between *Pee Mak*'s success within Southeast Asia and the film's performance outside this region. As the previous quote from *The Guardian* indicated, *Pee Mak* did not enjoy wide success outside of Southeast Asia, and particularly not in Europe and America, where, while well-received, the film was largely confined to niche festival audiences. Indeed, as the UK-based newspaper indicated, the film was 'too geared to Thai palates to travel all the way around the globe' (Hoad, 2013), indicating how this Southeast Asian version of horror holds very specific appeal within the region.

Modernity as Attractive in Thai Horror in Southeast Asia

Despite this high degree of cultural proximity between horror films in this region, the social depictions and subject matter of many Southeast Asian horror films can also be quite different to that of popular Thai horror films. In particular, Thai horror's image of Asian modernity and urban-ness throughout the 2000s and early 2010s (as discussed in the previous chapter) is different to the depictions in horror films from some other Southeast Asian nations at this time. Such difference can also be a source of attraction for consumers alongside that of cultural similarity (Chua, 2004). Indeed, a close examination of this difference and a comparison suggests that Thai horror may actually offer an alternative depiction for the modern urban-based Southeast Asian viewer who, particularly in the 2000s and early 2010s, was perhaps not adequately represented by horror films in other Southeast Asian nations.

As Trauma theory suggests, horror functions to mediate and engage with suppressed traumatic social events and upheaval. While Vietnamese horror largely did not come into fruition until later in the 2010s due to censorship issues, we can certainly see how horror from the 2000s in Malaysia was much more focused upon the issues and contradictions associated with rural and suburban village life and community at this time. For example, high-grossing Malaysian horror films such as *Hantukaklimahbalikrumah*, *Jangan Pandang Belakang* and *Hantu Bonceng* seem to portray a situation that is much less 'international' and 'modern' in terms of its subject matter and far more 'localised' in terms of its depiction of a particular social group and situation. These films focus upon *kampong* (village) life and the suburban Malay environment, rather than the isolated condos and gated communities of Thai horror since the millennium. In contrast to the international and pan-Asian depictions of 2010s Thai horror (and similar to the Thai films explored in Chapter 7), stories often involve characters coming together and defeating threats against their community, so maintaining the status quo and reaffirming rural life (often against the increasing fragmentation associated with modernity and urbanisation). For instance, the high-grossing 2010 comedy-horror *Hantukaklimahbalikrumah* is set in the village *Kampong Pisang*, to which the protagonist Husin returns from working in Singapore and tries to find out what happened to his neighbour.

These depictions contrast with recent Thai horror films from around the same time, in which the 'wounds' addressed are those associated with the pressures of existing as part of the urban middle-class.[3] Both the high-quality 'global' aesthetics and the pan-Asian urban depictions of Thai horror are very relevant to the wider socio-economic experience across Southeast Asia since the millennium. Similar to Thailand, the urban populations of countries such as Malaysia, Indonesia and Vietnam have increased substantially since the 1970s and rose very quickly throughout the 1980s and 1990s. The rate of urbanisation and consumption across the region is also very high and the wider population is overall fairly young, with an extremely high use of social media (JWT Asia Pacific and A. T. Kearney, 2013). Traditionally rural-based populations have been increasing dramatically over the past twenty years in urban areas and major cities of the region.

Thai horror addresses issues of relevance to this new middle-class Southeast Asian consumer, focusing upon an urbanised pan-Asian existence and its associated anxieties. The emphasis upon modernity addresses the Southeast Asian consumer as a global citizen and a consumer of global pop culture, rather than an individual in a contextually-specific rural/suburban situation. As explored in the previous chapter, recent Thai horror films are often set in urban areas and address issues relevant to the city-dweller: protagonists live in apartment blocks, must work or study hard and worry about how to pay the rent. The subject matter also addresses the inherent frustrations and unfairness of city life and, in particular, the hidden underside of exploitation and oppression that horror can address so well.

Thai horror's emphasis upon high-quality aesthetics, an urban *mise-en-scène*, and also the incorporation of comedy numbers and 'local' spirits is evidently a winning combination in Southeast Asia. Such characteristics are all evident in *Pee Mak*, which, judging by this film's extraordinary regional success, seems to offer a very relevant and highly entertaining representation for the modern Southeast Asian consumer of the 2010s. Indeed, the film seems to offer a nostalgia-inflected portrayal relevant across modern Southeast Asia, and one that allows a working-through of the anxieties associated with contemporary life.

Southeast Asia and ASEAN Identity

The success of Thai horror in this region is also particularly important as an example of Southeast Asian cultural proximity at a very significant time. Indeed, Thai horror was popular not only before the increased conglomeration of the region, but also at a moment when the bilateral relations and awareness between these countries was all being (re)formed. With the rise and conglomeration of the Association of Southeast Asian Nations (ASEAN) in the 2010s, the amalgamation of this region became increasingly important to the various governments. The region rose in economic prominence as a future economic and cultural hub, and one carving its own inter-Asian cultural flows that can challenge both the traditional Western and more recent East Asian dominance. Regional relations began to change fast due to increased ASEAN integration under the emerging ASEAN Economic Community which came into effect in late 2015 (Ishikawa, 2021), while Inter-ASEAN tourism across the region also increased significantly. Research in the 2010s also outlines these developing links, with scholars indicating that ASEAN people began to feel a strong cultural connection across the region at this time and believed that they shared key values (JWT Asia Pacific and A. T. Kearney, 2013).

Regional authorities recognised inter-ASEAN cultural exchange as particularly important due to the role such links could play in creating and furthering the much-desired economic networks, including the need for regional cooperation around 'urbanisation issues' (Soerakoesoemah and Thuzar, 2012). Initiatives therefore sought to increase cultural contact between the ASEAN nations, particularly given how such links had been noted as extremely weak prior to the 2010s (see Ravenhill, 2008 for a full discussion of the economic agenda behind – and problems facing – ASEAN integration at this time). Developing cultural connections in order to cultivate an ASEAN-based identity was encouraged, evident in initiatives such as the 'ASEAN Strategic Plan for Culture and Arts 2016–2025' (The ASEAN Secretariat, 2016). Educational initiatives were pushed in schools and colleges by various governments, often with a focus upon promoting regional-based knowledge such as learning the languages, histories and geographies of other ASEAN countries.

Such timing further suggests that Thai film, and (given its regional prominence) Thai horror in particular, has been a significant influence in this emerging regional identity and awareness amongst consumers. Film has certainly played a key role in forming an ASEAN cultural identity: the many ASEAN-titled film festivals, launched very soon after the substantial regional success of *Pee Mak*, are a very visible and obvious promotion of this identity. Such festivals include the biennial ASEAN International Film Festival and Awards (the AIFFA, which debuted in 2013), which stated one of its objectives as being to 'help promote our culture, tradition and heritage towards a convergence of ASEAN' (AIFFA, 2012). Organisers even state that when awarding films 'a criteria AIFFA jury looks for is the film has to explore and promote the ASEAN way of life', though this 'way of life' is not actually defined (Begum, 2019). In Thailand, the Bangkok ASEAN Film Festival was launched in 2015 and is sponsored by the Thai Ministry of Culture. Further demonstrating the significance of promoting the ASEAN initiative to the governments of the region (and internationally), the Indonesian Film Festival in The Netherlands, held every year since 2015 and organised by the Indonesian Embassy in The Hague, even changed itself to the ASEAN Film Festival in 2017 (Matahari Media, 2017). Universities internationally (including The School of Oriental and African Studies in London) and domestically (such as Ramkhamhaeng University in Thailand) also designed and held their own ASEAN film festivals, highlighting how such educational establishments see film as a means to position themselves as part of this geo-political agenda.

The increased attention towards the Southeast Asian regional film market, much of which mentions the success and reputation of Thai horror (and which is evident in initiatives such as the prior-mentioned film festivals), is heavily entwined within the post-2010 development of horror throughout the region. This is particularly true in Vietnam, which, due to censorship issues, did not develop a recognisable domestic horror industry and model until recently. In the late 2010s and following the success of Thai horror in the country, Vietnamese horror films are now prevalent and seem to notably follow the modernity-inflected model represented in Thai horror. For instance, *The Ancestral* depicts an urban-based family journeying back to a rural ancestral home. Yet similar to *Laddaland*, this haunted-house tale also becomes a psychological examination of grief, family dysfunction and mental illness, manifesting in mental disorders such as sleep paralysis. Further demonstrating the film's similarity to Thai horror's 'model', one of the top Google searches associated with the film is 'Is The Ancestral movie Thailand?[sic]'. Recent Vietnamese teen horror films also demonstrate a strong thematic and stylistic link to Thai horror: *Thang Máy* (Peter Mourougaya, 2020) tells the story of a haunted elevator in an abandoned hospital, depicting derelict urban buildings in a similar *mise-en-scène* to that of *The Promise* (Sophon Sakdaphisit, 2017), while *Dream Man* (Roland Nguyen, 2018) embraces social media and becomes a teen slasher similar to *The Swimmers* and *Art of the Devil 2*. Vietnamese horror *The Guardian* (Victor Vu, 2021) depicts popstars using magic to be successful in this very modern and urban industry, with a high-quality *mise-en-scène* of music videos and designer goods.

Inter-ASEAN co-productions are also becoming a feature in the region, notably beginning with horror and romantic comedy, the two genres that, as argued in the previous chapter, are most embedded in everyday urban life. Thai-Vietnamese co-productions include the 2015 horror production *Oan Hon* (Troy Le, 2015) and the romantic comedy *La May Tren Bau Troi Ai Do* (Thanadet Pradit, 2022). Thai actor and director Troy Le even stated when making *Oan Hon* that 'the taste of Vietnamese and Thai audiences is the same', and further stressed the popularity of Thai horror films in Vietnam (Hanoi Times, 2015). One Singapore blogger reviewing Vietnamese horror film *Conjuring Spirit* after its Singapore release even comments 'you might thought [sic] that this is a Thai horror film' (Evilbean, 2015). These commonalities are therefore evident in both thematic trends in horror as well as comments addressing the similarities of films. Both indicate that cultural products in the region are addressing key concerns, specifically the anxieties and traumas attached to rapid urbanisation. This model of horror in particular then becomes a significant indication of the similar needs across the region regarding the effects of rapid urbanisation, and becomes potential evidence of the need for regional cooperation around these growing issues.

International Growth

Along with such regional success and significance, Thai film has also reached a new level of global prominence. The post-1997 New Thai industry has always to an extent been popular on the international festival circuit, and many filmmakers have sought such success. Within Southeast Asia, Thai film was always the industry with the most significant international presence, particularly in Europe and America. Outside of the more globally prominent film industries of Hong Kong, Japan and South Korea, it was post-97 New Thai films that were most often found on DVD racks and in film festivals worldwide during the 2000s. Horror played a notable role in carving this international presence: as discussed in Chapter 3, the 1999 film *Nang Nak* was one of the first Thai films to achieve widespread international acclaim, winning twelve awards at a variety of international festivals. Such success can be attributed to the film's higher production values than previous Thai horror films, all of which impressed festival audiences (see Knee, 2005; Ingawanij, 2006; Knee and Chaiworaporn, 2006 for in-depth accounts of this change).

However, in the late 2010s and early 2020s, Thai film's international success has increased significantly to the extent that Nikkei Asia even ran a feature on Thai film in which the news-site refers to the Thai industry as 'Southeast Asia's most vibrant film industry' (Rithdee, 2021b). As in previous decades, Thai film's international success includes a strong focus upon horror. In the last two years, a host of English-language websites from around the world now list Thai horror films, with titles such as '13 Scariest Thai Horror Movies You Need to Watch' (Supateerawanitt, 2022), '15 Best Thai Horror Movies' (Daw, 2022), '10 Thai Horror Movies That'll Give You Nightmares' (Dei, 2021), 'Top 10 Best Thai Horror Movies' (Riordan, 2022), and '5 Thai Horror Films on Netflix That Will Absolutely Terrify You' (Dass, 2021).

This sudden increase in international prominence can be attributed to Thailand's particularly fast adoption of digital technology and, specifically, online streaming websites. Since the 2010s Thailand already possessed a robust digital infrastructure with the highest internet and social media usage in Southeast Asia. In 2017 there was a subscription video-on-demand (SVOD) platform boom in Southeast Asia, particularly in Thailand and Indonesia, which both experienced significant growth in this area. In 2018, Thailand generated a significant proportion of the world's broadcasts of Facebook Live (11.26 per cent), a livestreaming service launched in 2015 (for which it also constitutes 8 per cent of the viewers), and the country is behind only the US and Vietnam in terms of its global percentage of broadcasters (Raman et al., 2018).

On the back of Thailand's substantial digital infrastructure, 'Over-The-Top'[4] (OTT) platforms also became particularly popular in the country. In Thailand, OTT platforms tend to be consumed via smartphones and are now more popular among Thai viewers than traditional television. Netflix reached Thailand in early 2016 and was one of the first OTT video streaming platforms in the country. HBO Go launched in Thailand in mid-2020 while Disney+ and Hotstar arrived in Thailand mid-2021, partnered with local telecommunications provider AIS. Amazon Prime Video arrived in 2020 (Maneechote, 2021), while Asia-based Viu and Iflix are also available, alongside local platforms such as Monomaxx, Hollywood HDTV, Bugaboo, MV Hub, Danet and Doonee. The nation also possesses the highest consumer percentage in Southeast Asia of AVOD (advertising-based video-on-demand), a service popular in both rural and urban areas thanks to its affordability (helped by 5G).

Thai filmmakers and studios were quick to embrace this new avenue for both production and distribution, working with both local and international providers. Indeed Thailand is now considered 'a leading regional OTT content producer' (SpotX, 2021), with the COVID-19 pandemic increasing this already very high viewership. Netflix in particular welcomes such collaboration, in keeping with the organisation's dual approach to encompassing both the local and the global. Netflix Thailand offers an extremely diverse content library that is 'a hybridization of global and local elements'. The most popular products in this content-pool are from South Korea and Thailand as well as the UK and US (Ramasoota and Kitikamdhorn, 2021), reflecting the previous proliferation of European, American and East Asian popular culture in the country.

Cooperation with international OTT providers such as Netflix offers an opportunity for Thai filmmakers and studios to reach international audiences in a much wider and more direct capacity than before. Within this pool of available films, Thai horror remains extremely prominent, with the Netflix Thailand site containing a copious amount of local horror productions. Horror itself has also played a significant part in this relationship, with the 2021 horror production *The Maid* (Lee Thongkham, 2020) even sold straight to Netflix after the COVID-19 pandemic prevented cinema screenings (Ramasoota and Kitikamdhorn, 2021: 7).

Such collaboration is not limited to screenings only, but also involves actively commissioning and designing Thai content. This includes new forms of serialised Thai horror such as the HBO Asia-created segments and episodes on shows such as *Folklore* ('Broker of Death' S2. E3. Sitisiri Mongkolsiri, 2018) and HBO's *Halfworlds* (Season 2, Ekachai Uekrongtham, 2016), and the horror/mystery/supernatural series *The Stranded* (Sophon Sakdahisit, 2019). The latter was the result of a collaboration between Netflix and GMM and was heavily promoted as the first Thai original series produced by Netflix. As the first internationally proliferated serialised version of Thai horror, the show was specifically designed to introduce Thai series to the international market in a similar way to that of Scandinavian and South Korean dramas on Netflix. Reflecting the global success and prominence of Thai horror, the series was widely promoted through director Sophon Sakdaphisit's previous productions of *Laddaland* and *The Promise*.

Folk Horror

Such international success came quickly after (and in some cases alongside) the aforementioned wider regional ASEAN success. It is therefore perhaps surprising that very recent Thai horror films of the late 2010s and early 2020s tend to move away from depicting the urban-inflected anxiety that had become so popular and relevant in horror across Southeast Asia. As argued in the previous chapter as well as quoted from Ancuta (2014), one recognisable change in Thai horror of the 2010s was that films did not tend to attribute horrific events entirely to the supernatural. As part of the industry's wider engagement with the trauma of rapid modernity, economic crisis and political instability, horror films instead sought to attribute strange events to unclear origins and even non-supernatural occurrences, such as mental illness, poverty, family dysfunction and economic difficulties. Such an emphasis reflected the wider trauma and need to 'work through' the changes ensuing from rapid modernity and urbanisation. Local and regionally successful films such as *The Swimmers*, *The Promise* and *Laddaland* all place far less emphasis upon spirits and spirit beliefs in their narratives. Even *Pee Mak*, a film centered around the spirit Mae Nak, moves the emphasis away from this supernatural spirit, instead becoming a buddy comedy and a romance.

Yet in the digital era there is a new development in Thai horror. Films now seem to move away from the tower blocks of *The Promise*, the mental illness and consumer pressures of *Laddaland* and the urban-based teenagers of *The Swimmers*. Horror of the late 2010s and early 2020s instead places a strong emphasis upon 'folk horror'. This term is increasingly deployed in both popular and academic descriptions of horror, in part due to the success and prominence of the UK/US folk horror film *Midsommar* (Ari Aster, 2019). Together with a glut of similar films throughout the 2010s, this film made up a recent 'wave' of folk horror in the UK and US (Keetley, 2020). Indeed, popular film websites such as IMDB now list folk horror films while bloggers and critics deploy this term in articles and reviews. The term itself has been in use for around fifty years and tends to refer to the depiction of a supposedly unspoiled traditional and often rural setting that is pitted against modernity, a trope that has long been staple in the horror genre. The narratives of folk horror often depict the uncovering of ancient artifacts and/or spirits that are attached to forms of collective beliefs and accompanying rituals, all of which are somewhat ambiguous in their relationship to 'normality' (Keetley, 2020). The unwitting protagonists stumble into this initially normal-seeming situation and quickly become trapped within these ancient structures of belief. This form of horror encompasses notions of community and tradition, being rooted in crafting a (often invented) local community that is 'bound together by inherited tales' (Keetley, 2017).

While the spirits and beliefs of Thai folklore have always been present in Thai horror films of the contemporary industry, these depictions have generally been quite different to the definition and understanding of folk horror. In the New Thai industry, spirits in films such as *Shutter*, *Coming Soon*, *Buppha Ratri* and *Ghost Game* (Sarawut Wichiensarn, 2006) are largely detached from any framework of a collective culture and associated values. The complex social rituals that infuse this sub-genre are absent. Likewise, films such as *Nang Nak*, which do contain some representations of collectivity and ritual, focus much more upon issues of heritage and romance and do not devote much narrative space towards constructing a community. When ritualistic elements do exist in these films, such as the Khmer spells chanted by Miss Panor in *Art of the Devil 2*, they are very much peripheral to the central narrative and tend to remain within an individual, rather than being representative of a wider presence that can clash or threaten 'normality' (Keetley, 2020: 22). Indeed, in all these films the wider threat is contained within a single individual and/or entity.

In contrast, very recent Thai horror films such as *The Medium/Rang Song* (Banjong Pisanthanakun, 2021), *Krasue: Inhuman Kiss* (Sittisiri Mongkolsiri, 2019), *The Maid, Reside/Singsu* (Wisit Sasanatieng, 2018) and *The Whole Truth/Pritnarulon* (Wisit Sasanatieng, 2021), seem to embrace the characteristics of folk horror and embody the narrative structures and wider settings identified by Keetley (2020). Such films position their spirits and protagonists very differently, focusing strongly upon wider structures of social control and ritualistic cultish behavior, all of which depicts a community that somehow threatens, or calls into question, normality. For example, *The Medium* locates its story of spirit-possession to the communities of Northeastern Isaan, purporting to be the footage of a documentary crew who have come from outside of this minority region and become tangled within its rituals. Similarly, in *Krasue: Inhuman Kiss* the film takes place in a village and depicts a community (complete with flaming torches) trying to hunt down the Krasue spirit while the protagonists (one of which is actually a Krasue) try to escape. *The Maid*, while telling a very standard ghost story of abuse and revenge, is an artistic depiction of a seemingly innocent maid serving an abusive richer family, whose sexual predilections and strange living conditions are decidedly cultish. *Reside* focuses strongly upon ritual, telling a story of possession that includes extensive scenes of chanting around corpses and involves a cult-like centre with a female leader referred to as 'mother'. Similar to *The Maid*, *The Whole Truth* also takes place within a single family, with the grandchildren protagonists questioning their reality and trying to find out the truth about their own family by peering through a mysterious hole in a wall.

Authenticity

In the new Thai industry, this switch to folk horror can (ironically) be attributed to the further movement of these cultural products away from the rural and working-class Thais such narratives purport to represent. This deployment of and interest in folk horror appears to be a significant means by which to engage the key desired audiences of both global viewers and a new generation of (almost entirely) urban-based middle-class Thais. Certainly, one strong characteristic of folk horror is the reinvention of a 'primitive' collective culture complete with folklore that is presented as 'authentic' in the face of (global) modernity (Keetley, 2020). Reconstituting supernatural customs and wider rituals of collective belief becomes a means to construct an 'authentic' representation of Thai-ness and Thai culture for this viewer.

Such a construction is particularly attractive to a modern and globalised urban-based middle-class Thai audience which, in the digital era, is increasingly disconnected from this authenticity and its collective community. Cultural products offer the opportunity for 'authenticity by appreciation' (Hahl et al., 2017: 833), whereby appreciating and consuming products associated with a 'lowbrow status' becomes a means to address the supposed 'authenticity-insecurity' of social elites. 'High status actors' (social elites) are understood to often be insecure about their own authenticity because their desire to achieve and maintain a high-status position is regarded as morally problematic. As products that are supposedly not motivated by attaining and conforming to highbrow standards and elite audiences (Hahl et al., 2017: 829), 'lowbrow culture' is often constructed as an 'authentic' representation of a society and so becomes appealing to these social elites.

Given that the supernatural has long been associated with the rural lower-classes in Thailand (as demonstrated in Chapter 1), Thai spirit beliefs and horror films are often associated with 'lowbrow' culture. Indeed, despite the big-budget New Thai industry, Thai films have often been associated with the post-war 16mm era and its audiences, becoming constructed in popular consciousness as a form of 'authentic' local opposition to Hollywood. For consumers who are members of some social elites, demonstrating appreciation for cultural products that can be designated as 'authentic lowbrow culture' functions as a means to address insecurities over identity (Hahl et al., 2017). A rapidly modernising society such as Thailand also exacerbates this problematic position as rapid modernity encourages such status-related ambitions, often to the cost of increasing inequality. It is also easy to surmise, given the dramatic political and social class divisions in Thailand as well as the (at times outright) contempt demonstrated towards lower-class Thais from the middle-classes (as explored in Chapter 8), how such individuals are further disconnected from the 'lowbrow' discourses that signal authenticity.

Notably, the modernity-inflected themes of films such as *The Promise* are much more universal and so cannot provide this supposedly authentic culturally-specific insider knowledge. Likewise, the slapstick comedic scares of the highly successful *Pee Mak* that were so popular in Thailand and across Southeast Asia are also absent from folk horror. Instead, ritualistic networks of collective supernatural beliefs provide an authentic 'window' into Thai culture, all of which is evident in reviews and comments that display a need to connect oneself to the collectivity and authenticity of folk horror. Film critic Kong Rithdee stresses the term 'our' when describing these films, placing strong emphasis upon folklore in horror films as a form of lasting identity for Thai and Southeast Asian people: 'It's our default mode, our modus operandi, it's what audiences in this part of the world grew up with' (Rithdee, 2021). Comments around *The Stranded* also tend to focus upon these elements as making the series truly 'Thai'. Director Sophon makes claims as to the exclusive nature and inherent Thai-ness of spirit beliefs: 'we may make this for global audiences, but don't forget the story and characters are in Thailand ... we have our own unique things' (Mahavongtrakul, 2022). Similar comments position the supernatural as offering viewers a 'window' of cultural authenticity, but, with shades of self-Orientalised discourses, constructing Thai culture and people as 'mysterious': 'Good locally produced scares, usually adapted from true stories and urban legends, are a great window into Thai society, allowing the audience to unearth hidden, mysterious truths about Thai people and culture' (Supateerawanitt, 2022).

Likewise, for the international viewer, watching and appreciating such films also enables one to become a 'cultural insider' with authentic and intimate knowledge of Thailand. For such viewers, consuming these films can be a means to construct oneself as a cosmopolitan and globally-knowledgeable citizen with an 'intercultural aptitude', the signifier of sophistication that is so attractive today (Matthews, 2007: 49). This emphasis upon cosmopolitanism also reflects wider changes in the construction of Thailand internationally. In previous decades, films and television shows depicting Thailand for international audiences tended to follow sensationalist and quasi-Orientalist constructions, evident in films such as *The Man With the Golden Gun* (Guy Hamilton, 1974), *The Beach* (Danny Boyle, 2000) and *Bridget Jones: The Edge of Reason* (Beeban Kidron, 2004). Stereotypical narratives and characters revolved around drugs, prostitution, sandy beaches and the salacious hyper-sexualisation of Thai/Asian women, all of which took place against a background of general developing-world chaos.

Asian horror films promoted in Europe and North America from the late 1990s until the early 2010s were entwined within this quasi-Orientalist discourse that was most evident in the popular Asia Extreme brand of the late 1990s and early 2000s. During the 2000s, international festivals and global cinephiles in the West were hungry for more incarnations of what was often marketed as 'extreme' Asian cinema, spurred on by the success of Japanese and Korean horror films (Pett, 2017). Thailand's attachment to this construction is evident in collections such as the 2014 DVD release 'ASIA EXTREME Volume 3: Thai Horror Films'. This collection even contains two films by non-Thai white male directors, one of which depicts sex workers, so completing this salacious and exoticised outsider gaze.

Now however, the promotion of Thai horror internationally is very much attached to a construction of sophisticated cosmopolitan globality. Online articles pose questions such as 'Are You Really a Horror Movie Fan if You Have Not Explored Films from Different Countries?' (Dass, 2021) and 'If you're a fan of horror, you shouldn't shy away from subtitles. You shouldn't watch movies made exclusively in the area where you live. You should branch out and expose yourself to films from around the world' (Riordan, 2022).

Platforms such as Netflix are also aware of the global attraction of such 'authenticity'. Including 'local' and 'authentic' elements is a deliberate part of designing a series for the international market. At a promotional discussion of *The Stranded*, Erika North, director of International Originals at Netflix, clearly illustrates the importance of such a construction: 'what we see on Netflix is the more locally and authentically grounded the story is, the better its prospect to travel', with North citing Spanish and Scandinavian dramas as examples (Mahavongtrakul, 2019).

In English-language articles writers also claim that Thai horror can offer an authentic way to understand Thai culture for the non-Thai viewer, specifically through depicting spirits and associated beliefs. For instance, one article refers to Thai horror films as 'culture-driven' and implies that horror can offer a 'unique' and authentic 'window' into Thai culture for international viewers: 'Thai films are now being internationally recognized for their culture-driven, unique take on tales from beyond the grave' (Daw, 2022). Another states 'A lot of these horror movies are inspired by Thai folklore. The most common legends revolve around Mae Nak and Krasue' (Riordan, 2022). Likewise, promotional news reports for Parkpoom Wongpoom's 2022 short horror film *Those That Follow* (a film created with Apple and funded to demonstrate the capabilities of the iPhone's 'Cinematic mode') anchor the film within local beliefs as a means to further disseminate this text. Reports describe the film as 'rooted in Thai culture' and with a plot 'connected to local Thai belief' (Gupta, 2022).

A Resurgence of Social Divisions of Quality

As part of this emphasis upon folk horror in the digital era, there is also evidence of a resurgence of the earlier divisions and disdainful attitudes directed at Thai popular culture in the post-World War Two era. In the contemporary age of online streaming, in which urban-based middle-class Thais together with international viewers and markets are a priority audience, we see a construction of the regionally and nationally popular elements of visceral horror, and slapstick comedy in particular, as inferior. The folk horror films screened on international OTT platforms are positioned as somehow 'above' the comedy, graphic horror and engagement with modernity that has characterised Thai horror. Paradoxically, seeking authenticity seems to denigrate the long-term characteristics of Thai horror films, elements that were deeply embedded within this society and its audiences.

Certainly, while stressing the genre's 'authentic' engagement with Thai culture, Thai filmmakers and critics seem to bely the visceral history of the horror genre and its origins in this nation. Comments suggest that previous decades of Thai horror do not give insight into Thai culture similar to that offered by recent incarnations of folk horror. For instance, one critic describes the visceral comedy and comedy-horror elements as 'gimmicks', a term that implies a lack of sophistication and instead speaks of a shallow trick to gain popularity: 'Whereas jump-scares and tongue-in-cheek brouhaha may be the gimmick of the genre, Thai horror films go beyond' (Supateerawanitt, 2022). The term 'going beyond' also suggests doing more or achieving more than these 'gimmicks' can offer.

Film critics also seem to follow this general denigration of visceral and presentational elements. For instance, one critique of Wisit Sasanatieng's 2021 horror film *The Whole Truth* claimed that the film had 'too many subplots that have little to do with the overarching narrative' and 'the compelling premise is quickly zapped of all intrigue. Melodramatic acting and flimsy characters do little to entice you to keep watching' (Scott, 2022). In adopting folklore beliefs as part of *The Stranded*, director Sophon also contradictorily states: 'we shouldn't look down on our own legends and roots' (Mahavongtrakul, 2022), while paradoxically removing the visceral and comedic elements that form such 'roots'. Likewise, in lauding the authenticity of *The Medium*, Kong Rithdee praises the depiction of the spirit medium character who 'approaches her job with spiritual dignity – she doesn't give out lotto numbers or pretends [sic] to have a superpower, which is normally expected' (Rithdee, 2021). Such a comment pours scorn upon the social function of spirit mediums, and the reality of the ways in which they operate for the majority of local Thai people.

Mirroring the post-World War Two disdainful attitudes, such elements are generally constructed as inferior due to their association with local and regional viewers, rather than any specific engagement with notions of quality. Thai critic Cod Satrusayang scathingly refers to products popular with 'the masses', stating 'for the most part Thai films have been produced and created for the masses (in Thailand) and have failed to travel internationally. One only has to look at the over-acted and overly formulaic soap operas of the various TV networks to understand how poor the quality control and creative process is' (Satrusayang, 2022). This statement denigrates local audiences while lamenting Thai products that do not have non-Thai appeal as a 'failure'. Likewise, Cod's statements about 'formulaic soap operas' as 'poor' is an absurd judgement, given that such products are highly successful, that this genre is known to be associated with staple narrative 'formulas' and that acting within such entertainment products has always been governed by a histrionic performance code.

Conclusion

As the final chapter in this volume, Chapter 9 has explored the popularity and form of Thai horror overseas. The Thai incarnation of this genre has become a significant regional and international phenomenon, particularly within Southeast Asia, where these films have carved a strong and positive reputation in countries such as Malaysia, Vietnam, Singapore and Indonesia. The chapter explored how this national genre has become and can be understood as a specifically Southeast Asian version of horror, one that is evident in high-grossing successes such as *Pee Mak*, with its visceral and comedic moments and thematic emphasis upon the anxieties of rapid modernity and urban living. Close analysis demonstrates that such cultural similarity can be found across Southeast Asia, in the horror films of prominent industries such as Vietnam, Indonesia and Malaysia. Thai horror therefore becomes a potential example of cultural proximity and a vehicle for ASEAN identity in this region at a moment when this geo-political conglomeration was significant for authorities and consumers.

After outlining such success, the chapter then indicated how we can also see a surprising thematic change in Thai horror when moving into the digital age of the 2020s. This change takes the form of a shift away from the regionally popular emphasis upon the effects of urbanisation and modernity. Films instead embrace the globally recognised characteristics of folk horror, including an emphasis upon collective beliefs and rituals. The chapter argued that this construction was related to attracting and targeting an international viewer as well as seeking a distinctive national identity based upon 'authentic' lowbrow culture for the globalised middle-class Thai viewer. Such an emphasis then leads to a devaluation of the visceral characteristics honed since the post-war era which are very much part of the regional popularity of Thai horror, indicating how internal social divisions continue to be a part of the Thai industry today.

Notes

Parts of this chapter have been previously published as Ainslie, M. (2015), 'Thai Horror Film in Malaysia: Urbanization, Cultural Proximity and a Southeast Asian Model', *Plaridel: A Philippine Journal of Communication, Media, and Society*, 12(2).

1. Such threads are largely in English and are written in local colloquial dialects.
2. While this is actually a South Korea-Thailand-Singapore-USA coproduction, commentators notably refer to it purely as Thai, demonstrating how this connection displaces any other association in both its marketing and reception.
3. In keeping with these 'local' depictions, Malaysian films do not have an established presence internationally beyond Indonesia, Brunei, the Philippines and Singapore (the latter of which caters largely to the Malay community and the former two

in which it can rely upon linguistic and cultural similarities in a similar way to the relationship between Thailand, Laos and Cambodia). There are generally no Malaysian films available on the European and American DVD racks upon which Thai cinema has carved a place, and few festivals host Malaysian films beyond the niche independent and art cinema from celebrated auteurs such as the late Yasmin Ahmad.
4. This refers to a media provider that broadcasts content directly to viewers via the internet, so bypassing traditional controllers such as television platforms.

CONCLUSION

This book has explored the stylistic, thematic and political characteristics of Thai cinema from the post-World War Two era up into the recent twenty-first century. Examining horror films in particular, the book outlined how this frequent and popular genre becomes a vehicle to articulate the various stylistic and thematic changes undergone by Thai cinema in the previous decades. Analysis traced how these various characteristics altered across the decades, connecting such changes to the complex and socially divided nature of contemporary Thailand. The book therefore indicates how the wider Thai context engendered very different entertainment forms and varying ideological positions. Likewise, the analysis indicated how films (and horror in particular) became a cogent means to address Thai cinema's wider relationship to both authorities and viewers.

To this end, the first two chapters of the book explored the development of horror films since the 1960s and up into the 1990s, before the establishment of the post-1997 New Thai industry. Chapter 1 began by conducting an analysis of Thai film in the post-war era, known as the 16mm era, and in particular a case study of the popular horror genre. The book outlined how these productions blended many genres in single films and were less concerned with eliciting the primary emotions of fear and disgust that are usually associated with the horror genre. Such productions tended to follow a causal narrative structure and did not prioritise suspense, while also inserting the supernatural liberally into productions without violating any notion of 'Natural Law'. The book also highlighted how these early productions catered for a communal audience and so tended not to replicate the cinematography and editing structures associated with the horror genre and its isolated viewers. Chapter 2 then indicated how such characteristics continued in Thai films of later decades, existing alongside the various (and quite radical) industrial, political and economic changes taking place. These included increased appeal to urban-based viewers, advances in film quality due to improved technology and the incorporation of an Americanised modern *mise-en-scène* and film style. Such changes laid the later foundations from which the post-97 New Thai industry was to grow.

These opening chapters also examined Thai film thematically, arguing that horror in particular operated as a traumatic form of mediation during times when societal norms were questioned by rapid social change. The book demonstrated that such engagement tended to focus upon the depiction of women, reflecting the challenges to traditional gender roles during modernisation and economic development. Films alternatively operated as both a conservative affirmation of traditional constructions as well as a progressive acknowledgement and a means to give voice to subaltern positions.

Subsequent chapters then moved into the post-97 contemporary New Thai industry, exploring both the changing stylistic characteristics of Thai films as well as the shifting political relationship to the state. Chapter 3 indicated how the heritage horror film *Nang Nak* (Nonzee Nimibutr, 1999) offered a conservative affirmation of traditional social roles after the 1997 economic crisis. Chapter 4 likewise addressed how films such as *Zee Oui* (Nida Sudasna and Buranee Ratchaiboon, 2004) and *Laa Thaa Phii/Ghost Game* (Sarawut Wichiensarn, 2006) sought to reinforce nationalistic Thai-ness through constructing a reactionary portrayal of a monstrous Other.

However, later chapters then explored the various ways in which New Thai films also tended to question and undercut such reactionary portrayals. Chapter 5 examined the ways in which a corpus of films labelled as the 'Vengeful Ghost Films' addressed the abuse of lower-class women after the 1997 economic crisis. Films depicted a traumatised young female ghost returning from the afterlife and holding her abusers to account. Chapter 6 then followed such analysis with an examination of the depiction of cinematic technology in contemporary Thai horror films. The chapter argued that this (self-)reflexivity functioned as a further critique of social inequality and engagement with socially-marginalised perspectives. Chapter 7 extended such analysis by addressing films of the New Thai industry that embraced the film style of the post-World War Two era, a reminder of the importance of the provincial audience through the continuing influence of their entertainment preferences.

After this in-depth analysis of the New Thai industry throughout the 2000s, the final two chapters then moved on to explore more recent Thai cinema, whereby this industry now exists as part of a 'fully developed' nation and a wider corpus of regional horror films. Chapter 8 outlined how Thailand in the late 2010s is considered to have transitioned to an upper-income nation. Analysis indicated how Thai horror now frequently examines the effects of social alienation, reflecting a context of rapid modernity and rampant consumerism. This engagement is comparable to East Asian models of horror that are also concerned with such 'turbo-modernity'. However the chapter also indicated how such depictions differ in light of the complex political position of the Thai middle-classes, who remain particularly isolated given their reactionary alignment with the state throughout the past decade.

The final chapter then moved outside of Thailand to examine how Thai horror and its 'modern' incarnation has become the standard regional representation of this genre, with a significant reputation and high level of popularity in other Southeast Asian countries. Cultural proximity is also evident in horror films made in countries such as Vietnam and Malaysia, carving a form of regional cultural identity at a significant moment during these nations' conglomeration under the geo-political banner of ASEAN. The second part of this final chapter then moved on to examine the changes and global expansion of Thai horror in the digital era. While this new technology impacted upon horror stylistically, the chapter also noted how thematically, recent productions engaged much more with subject matter that could be labelled as 'folk horror', a potential reaction to the destabilisation of national identity in the aftermath of rapid modernity.

Through such close analysis, the book provided a new international case study of the horror genre, and one very different to the exploration of Western and East Asian incarnations that have previously dominated studies of this genre. The emphasis upon issues such as the changing position and preferences of audiences, the influence of prior-existing entertainment forms, the social discourses around women and 'Others' as well as the complex position of the middle-classes and provincial Thais all highlight the specificity of this model of horror. Likewise, the final chapter also expanded such analysis to address how this can be understood as a regionally specific model, an important development in light of the increasing international influence of ASEAN in world politics today.

The book has ramifications for the study of non-EuroAmerican cinema in general. Specifically such analysis invites interrogation as to how film theory developed from Hollywood and European cinema should be deployed to investigate films and industries that have developed outside of this context. As a means to address such concerns and avoid the tensions and pitfalls of orientalism when assessing Thai culture within the global context, the book has been underpinned throughout by empirical data. As outlined in the Introduction by Peter A. Jackson, such empirically-based 'locally grounded enquiry' is crucial when deploying theory from one context to another. The book deployed this in the field of film studies, conducting a translation of theoretical frameworks that is based upon empirical data and information. This enabled me to assess when and how theory can be used to analyse Thai film.

This 'translation' of theory also illustrated how the analysis of cultural products in diverse nations cannot and must not be conducted purely within the boundaries of the nation and nationality. By this I mean that the study of Thai texts cannot be divorced from a study of the different social groups within the nation and defined purely by national boundaries. The book has indicated how the formal and thematic parameters of Thai films are influenced by and vary greatly according to the wider concerns and preferences of different communities and historical periods. Films cater for and exist alongside radically different social groups, whether upholding a dominant ideology or functioning as a lower-class means to disrupt and/or negotiate this. Likewise, the final chapter illustrated how Thai film must now also be viewed within a wider corpus of Southeast Asian cinema, particularly when addressing the incarnation of genres such as horror, which become regionally (rather than nationally) very specific and hold strong evidence of cultural proximity.

Finally, the book demonstrated that ethnicity, cultural background and, most importantly, social class must all be taken into account when exploring Thai entertainment. This nation was created from a collection of diverse communities with rich histories and cultural traditions, all of whom responded to and consumed media in their own way. Likewise, the contemporary nation also grapples with wider issues involving lasting inequality and political upheaval. Such diversity is particularly significant in the contemporary age when Thai cultural products are pulled between the preferences and agendas of these social groups. My examination of the Thai film industry and Thai horror in particular has indicated that Thai films are shaped by their relationship to these various communities and must be explored through such a perspective, not simply and solely designated through the nation.

BIBLIOGRAPHY

AIFFA (2012) *Celebrate ASEAN Movies at AIFFA 2021*. Available at: https://asean filmfestival.com/index.php/about-us/ (Accessed 16 May 2023)
Akkarakul, N., Paitoonpong, S. and Rodsomboon, S. (2009) *Impact of the Financial Crisis on Women in Thailand. Oxfam Research Report*. August. Thailand: Oxfam GB.
Altman, R. (1999) *Film/Genre*. London: British Film Institute.
Ancuta, K. (2011) 'Global Spectrologies: Contemporary Thai Horror Films and the Globalization of the Supernatural', *Horror Studies*, 2(1), pp. 131–144.
Ancuta, K. (2014) 'Spirits in Suburbia: Ghosts, Global Desires and the Rise of Thai Middle-class Horror', *Horror Studies*, 5(2), pp. 233–247.
Ancuta, K. (2016) 'That's the Spirit! Horror Films as an Extension of the Thai Supernatural', in P. J. Braunlein and A. Lauser (eds) *Ghost Movies in Southeast Asia and Beyond*. Boston: Brill, pp. 123–140.
Anderson, W. W. (1989) 'Folklore and Folklife of Thailand Foreword', *Asian Folklore Studies*, 48(1–3).
Århem, K. and Sprenger, G. (2015) *Animism in Southeast Asia*. London and New York: Routledge.
Asian Development Bank (2017) *Asian Economies: Making the Transition to High Income*. 12 January. Available at https://www.adb.org/news/features/asian-econo mies-making-transition-high-income (Accessed 16 May 2023)
Bangkok Post (2006) *Cambodia Fumes at Disrespectful Thai Ghost Movie* 27 April.
Begum, M. (2019) 'ASEAN International Film Festival & Awards Enters its Fourth Edition', *The Jakarta Post*, 2 April. Available at: https://www.thejakartapost.com/life/2019/04/01/asean-international-film-festival--awards-enters-its-fourth-edition.html (Accessed 16 May 2023)
Bell, P. (1997) 'Thailand's Economic Miracle: Built on the Backs of Women', in V. Somswasdi and S. Theobold (eds) *Women, Gender Relations and Development in Thai Society*. Chiang Mai: Ming Muan Navarat Co. Ltd, pp. 55–82.

Benshoff, H. M. (1997) *Monsters in the Closet: Homosexuality and the Horror Film*. Manchester: Manchester University Press.

Beyond Hollywood (2002) *Nang Nak (1999) Movie Review*. Available at: http://www.beyondhollywood.com/nang-nak-1999-movie-review (Accessed 23 August 2009)

Birr, H. (2009) 'Put Your Hands Up and Sing: Cross-Cultural Film Reception and Fandom', *Projections*, (3/2), pp. 37–55.

Blake, L. (2008) *The Wounds of Nations: Horror Cinema, Historical Trauma and National Identity*. Manchester: Manchester University Press. Boehler, N. (2014), 'Staging the Spectral: The Border, Haunting and Politics in Mekong Hotel', *Horror Studies Journal*, 5(2), pp. 197–210.

Boonyaketmala, B. (1992) 'The Rise and Fall of the Film Industry in Thailand 1897–1992', *East West Film Journal*, 6/2, pp. 62–98.

Bordwell, D. (1985) *Narration in the Fiction Film*. Madison: University of Wisconsin Press, pp. 48–62.

Bourdieu, P. (1979) *La distinction: critique sociale du jugement*, Paris: Editions de minuit.

Brand, R. (2008) 'Witnessing Trauma on Film', in P. Frosh and A. Pinchevski (eds) *Media Witnessing: Testimony in the Age of Mass Communication*. London and New York: Palgrave Macmillan, pp. 198–215.

Braunlein, P. J. (2016) 'Cinema-Spiritualism in Southeast Asia and Beyond', in P. J. Braunlein and A. Lauser (eds) *Ghost Movies in Southeast Asia and Beyond*. Boston: Brill, pp. 1–39.

Brown, T. (2006) *Art of The Devil 2 Review*. Available at: http://twitchfilm.net/archives/006710.html (Accessed 1 June 2011)

Brown, W. (2015). 'Politicizing Eye-tracking Studies of Film', *Refractory: A Journal of Entertainment Media*, 25.

Broxton, J. (2014) 'VENGEFUL HEART (QUA TIM MÁU) – Christopher Wong and Garrett Crosby', *Movie Music UK*. 14 February. Available at https://moviemusicuk.us/2014/02/14/vengeful-heart-qua-tim-mau-christopher-wong-and-garrett-crosby/ (Accessed 16 May 2023)

Brzeski, P. (2013) 'Southeast Asia 2013 in Review: "Pee Mak" Huge in Thailand, "Iron Man 3" Lands in Myanmar', *The Hollywood Reporter*. 27 December. Available at: https://www.hollywoodreporter.com/news/general-news/southeast-asia-2013-review-pee-667738/ (Accessed 16 May 2023)

Bulman, D., Eden, M., Nguyen, H. (2017) 'Transitioning from Low Income Growth to High-Income Growth: Is There a Middle-Income Trap?', *Journal of the Asia Pacific Economy*, 22(1), pp. 5–28.

Burnard, P. Naiyapatana, W. and Lloyd, G. (2006) 'Views of Mental Illness and Mental Health Care in Thailand: A Report of an Ethnographic Study', *Journal of Psychiatric and Mental Health Nursing*, 13, pp. 742–749.

Buruma, I. (1983), 'Thailand's Filmmakers Sink in a Morass of Money vs Artistry', *Far Eastern Economic Review*, 122(43), pp. 53–54.

Callahan, W. A. (2003) 'Beyond Cosmopolitanism and Nationalism: Diasporic Chinese and Neo-Nationalism in China and Thailand', *International Organization*, 57(3), pp. 481–517.

Carroll, N. (1990) *The Philosophy of Horror or Paradoxes of the Heart*. London and New York: Routledge.

Chaiworaporn, A. (2001) 'Thai Cinema Since 1970', in D. Hanan (ed.) *Film in South East Asia: Views from The Region*. Hanoi: South East Asia Pacific Audio Visual Archives Association, pp. 141–162.

Chaiworaporn, A. (2006) 'M.A.I.D.', in *Udine Far East Film 8 Festival Program 2006*. Udine: Nickelodeon, p. 114.

Chaiworaporn, A. (2007) 'The Year of Conflict and Diversity: Thai Cinema In 2006', in *Udine Far East Film 9 Festival Program 2007*. Udine: Nickelodeon, pp. 71–75.
Chaiworaporn, A. (2008) 'A Case of Wait and See: Thai Cinema in 2007', in *Udine Far East Film 10 Festival Program 2008*. Udine: Nickelodeon, pp. 79–83.
Chaiworaporn, A. and Knee, A. (2006) 'Thailand: Revival in an Age of Globalization', in A. T. Ciecko (ed.) *Contemporary Asian Cinema*. New York: Berg, pp. 58–70.
Chiang, W. (2012). 'The Suppression of Emotional Expression in Interpersonal Context', *Bulletin of Educational Psychology*, 43, pp. 657–680.
Christian, J. L. (1941) 'Thailand Renascent', *Pacific Affairs*, 14(2), pp. 184–197.
Chua, B. H. (2004) 'Conceptualizing an East Asian Popular Culture', *Inter-Asia Cultural Studies*, 5, pp. 200–221.
Chua, B. H. (2015) 'Korean Pop Culture: Emergent Genre of East Asian Pop Culture?', in M. Ainslie and J. Lim (eds) *The Korean Wave in Southeast Asia: Consumption and Cultural Production*. Kuala Lumpur: SIRD, pp. 175–192.
Chung, H. S. (2014) 'Acacia and Adoption Anxiety in Korean Horror Cinema', in D. Martin and A. Peirse (eds) *Korean Horror Cinema*. Edinburgh: Edinburgh University Press, pp. 87–100.
Clover, C. J. (1993) *Men Women and Chainsaws: Gender in the Modern Horror Film*. London: BFI Publishing.
Corera, G. (1997) *Thailand: The Crisis Starts*. Available at: http://news.bbc.co.uk/1/hi/special_report/1997/asian_economic_woes/34487.stm (Accessed 23 October 2005)
Coughlin, R. J. (1955) 'The Chinese in Bangkok: A Commercial-Oriented Minority', *American Sociological Review*, 20(3), pp. 311–316.
Creed, B. (1993) *The Monstrous Feminine: Film, Feminism and Psychoanalysis*. London: Routledge.
Curzon, G. (1893) 'Miscellaneous Extracts, etc', *Manchester Times*, April 21.
Dass, C. (2021) '5 Thai Horror Films on Netflix That Will Absolutely Terrify You', *Tatler*. 9 July. Available at: https://www.tatlerasia.com/culture/entertainment/sg-thai-horror-films-netflix (Accessed 16 May 2023)
Daw, D. (2022) '20 Best Thai Horror Movies', *ScreenRant*. 9 October. Available at: https://screenrant.com/best-thai-horror-movies/ (Accessed 16 May 2023)
Dei, F. (2021) 'Netflix and Chills: 10 Thai Horror Movies That'll Give You Nightmares', *Klook*. 1 May. Available at: https://www.klook.com/en-PH/blog/horror-movies-thai/ (Accessed 16 May 2023)
Errasti, J. M., Amigo Vázquez, I., Villadangos, M. and Morís, J. (2018) 'Differences Between Individualist and Collectivist Cultures in Emotional Facebook Usage: Relationship with Empathy, Self-esteem, and Narcissism', *Psicothema*, 30(4), pp. 376–381.
Estrada, G., Xuehui, H., Donghyun, P. and Shu, T. (2017) 'Asia's Middle-Income Challenge: An Overview', *Asian Development Bank ADB Economics Working Paper Series* No. 525. Available at: www.adb.org/sites/default/files/publication/381381/ewp-525.pdf (Accessed 16 May 2023)
Evilbean (2015) *Vietnamese Horror Movie – Conjuring Spirit*. Available at: http://www.talkingevilbean.com/2015/05/vietnamese-horror-movie-conjuring-spirit.html?m=0 (Accessed 17 May 2023)
Ferrarese, M. (2021) '"New Kinds of Monsters": The Rise of Southeast Asian Horror Films', *AlJazeera*. Available at: https://www.aljazeera.com/news/2021/6/2/zombie-films-breathe-new-life-into-malaysian-and-indonesia-horror (Accessed 16 May 2023)
Formoso, B. (1996) 'Hsiu-Kou-Ku: The Ritual Refining of Restless Ghosts Among the Chinese of Thailand', *The Journal of the Royal Anthropological Institute*, 2(2), pp. 217–234.

Fouquet, G. (2006), 'Trente ans de séances de cinema' ('30 Years of Screening'), in M. Bastian (ed.), *Le cinéma thaïlandais (Thai Cinema)*. Lyon: Asiexpo, pp. 42–59.
Freeland, C. (2000) *The Naked and the Undead: Evil and the Appeal of Horror*. Oxford: Westview Press.
Gelder, K. 2000. *The Horror Reader*. London and New York: Routledge.
Glassman, J. (2010) 'Commentary', *Environment and Planning A*, 42(4), pp. 765–770.
Grodal, T. and Kramer, M. (2010) 'Empathy, Film, and the Brain', *Recherches sémiotiques/Semiotic Inquiry*, 30, pp. 19–35.
Gunew, S. (2009) 'Subaltern Empathy: Beyond European Categories in Affect Theory', *Concentric: Literary and Cultural Studies*, 35(1), 11–30.
Gunning, T. (1991) *D. W. Griffith and the Origins of American Narrative Film*. Urbana and Chicago: University of Illinois Press.
Gupta, M. S. (2022) '"Shutter" Director Parkpoom Wongpoom's Latest Horror Film was Shot Entirely on an iPhone 13 Pro', *Lifestyle Asia*, 6 May. Available at: https://www.lifestyleasia.com/sg/culture/entertainment/parkpoom-wongpoom-thai-horror-film-those-that-follow-shot-on-apple-iphone-13-pro-released/ (Accessed 16 May 2023)
Hahl, O. Zuckerman, E. W. and Minjae, K. (2017) 'Why Elites Love Authentic Lowbrow Culture: Overcoming High-Status Denigration with Outsider Art', *American Sociological Review*, 82(4), pp. 828–856.
Hamid, F. (1992) 'Hot-Air Balloons Join Crowded Outdoor Scene in Thailand', *Asian Advertising & Marketing*. May. Travel and Trade Publishing (Asia) Ltd., pp. 40–42.
Hamilton, A. (1993) 'Video Crackdown, or The Sacrificial Pirate: Censorship and Cultural Consequences in Thailand', *Public Culture*, 5, pp. 515–531.
Hamilton, A. (1994) 'Cinema and Nation: Dilemmas of Representation in Thailand', in Dissanayake, W. (ed.) *Colonialism and Nationalism in Asian Cinema*. Indiana: Indiana University Press, pp. 141–161.
Hanich, J. (2010) *Cinematic Emotion in Horror Films and Thrillers: The Aesthetic Paradox of Pleasurable Fear*. New York: Routledge.
Hanich, J. (2018) *The Audience Effect: On the Collective Cinema Experience*. Edinburgh: Edinburgh University Press.
Hanich, J. (2022) 'An Invention with a Future: Collective Viewing, Joint Deep Attention, and the Ongoing Value of the Cinema', in K. Stevens (ed.) *Oxford Handbook of Film Theory*. Oxford: Oxford University Press, pp. 590–609.
Hanoi Times (2015) VN, Thai Filmmakers Work on Horror Flick. 2 February. Available at: https://hanoitimes.vn/vn-thai-filmmakers-work-on-horror-flick-15879.html (Accessed 16 May 2023)
Hansen, M. (1994) 'Early Cinema, Late Cinema: Transformations of the Public Space', in L. Williams (ed.) *Viewing Positions: Ways of Seeing Film*. New Brunswick: Rutgers University Press, pp. 134–152.
Hansen, M. (2000) 'The Mass Production of the Senses: Classical Cinema as Vernacular Modernism', in C. Gledhill and L. Williams (eds) *Reinventing Film Studies*. London: Arnold, pp. 332–350.
Heller-Nicholas, A. (2014) *Found Footage Horror Films: Fear and the Appearance of Reality*. Jefferson: McFarland.
Hewison, K. (1999) *After the Asian Crisis: Challenges to Globalization*. New South Wales: University of New England.
Higgins, S. (2008) 'Suspenseful Situations: Melodramatic Narrative and the Contemporary Action Film', *Cinema Journal*, 47(2), pp. 74–96.
Higson, A. (2000) 'The Limiting Imagination of National Cinema', in Hjort, M. and MacKenzie, S. (eds) *Cinema and Nation*. London and New York: Routledge, pp. 63–74.

Higson, A. (2003) *English Heritage, English Cinema*. Oxford: Oxford University Press.
Hill, J. (1999) *British Cinema in the 1980s*. Broadbridge: Clarendon Press.
Hoad, P. (2013) 'Thai Horror Film-makers Sink Teeth into South-east Asian Market', *The Guardian*. 16 April. Available at: https://www.theguardian.com/film/2013/apr/16/thai-horror-film-pee-mak (Accessed 16 May 2023)
Hofstede (2017) *Hofstede Insights: Thailand*. Available at: https://www.hofstede-insights.com/country/thailand/ (accessed 25 January 2022)
Hunt, L. (2000), 'A (Sadistic) Night at the Opera: Notes on the Italian Horror Film', in K. Gelder (ed.) *The Horror Reader*. London: Routledge, pp. 324–335.
Hutchings, P. (2004) *The Horror Film*. Essex: Pearson Education Limited.
Imada, T. (2012). 'Cultural Narratives of Individualism and Collectivism: A Content Analysis of Textbook Stories in the United States and Japan', *Journal of Cross-Cultural Psychology*, 43(4), pp. 576–591.
Ingawanij, M. A. (2006) 'Un-Thai Sakon: The Scandal of Teen Cinema', in *South East Asia Research* 14(2), pp. 147–177.
Ingawanij, M. A. and MacDonald, R. L. (2005) 'The Value of an Impoverished Aesthetic: The Iron Ladies and its Audiences', *South East Asia Research*, 13(1), pp. 43–56.
Ishikawa, K. *(2021) 'The ASEAN Economic Community and ASEAN* Economic Integration', Journal of Contemporary East Asia Studies, 10(1), pp. 24–41.
Jackson, P. A. (2005) 'Semicoloniality, Translation and Excess in Thai Cultural Studies', *South East Asia Research*, 13(1), pp. 7–41.
Jackson, P. A. (2014) *Ascendant Doctrine and Resurgent Magic in Capitalist Southeast Asia: Paradox and Polarisation as 21st Century Cultural Logic*. In: DORISEA Working Paper Series No. 6.
Jenmana, T. and Gethin, A. (2019) 'Extreme Inequality, Democratisation and Class Struggles in Thailand,' *WID.world Issue Brief 2019–1*. March. Available at https://wid.world/document/extreme-inequality-democratisation-and-class-struggles-in-thailand-wid-world-issue-brief-2019-1/ (Accessed 17 May 2023)
Jitsuchon, S. (2012) 'Thailand in a Middle-income Trap', *Thailand Development Research Institute Quarterly Review*, 27(2), pp. 13–20.
Jirattikorn, A. (2008) 'Pirated Transnational Broadcasting: The Consumption of Thai Soap Operas among Shan Communities in Burma', *Sojourn* 23(1), pp. 30–62.
JWT Asia Pacific and A. T. Kearney (2013) *ASEAN Consumers and the AEC JWT Asia Pacific*. Available at http://d3ftitl17j4lal.cloudfront.net/a4bd1048-007c-45ec-ad51-85fdc2411e76-all_documents.pdf (Accessed 17 May 2023)
Jung, S. (2006) 'Bae Yong-Joon, Hybrid Masculinity and the Counter-coeval Desire of Japanese Female Fans', *Participations*, 3(2).
Karim, W. J. (1995) 'Bilateralism and Gender in Southeast Asia', in W. J. Karim (ed.) *'Male' and 'Female' in Developing Southeast Asia*. Oxford: Berg Publishers, pp. 35–77.
Kastanakis, M., Kastanakis, N. and Voyer, B. G. (2014) 'The Effect of Culture on Perception and Cognition: A Conceptual Framework', *Journal of Business Research*, 67, pp. 425–433.
Keetley, D. (2020) 'Introduction: Defining Folk Horror', *Revenant: Critical and Creative Studies of the Supernatural*, 5, pp. 1–32.
Keyes, C. F. and Tanabe, S. (eds) (2002) *Cultural Crisis and Social Memory: Modernity and Identity in Thailand and Laos*. London: Routledge.
Kitiarsa, P. (1999) *You May Not Believe, But Never Offend the Spirits: Spirit-medium Cult Discourses and the Postmodernization of Thai Religion*. Ph.D. University of Washington.
Knee, A. (2005) 'Thailand Haunting: The Power of the Past in the Contemporary Thai Horror Film', in S. J. Schneider and T. Williams (eds) *Horror International*. Detroit: Wayne State University Press, pp. 141–159.

Koanantakool, P. C. (1989) 'Relevance of the Textual and Contextual Analysis in Understanding Folk Performance of Modern Society: A Case of Southern Thai Shadow Puppet Theatre', *Asian Folklore Studies*, 48, pp. 31–57.

Korea Foundation (2011) *2011 Annual Report*. Seoul: Korea Foundation.

Kristeva, J. (1982) *Powers of Horror: An Essay on Abjection*. Guildford: Colombia University Press.

Ksiazek, T. B. and Webster, J. G. (2008) 'Cultural Proximity and Audience Behavior: The Role of Language in Patterns of Polarization and Multicultural Fluency', *Journal of Broadcasting & Electronic Media*, 52(3) pp. 485–503.

Le, N. (2021) '"HÙ!" — A Vietnamese Horror Primer', *Fangoria*. 1 March. Available at: https://www.fangoria.com/original/vietnamese-horror/ (Accessed 17 May 2023)

Lee, H. (2014) 'Family, Death and the Wonhon in Four Films of the 1960s 23 Hyangjin Lee', in D. Martin and A. Peirse (eds) *Korean Horror Cinema*. Edinburgh: Edinburgh University Press, pp. 23–34.

Lee, N. J. Y. (2014) 'Apartment Horror: Sorum and Possessed', in D. Martin and A. Peirse (eds) *Korean Horror Cinema*. Edinburgh: Edinburgh University Press, pp. 101–113.

Leeder, M. (2017) *The Modern Supernatural and the Beginnings of Cinema*. London: Palgrave.

Leona (2022) '12 Recommendations for the Latest and Scariest Thai Horror Movies 2022', *Indonesia Posts English*. Available at: https://indonesia.postsen.com/movies/155470/12-Recommendations-for-the-Latest-and-Scariest-Thai-Horror-Movies-2022.html (Accessed 17 May 2023)

Leona (2022) '12 Recommendations for the Latest and Scariest Thai Horror Movies 2022' *Indonesia Posts English*. Available at: https://indonesia.postsen.com/movies/155470/12-Recommendations-for-the-Latest-and-Scariest-Thai-Horror-Movies-2022.html (Accessed 17 May 2023)

Lertchoosakul, K (2021) 'The Paradox of the Thai Middle Class in Democratisation', *TRaNS: Trans-Regional and-National Studies of Southeast Asia*, 9, pp. 65–79.

Levi, N. and Rothberg, M. (2003) *The Holocaust: Theoretical Readings*. Edinburgh: Edinburgh University Press.

Liew, K. K. (2015) 'Into the Heart of the Korean Wave in Banjong Pisanthanakun's *Hello Stranger* and Poj Arnon's *Sorry, Sarangheyo*', in M. Ainslie and J. B. Y. Lim (eds) *The Korean Wave in Southeast Asia*. Selangor: SIRD.

Lim, N. (2016) 'Cultural Differences in Emotion: Differences in Emotional Arousal Level between the East and the West', *Integrative Medicine Research*, (20), pp. 105–109.

Limoges, J-M. (2009) 'The Gradable Effects of Self-Reflexivity on Aesthetic Illusion in Cinema', in W. Wolf, K. Bantleon and J. Thoss (eds) *Metareference across Media Theory and Case Studies*. New York: Rodopi, pp. 391–408.

Louie, K. (2012) 'Popular Culture and Masculinity Ideals in East Asia, with Special Reference to China', *Journal of Asian Studies*, 71(4), pp. 929–943.

Lowenstein, A. (ed.) (2005) *Shocking Representation*. New York: Columbia University Press.

Lowenstein, A. (2010) 'Living Dead: Fearful Attractions of Film', *Representations* 110(1), pp. 105–128.

Lu, J., Liu, X. and Cheng, Y. (2019) 'Cultural Proximity and Genre Proximity: How Do Chinese Viewers Enjoy American and Korean TV Dramas?' *SAGE Open*, 9(1).

Mahavongtrakul, M. (2019) 'Netflix Embraces Thai-ness', *Bangkok Post*. 22 September. Available at: https://www.bangkokpost.com/life/arts-and-entertainment/1755679/netflix-embraces-Thai-ness (Accessed 17 May 2023)

Maneechote, P. (2021) 'The Four Major Streaming Services in Thailand: Which one is for You?', *Thai Enquirer*. 14 June. Available at: https://www.thaienquirer.com/28532/the-four-major-streaming-services-in-thailand-which-one-is-for-you/ (Accessed 17 May 2023)

Masuda, T., Gonzalez, R., Kwan, L. and Nisbett, R. E. (2008). 'Culture and Aesthetic Preference: Comparing the Attention to Context of East Asians and Americans', *Personality and Social Psychology Bulletin*, 34(9), pp. 1260–1275.

Matahari Media (2017) *ASEAN Film Festival (AFF) and Indonesian Film Festival (IFF) in The Netherlands*. Available at: https://www.mataharimedia.nl/indonesian-film-festival-iff-in-nederland/ (Accessed 17 May 2023)

Matthews, J. (2007) 'Eurasian Persuasions: Mixed Race, Performativity and Cosmopolitanism', *Journal of Intercultural Studies*, 28(1), pp. 41–54.

McKinney (2022) '14 Most Terrifying Indonesian Horror Movies', *The Uncorked Librarian*. 11 October. Available at: https://www.theuncorkedlibrarian.com/indonesian-horror-movies/ (Accessed 17 May 2023)

Mills, M. B. (1995) 'Attack of the Widow Ghosts: Gender, Death, and Modernity in Northeast Thailand', in A. Ong and M. G. Peletz (eds) *Bewitching Women, Pious Men: Gender and Body Politics in Southeast Asia*. London: University of California Press, pp. 224–273.

Neale, S. (2000) *Genre and Hollywood*. London and New York: Routledge.

Neale, S. (2004) 'Halloween: Suspense, Aggression and the Look', in B. K. Grant and C. Sharrett (eds) *Planks of Reason: Essays on the Horror Film*. Lanham: Scarecrow Press Ltd, pp. 356–369.

Ngo, T. H. (2015) 'Korean Masculinity in TV Dramas and Local Fantasies: A Case Study of Full House and Its Vietnamese Remake Ngôi Nhà Hạnh Phúc', in J. Lim and M. J. Ainslie (eds) *The Korean Wave in Southeast Asia: Consumption and Cultural Production*. Kuala Lumpur: SIRD, pp. 133–154.

Nguyen, T. (2017) 'Quan Am and Mary: Vietnamese Religious, Cultural, and Spiritual Phenomena', *Buddhist-Christian Studies* 37, pp. 191–208.

Nisbett, R. E. and Masuda, T. (2003) 'Culture and Point of View', *Proceedings of the National Academy of Sciences of the United States of America*, 100(19), pp. 11163–11175.

Noh, J. (2013) 'Pee Mak Scares up Thai Box Office', *ScreenDaily*. 9 April. Available at: https://www.screendaily.com/pee-mak-scares-up-thai-box-office/5053724.article (Accessed 17 May 2023)

Nusair, D. (2004) *Toronto International Film Festival 2004 – UPDATE #9*. Available at: http://www.reelfilm.com/tiff0409.htm#rahtree (Accessed 23 August 2009)

Pajee, P. (2003) 'What Made Him Tick?' *The Nation*, 31 March.

Pajee, P. (2013) 'Ghosts from Some of Thailand's Best-loved Horror Flicks will Haunt Sentosa for Halloween', *The Nation*. 5 August. Available at: https://www.nationthailand.com/life/30211963 (Accessed 17 May 2023)

Parivudhiphong, A. (2005) 'What Lurks Beneath the Horror', *Bangkok Post*, 24 Aug.

Parkes, C. (2000) *Thailand Handbook*. Emeryville: Avalon Travel Publishing.

Patsorn, S. (2004) 'Thai Cinema as National Cinema: An Evaluative History'. Ph.D. thesis, Murdoch University.

Pett, E. (2017) 'Transnational Cult Paratexts: Exploring Audience Readings of Tartan's Asia Extreme Brand', *Transnational Cinemas*, 8(1), pp. 35–48.

Phongpaichit, P. and Baker, C. (1998) *Thailand's Boom and Bust*. Chang Mai: Silkworm Books.

Phongpaichit, P. (2001) 'Developing Social Alternatives: Walking Backwards into a Khlong', in P. Warr (ed.) *Thailand Beyond the Crisis*. London: Routledge, pp. 161–183.

Phongpaichit, P. and Baker, C. (2008) *The Spirits, The Stars and Thai Politics*. Copy of an unpublished paper presented to the Siam Society, 2 December.

Pongsapich, A. (1997) 'Feminism Theories and Praxis: Women's Social Movement in Thailand', in V. Somswasdi and S. Theobold (eds) *Women, Gender Relations and Development in Thai Society Volume 1*. Chiang Mai: Ming Muan Navarat Co. Ltd., pp. 3–51.

Pornwasin, A. (2013) 'The Net Catches Pee-Mak Fever', *The Nation*. 12 April. Available at: https://www.nationthailand.com/in-focus/30204006 (Accessed 17 May 2023)

Raisz, A. (2017) 'Privatizing Peri-urbanization: Gated Communities, Social Fragmentation, and "Modernization" in Greater Buenos Aires, Argentina', May 1. GEOG–494: Global Urbanism, pp. 1–24.

NA (2013) *Pee Mak* [blog post]. 15 July. Available at: http://komplikasiduniawi.blogspot.my/2013/07/pee-mak.html (Accessed 17 May 2023)

Raman, A., Tyson, G. and Sastry, N. (2018) 'Facebook (A)Live?: Are Live Social Broadcasts Really Broadcasts?' *WWW '18: Proceedings of the 2018 World Wide Web Conference*. April, pp.1491–1500.

Ramasoota, P. and Kitikamdhorn, A. (2021) '"The Netflix Effect" in Thailand: Industry and Regulatory Implications', *Telecommunications Policy*, 45(7).

Randhawa, N. (2011) 'Malaysian Horror Controversy', *Yahoo News*. 17 October. Available at: https://sg.news.yahoo.com/malaysian-horror-controversy-094400054.html (Accessed 17 May 2023)

Ravenhill, J. (2008) 'Fighting Irrelevance: An Economic Community "with ASEAN Characteristics"', *The Pacific Review*, 21(4): 469–488.

Realo, A. and Luik, M. (2002) 'On the Relationship between Collectivism and Empathy in the Context of Personality Traits', *TRAMES*, 6(56/51), p. 3, pp. 218–233.

Reid, A. (2014) 'Patriarchy and Puritanism in Southeast Asian Modernity', in *DORISEA Working Paper*, Series No. 8.

Reynolds, C. J. (2002) *National Identity and Its Defenders: Thailand Today*. Chiang Mai: Silk worm Books.

Riordan, Holly (2022) 'Top 10 Best Thai Horror Movies', *Creepy Catalogue*. 22 February. Available at https://creepycatalog.com/best-thai-horror-movies-list/ (Accessed 17 May 2023)

Rithdee, K. (2004a) 'Manmade Monsters', *Bangkok Post*, 29 October.

Rithdee, K. (2004b) 'Murderous Martyr', *Bangkok Post*, 5 November.

Rithdee, K. (2004c) 'Review', *Bangkok Post*, 5 November.

Rithdee, K. (2005) 'Eternally Exotic', *Bangkok Post*. 7 October.

Rithdee, K. (2008) *Remembering the MASTER*. Available at: http://www.thaifilm.com/articleDetail_en.asp?id=114 (Accessed 12 October 2009)

Rithdee, K. (2013) 'Films Write History, Always and Forever', *Bangkok Post*. 6 April. Available at: https://www.bangkokpost.com/thailand/politics/344179/films-write-history-always-and-forever (Accessed 17 May 2023)

Rithdee, K. (2021a) 'Into the Devil's Lair', *Bangkok Post*. 5 November. Available at: https://www.bangkokpost.com/life/arts-and-entertainment/2210099/into-the-devils-lair (Accessed 17 May 2023)

Rithdee, K. (2021b) 'Thai Films Struggle at Home amid International Praise', *Nikkei Asia*. 8 September. Available at https://asia.nikkei.com/Life-Arts/Arts/Thai-films-struggle-at-home-amid-international-praise

Roby, F. T. (2000) 'King Kong and the Monster in Ethnographic Cinema', in K. Gelder (ed.) *The Horror Reader*. London: Routledge, pp. 242–250.

Ruth, R. A. (2011) *In Buddha's Company: Thai Soldiers in the Vietnam War*. Honolulu: University of Hawai'i Press.

Satrusayang, C. (2022) 'Thai Film Crews are Sought After Across the World, Why then do Thai Films Lag so Far Behind?', *Thai Enquirer*. 14 February. Available at https://www.thaienquirer.com/37473/thai-film-crews-are-sought-after-across-the-world-why-then-do-thai-films-lag-so-far-behind/ (Accessed 17 May 2023)

Schneider, A. (2009) '"Hum aapke hain koun...!" An Example of the Coding of Emotions in Contemporary Hindi Mainstream Film', *Projections*, 3(2), pp. 56–70.

Scott, B. (2022) 'Every Netflix Exclusive Horror Movie Ranked Worst To Best', *Slashfilm*. 13 July. Available at: https://www.slashfilm.com/926852/every-netflix-exclusive-horror-movie-ranked-worst-to-best/?utm_campaign=clip (Accessed 17 May 2023)

Shariman, M. (2010, January 6). *License to Scare* [blog post]. Retrieved from http://malaysiacinema.blogspot.com/2010/01/licence-to-scare.html (Accessed 17 May 2023)

Shim, D. (2008) 'The Growth of Korean Cultural Industries and the Korean Wave', in B. H. Chua and K. Iwabuchi (eds) *East Asian Pop Culture: Analyzing the Korean Wave*. Hong Kong: Hong Kong University Press, pp. 15–32.

Siburapha (1990) *Behind the Painting and Other Stories*, translated by David Smyth. Oxford: Oxford University Press.

Siriyuvasak, U. (2000), 'The Ambiguity of the "Emerging" Public Sphere and the Thai Media Industry', in S. Goonasekera, J. Servaes and G. Wang (eds) *The New Communications Landscape: Demystifying Media Globalization*. London: Routledge, pp. 96–212.

Soerakoesoemah, R. and Thuzar, M. (2012) 'Promoting an Integrated Approach to Urbanization in ASEAN Countries', in Y. K. Sheng and M. Thuzar (eds) *Urbanization in Southeast Asia: Issues and Impacts*. Singapore: ISEAS Publishing, pp. 361–372.

Song, G. (2016), 'Changing Masculinities in East Asian Pop Culture', *East Asian Forum Quarterly*, 8(2), pp. 3–5.

Spotx (2021) 'Thailand', *OTT is for Everyone APAC*. Available at: https://spotxinc.showpad.com/share/v7H2KzcXBJNA7UV21Im51?__hstc=172284156.5c21a64224bae545c1925d4bdd016c7e.1584466911071.1615312065047.1615328096702.419&__hssc=172284156.1.1615388497893&__hsfp=1082933769&hsCtaTracking=4b127f92-b1c6-49b5-829d-a1ab64ce9ead%7C29a4adb0-9575-4ee8-b2bf-2806c18e163c&utm_source=LI&utm_medium=cpc&utm_campaign=paidthailand (Accessed 17 May 2023)

Srinivas, L. (2016) *House Full – Indian Cinema and the Active Audience*. Chicago: University of Chicago Press.

Streckfuss, D. (2012), 'An "Ethnic" Reading of "Thai" History in the Twilight of the Century-Old Official "Thai" National Model', *Southeast Asia Research* 20(3), pp. 305–27.

Sukawong, D. (2001) *A Century of Thai Cinema*. London: Thames and Hudson, 2001.

Supateerawanitt, A. (2022) '18 Scariest Thai Horror Movies You Need to Watch', *Time Out*. 12 October. Available at: https://www.timeout.com/bangkok/movies/best-thai-horrors-movies (Accessed 17 May 2023)

Suwanlert, S. (1976) 'Neurotic and Psychotic States Attributed to Thai "*Phii* Pop" Spirit Possession', *Australian and New Zealand Journal of Psychiatry*, 10/1A, pp. 119–123.

Suwanlert, S. and Vissuthikosol, Y. (1980) '*Phii* Pha: Folk Group Psychotherapy in Northeast of Thailand', *Journal of Psychiatric Association of Thailand* 25(3–4), pp. 234–238.

Tamborini, R. and Weaver, J. B. (1996) 'Frightening Entertainment: A Historical Perspective of Fictional Horror', in R. Tamborini and J. B. Weaver (eds.) *Horror Films: Current Research on Audience Preferences and Reactions*. Mahwah: Lawrence Erlbaum Associates, pp. 1–14.

BIBLIOGRAPHY

Tan, E. S. (1996) *Emotion and the Structure of Narrative Film: Film as an Emotion Machine*. Mahwah: Lawrence Erlbaum Associates.

Tanabe, S. (2002) 'The Person in Transformation: Body, Mind and Cultural Appropriation', in C. F. Keyes and S. Tanabe (eds) *Cultural Crisis and Social Memory: Modernity and Identity in Thailand and Laos*. London: Routledge, pp. 43–67.

Thai Film Festival 2016 in HCM City (2016) 'Social News 29/9', *Vietnamnet Global*. 9 September.

Thai Film Festival Kicks Off in Ho Chi Minh City (2016) *Nhan Dan*. 1 October. Available at: https://en.nhandan.vn/thai-film-festival-kicks-off-in-ho-chi-minh-city-post45808.html (Accessed 17 May 2023)

Thai Horror Movie Well-received in Vietnam (2013) 'TUOITRENEWS', *Vietnam Life*. 3 July. Available at: https://vietnamlife.tuoitrenews.vn/news/ttnewsstyle/20130703/thai-horror-movie-well-received-in-vietnam/16894.html (Accessed 17 May 2023)

The ASEAN Secretariat (2016) *ASEAN Strategic Plan for Culture and Arts 2016–2025*. Jakarta: ASEAN Secretariat. Available at: https://asean.org/wp-content/uploads/2021/01/ASEAN-Strategic-Plan-for-Culture-and-Arts-2016-2025.pdf (Accessed 17 May 2023)

The Nation (2006) *Thai Football Comedy Fails to Score with Laos Officials*, May 16.

The Nation (2013) '*Pee Mak*' Leaps Language Barriers Around the World. 22 November. Available at: https://www.nationthailand.com/life/30220361 (Accessed 17 May 2023)

Thị Hiền, N. (2007) '"Seats for Spirits to Sit Upon": Becoming a Spirit Medium in Contemporary Vietnam', *Journal of Southeast Asian Studies*, 38(3), pp. 541–558.

Tiwahyupriadi, D. and Ayuningtyas, Y. (2022) 'Indonesian Horror Film: Deconstruction of Repetitive Elements of Indonesian Urban Legend for Cultural Revitalization, Creativity, and Critical Thinking', *International Conference on Art, Design, Education and Cultural Studies*. Surabaya: State University of Surabaya.

The World Bank (2022) 'Overview', *The World Bank In Thailand*. Available at: https://www.worldbank.org/en/country/thailand/overview (Accessed 17 May 2023)

Thompson, K. (1981) *Ivan the Terrible: A Neoformalist Analysis*. Princeton: Princeton University Press, pp. 287–295.

Tobias, S. F. (1977) 'Buddhism, Belonging and Detachment – Some Paradoxes of Chinese Ethnicity in Thailand', *The Journal of Asian Studies*, 36(2), pp. 303–326.

Tudor, A. (1974) *Theories of Film*. London: Secker and Warburg.

Uabumrungjit, C. (2001) 'Cinema in Thailand 1897 to 1970', in D. Hanan (ed.), *Film in South East Asia: Views from The Region*. Hanoi: South East Asia Pacific Audio Visual Archives Association, pp. 119–139.

Uabumrungjit, C. (2003a) 'Resurrection of The Knight', *Thai Film Festival*. Tokyo: The Japan Foundation Asia Center, pp. 40–45.

Uabumrungjit, C. (2003b) 'Thai Film History', *Thai Film Festival*. Tokyo: The Japan Foundation Asia Center, pp. 55–60.

Udo, S. (1990) 'The Situation in Thai Films and The Appearance of The Social-Consciousness Films', *Thai Film Festival*. March 9. Tokyo: Masaru Inoue, pp. 2–10.

Udomdet, M. (1990) *Thai Film Festival*. March 9. Tokyo: Masaru Inoue, pp. 54–59.

UNESCO (1982) *Transnational Communication and Culture Industries*. Paris: United Nations Educational, Scientific and Cultural Organisation.

Unger, L. (1944) 'The Chinese in Southeast Asia', *Geographical Review* 34(2), pp. 196–217.

Ungpakorn, G. J. (2009) 'Class Struggle between the Coloured T-Shirts in Thailand', *Journal of Asia Pacific Studies*, 1(1), pp. 76–100.

Van Esterik, P. (2000) *Materializing Thailand*. Oxford: Berg.

Van Klinken, G. and Berenschot, W. (2014) *In Search of Middle Indonesia: Middle Classes in Provincial Towns*. Boston: Brill.

Vichit-Vadakan, J. (1977), 'Thai Movies as Symbolic Representation of Thai Life', *Journal of Social Sciences*, 14(1), pp. 32–48.

Willemen, P. (2006) 'The National Revisited' in V. Vitali and P. Willemen (eds) *Theorising National Cinema*. London: BFI, pp. 29–43.

Williams, L. (1991), 'Film Bodies: Gender, Genre and Excess', *Film Quarterly*, 44(4), pp. 2–13.

Williams, L. (2002), 'Discipline and Fun: *Psycho* and Postmodern Cinema', in C. Gledhill and L. Williams (eds) *Reinventing Film Studies*. London and New York: Arnold, pp. 351–378.

Winichakul, T. (1994) *Siam Mapped: A History of the Geo-Body of a Nation*. Honolulu: University of Hawai'i Press.

Winichakul, T. (2000) '"The Quest for 'Siwilai'": A Geographical Discourse of Civilizational Thinking in the Late Nineteenth and Early Twentieth-Century Siam', *The Journal of Asian Studies*, 59(3), pp. 528–549.

Wise, K. (2013) 'Scaring up Laughter', *The Nation*. 4 April. Available at: https://www.nationthailand.com/life/30203368 (Accessed 17 May 2023)

Wong, S. (2022) 'Horror Features Top Box Office in Taiwan, Vietnam and Thailand', *Screendaily*. 1 April. Available at: https://www.screendaily.com/news/horror-features-top-box-office-in-taiwan-vietnam-and-thailand/5169263.article (Accessed 17 May 2023)

Woofter, K. and Stokes, J. (2014) 'Once More into the Woods: An Introduction and Provocation', *Slayage* 10(2)/11(1), pp. 36–37, p. 3.

Wood, R. (2004) 'An Introduction to the American Horror Film', in B. K. Grant and C. Sharrett (eds) *Planks of Reason: Essays on the Horror Film*. Lanham: Scarecrow Press Ltd, pp. 107–141.

Young, E. (2000) 'Here Comes the Bride: Wedding Gender and Race in *Bride of Frankenstein*', in K. Gelder, (ed.) *The Horror Reader*. London: Routledge, pp. 128–142.

Yu, L. (1936) 'Twin Loyalties in Siam', *Pacific Affairs* 9(2), pp. 191–200.

Zee Oui Film Website (2004) Available at: http://www.pantip.com/cafe/chalermthai/newmovie/Zee oui/zee.html [(Accessed 14 April 2007)

Zappei, J. (2012) 'Horror Films Rise from the Dead in Malaysia', *Daily News Egypt*. 27 March. Available at https://dailynewsegypt.com/2012/03/27/horror-films-rise-from-the-dead-in-malaysia/ (Accessed 17 May 2023)

INDEX

References to notes are indicated by n.

4bia/Si Phraeng (Youngyooth
 Thongkonthun, Banjong
 Pisanthanakun, Parkpoom
 Wongpoom, Paween Purijitpanya,
 2008), 155, 169
16mm era, 9–10, 15–17, 41–2, 62,
 190–1
 and film form, 26–32, 50
 and horror genre, 18–24, 24–5
 and legacy, 48–9
 and lowbrow horror, 32–4
 and New Thai film, 88–90
 and provincial audience films, 144
 and vengeful ghost films, 117–23
 and viewing scenario, 34–41
 and women, 60–1, 76
*30+ Single on Sale/30+ Soht on
 Sale* (Puttipong Pormsaka
 Na-Sakonnakorn, 2011), 152
35mm film, 10, 17, 45, 49, 50, 57
*303 Klua Kla Akhat/303 Fear Faith
 Revenge* (Somching Srisupap, 1998),
 169
1976 coup, 46
*2499 Antapan Krong Muang/Daeng
 Birley and the Young Gangsters*
 (Nonzee Nimibutr, 1997), 67–8, 72

Abhisit Vejjajiva, 146
abject, 6, 33
abstract 'ideal', 4–5, 6
abuse, 44–5, 58–61, 62, 93–4; *see also*
 vengeful ghost films

Acacia (Park Ki-hyung, 2003), 158
advertising, 54, 63n5, 169
affect, 30–1, 33
agency, 10, 21, 22, 61, 76–7, 117, 153
Alexander (Oliver Stone, 2004), 7
Alien (Ridley Scott, 1979), 20
Altman, Rick, 31
America *see* United States of America
American cinema *see* Hollywood
Ancestral, The (Le-Van Kiet, 2021), 171,
 178–9
Ancuta, Katarzyna, 129, 130, 157
Anderson, Wanni Wibulswasdi, 27
Angkor Wat complex, 101
animism, 18, 19, 171–2
anti-Chinese-ness, 91–7, 104–6, 108
anti-Communists, 46
anxiety, 131–6
Art of the Devil 2/Long Khong (Kongkiat
 Khomsiri, 2005), 99–100, 111, 113,
 114, 115–17, 118–19
 and reviews, 119–20
 and Malaysia, 169
 and spirits, 183
ASEAN identity, 13, 177–9, 188, 192
Asia, Nikkei, 180
Asian financial crisis, 11, 69
Association of Southeast Asian Nations
 see ASEAN identity
ATM: Er Rak Error (Mez Tharatorn,
 2012), 152
attraction, 27, 29, 32, 35, 39, 144–5
 and *Baan Phii Pop*, 55

INDEX

attraction (*cont.*)
  and *Buppha Ratri*, 118–19
  and *Ghost Game*, 106, 107
  and *Nang Nak*, 79, 80, 82
  and *Zee Oui*, 105
audience, 13, 27–8, 34–41, 138–48
  and (self-)reflexivity, 126, 135–6
  and teen cycle, 65–7
  and urbanism, 151
  see also communal viewing; international audience
authenticity, 13, 95, 183–7

B-grade films, 44, 51–8, 138, 143
  and women, 58–61
Baan Phii Pop (Srisawat, 1989), 10, 44, 52–8, 61, 63n7
Baan Phii Pop 2008 (Bunharn Taitanabul, 2008), 140, 142–3, 144–6, 147–8
Baba, Shuhaimi, 174
'back to basics' movement, 69–70
Baker, Chris, 51, 99
Bakhtin, Mikhail, 37, 38
Bang Rajan (Thanit Jitnukul, 2000), 68, 72, 79, 89–90, 95, 111
Bangkok, 19, 34, 47, 178
  and cinemas, 16, 17, 37, 52
  and *The Promise*, 156–7, 161–2, 164
  and teen cycle, 65, 66
Bangkok Traffic (Love) Story/Rot Fai Fa Ma Ha Na Thoe (Adisorn Tresirikasem, 2009), 152
Battle Royale (Kinji Fukasaku, 2000), 98, 122
Beach, The (Danny Boyle, 2000), 7, 185
Beautiful Boxer (Ekachai Uekrongtham, 2003), 93
belief systems, 18, 85, 158, 171–2
Bell, Peter, 59, 112
Benh Vien Ma/Ghost Hospital (Vo Thanh Hoa, 2016), 173
Bhumibol of Thailand, King, 70
Blair Witch Project, The (Daniel Myrick and Eduardo Sánchez, 1999), 127
Blake, Linnie, 3, 6, 58

Body … Sop 19/Body (Paween Purijitpanya, 2007), 111, 113, 114, 117–18, 119, 168
Bodyguard, The (Petchtai Wongkamlao, 2004), 120
Boonchu series (1988–95), 66
Boonchu 9 (Bundit Rittakol, 2008), 140, 142
Bourdieu, Pierre, 34
boxing films, 168
Brand, Roy, 6
Braunlein, Peter J., 130
Bridget Jones 2: The Edge of Reason (Beeban Kidron, 2004), 7, 185
British Heritage films, 68–9
Brunei, 168
Buddhism, 19, 23, 85, 100, 171–2
  and *Nang Nak*, 75, 76, 77, 80–1
  and temple fairs, 92–3
  and women, 59–60
Buppha Ratri (Yuthlert Sippapak, 2003), 2, 111, 122, 169
  and horror-comedy, 172–3
  and international audience, 120, 121
  and spirits, 182
  and vengeful ghost, 113–14, 115, 116, 117–18, 119
Burma *see* Myanmar
Burmese, 90
Buruma, Ian, 32, 34
Bushido code, 58

Callahan, William, 96
Cambodia, 168
Cambodian characters, 6, 11, 97–103, 106–8
camera work *see* cinematography
cannibalism, 92, 94, 97, 106
capitalism, 20, 46, 58, 60, 85
carnivalesque atmosphere, 37, 38
Carroll, Noel, 5, 26
censorship, 128, 141, 176, 178
Chaibancha, Mitr, 45
Chaiworaporn, A., 47, 48, 51, 52, 141
Chalui (Adirek, 1988), 66
Champagne X, 66
chaobannok, 18, 73, 74

INDEX

Chaowarat, Petchara, 45
character types, 30–1, 42, 49, 56, 81–2; see also Cambodian characters; Chinese characters
Cheewasuthon, Somchai, 95
Cheuuat Gaawn Chim/Meat Grinder (Tiwa Moeithaisong, 2008), 157
Chiang Mai, 37
childbirth, 19, 72, 86, 169
China, 150, 154
Chinese characters, 6, 11, 91–7, 104–6, 108
Chit Sam Phat/The Second Sight (Pornchai Hongrattanaporn, 2013), 155, 158, 161
Choeung Ek killing fields, 102, 103
Chok Song Chan/Double Luck (Manit Wasuwat, 1927), 16
Christian, John L., 8
Christianity, 171–2
Chuean/Slice (Kongkiat Khomsiri, 2009), 157
Cinema Spiritualism, 130–1
cinemas, 16, 17, 34, 52, 84
  and environment, 36, 37
  and teen cycle, 65
cinematography, 34–5, 40, 42, 49
  and *Baan Phii Pop*, 56–7
  and *Nang Nak*, 80, 81, 82–3
  and provincial audience films, 146–7
  and (self-)reflexivity, 132–3
  and *Tone*, 46, 47, 49
class *see* elites; lower-classes; middle-classes
classical principle, 5
Clover, Carol, 58, 107
cognition, 30, 33
collective society, 10, 11, 30, 83–4, 87
  and B-grade films, 54
  and vengeful ghost films, 118, 119, 120–1
  and viewing scenario, 39, 40–1
colonialism, 8, 10, 33–4, 91, 98–9
comedy, 2, 31, 186–7; *see also* horror-comedy genre; romantic comedy; slapstick comedy

Coming Soon/Program Na Winyan Akat (Sopon Sakdaphisit, 2008), 111, 126, 132–6, 168, 169
  and pirate video, 138
  and spirits, 182
communal viewing, 10, 12, 35
  and B-grade films, 54
  and environment, 36, 37–9
  and provincial audience, 147
  and theatre, 41
Communism, 17, 19; *see also* anti-Communists
community, 69–70, 92–3; *see also* communal viewing
Conjuring Spirit (Van M. Phan, 2014), 179
consumerism, 149, 150–6, 163–4
corruption, 48
cosmopolitanism, 152, 153–6, 165, 185–6
costume, 80
counterculture, 45–6
country music (*luk thung*), 45
Couple in Two Worlds, A/Khu Thae Song Lok (Udom Udomroj, 1994), 66
Creed, Barbara, 6, 19
cross-culturalism, 4–5
Cultural Mandates, 80
culture, 2–3, 4–5, 6–8, 27–8, 81–2
  and ASEAN identity, 177–8
  and proximity, 170–5, 192
  and Southeast Asia, 168
  see also popular culture; youth culture
Curzon, George, 8

Dae Jung Geum/Jewel in the Palace (Lee Byung-hoon, 2003–4), 153
Dark Water (Takashi Shimizu, 2002), 122
Dek Hen Pee/Colic (Patchanon Thammajira, 2006), 169
Dek Hor/Dorm (Songyos Sugmakanan, 2006), 168
democracy, 46, 140, 160–1
Democrat Party, 140
'Developing Asia', 150, 151, 154, 160
dhamma, 18

207

INDEX

digital technology, 180–1, 192
disgust, 5
displacement, 45
Djoerig Salawe (Sahrul Gibran, 2022), 173
Dracula (film series), 4, 82
Dream Man (Roland Nguyen, 2018), 179
dubbing, 40, 41
DVDs, 103, 105, 119, 138–9, 179
  and extreme horror, 185
  and Southeast Asia, 168
  and vengeful ghost films, 120, 121

East Asia, 121–2, 149–50, 151–3, 154
economics, 13, 20
  and ASEAN, 177
  and crisis, 64, 69–70
  and growth, 51–2, 58–9, 60
  and middle-classes, 150–6
editing, 34–5, 40, 82
Elephant King, The (Grossman, 2006), 7
elites, 6, 10, 33–4, 138, 184
  and Cambodia, 100–1
  and lower classes, 141–2
  and nostalgia, 69
  and power, 98–9
  and rural society, 18
emotion, 28, 30–2, 39, 42, 49
  and B-grade films, 54–5, 56
  and *Nang Nak*, 83–4
empathy, 30, 83
empowerment, 10, 20–1, 22–3, 60–1
entertainment, 40, 41, 98, 138
eroticism, 56
escapism, 32
ethnicity *see* racism
Eurocentrism, 7, 10, 33–4, 42
Exorcist, The (William Friedkin, 1974), 4
exoticism, 7–8

Faed/Alone (Banjong Pisanthanakun and Parkpoom Wongpoom, 2007), 111, 169
family, 21, 158–9
Fan Chan/My Girl (Vitcha Gojiew et al., 2003), 68, 71

fear, 5, 24, 25
female sexuality, 6, 19, 21, 146
festivals, 40, 41; *see also* temple fairs
film festivals, 87n3, 119, 169, 178, 179–80
filmmakers, 33, 51, 44, 49–50, 62
filmmaking *see* technology
Final Girl theme, 107–8
finance, 27
folk horror genre, 13, 182–7, 188
Folklore (HBO series), 181
Formoso, Bernard, 95–6
Fouquet, Gerald, 37, 40
fourth wall concept, 126, 127, 135–6
Frankenstein (film series), 4
Freeland, Cynthia, 28
Friday the 13th (Sean S. Cunningham, 1980), 107

game shows, 98
gangster genre, 3
gender, 19, 20, 41; *see also* women
genocide, 102
genre, 26–7, 49, 50, 79, 83
  and proximity, 173–4
  see also comedy; horror genre
Ghibah (Monty Tiwa, 2021), 173
Ghost Game (Sarawut Wichiensarn, 2006), 11, 88–9, 91, 97–103, 106–9
  and (self-)reflexivity, 126
  and spirits, 182
  and Thai-ness, 191
Ghost Writer (Bene Dion, 2019), 173
ghosts, 1–2, 11–12, 42, 58
  and *Baan Phii Pop*, 53–4, 55
  and Mae Nak, 19, 21
  and *The Promise*, 157–8, 163
  and women, 59–60
  see also vengeful ghost films
globalisation, 160
Goh, David, 168–9
Great Britain, 68–9
Grossman, Seth, 7–8
Guardian, The (Victor Vu, 2021), 179
Gunew, Sneja, 33
Gunning, Tom, 27, 35

Halfworlds (HBO series), 181
Halloween (event), 168
Halloween (John Carpenter, 1978), 4, 20, 35, 107
Hanich, Julian, 36, 38, 40
Hansen, Miriam, 5, 26–7, 38
Hantu Bonceng (Ahmad Idham, 2011), 172, 173, 176
Hantukaklimahbalikrumah/KakLimah's Ghost Has Gone Home (Mamat Khalid, 2010), 173, 176
HBO, 180, 181
Heart Attack/Freelance: Ham puay ... Ham phak ... Ham rak mor (Nawapol Thamrongrattanarit, 2015), 152
Hello Stranger (Banjong Pisanthanakun, 2010), 152, 166n1
Heritage films, 11, 64, 67–9, 71–2, 89–90; see also *Nang Nak*
Hewison, Kevin, 69–71
Higgins, Scott, 29
highbrow, 33–4
Higson, Andrew, 4, 68
historical drama, 79, 153
Hollywood, 3, 15, 26–7, 29, 36
 and imports, 16, 17, 51
 and patriarchy, 60
 and rape revenge films, 58
 and *Shutter*, 122–3
Hom Rong/The Overture (Ittisoontorn Vichailak, 2004), 68
home environment, 21–2
homosexuality, 89
Hong Kong, 29, 51, 151–2, 154
horror-comedy genre, 172–5
horror genre, 1–2, 3–6, 191–2
 and 16mm era, 18–24, 41–2, 190–1
 and ASEAN identity, 178–9
 and *Baan Phii Pop*, 52, 53–4, 55
 and cosmopolitanism, 154–6
 and definition, 2–3, 24–5
 and East Asia, 29
 and economic growth, 149–56
 and international growth, 179–81
 and lowbrow, 32–4
 and middle-classes, 161–6
 and modernity, 175–7
 and New Thai, 64–5
 and the Other, 89–91
 and patriarchy, 60
 and *The Promise*, 156–9
 and provincial audience, 142–8
 and (self-)reflexivity, 126–9, 131–6
 and Southeast Asia, 167–75
 and viewing scenario, 34–5, 39
 and women, 58–61, 61
 see also folk horror genre; *Nang Nak*; vengeful ghost films
Hunger Games, The (Lawrence and Ross, 2012), 98
Hunt, Leon, 32
Hutchings, Peter, 2, 4
hybridity, 103–8

I Fine ... Thank You ... Love You (Mez Tharatorn, 2014), 152
I, Robot (Alex Proyas, 2004), 120
Indian cinema, 29–30, 38
Indonesia, 167, 168, 169, 170, 173
 and ASEAN identity, 178
 and belief systems, 172
 and film industry, 171
industrialisation, 19–20, 85
inequality see social inequality
Ingawanij, May Adol, 65–8, 79, 80, 97
international audience, 13, 78–9, 119–22, 179–81, 185
Islam, 171–2

Jaawn Khon (Daen Krisada, 1969), 22, 28–9
Jackson, Peter A., 7
Jaew/M.A.I.D. (Yongyuth Thongkongthun, 2004), 140, 141
Jan Dara (Nonzee Nimibutr, 2001), 68
Jangan Pandang Belakang (Ahmad Idham, 2007), 171, 172, 176
Jangan Pandang Belakang Congkak/ Don't Look Back, Congkak (Ahmad Idham, 2009), 173
Japan, 16, 29, 152, 154
 and *onryou* figure, 58, 122
 and *Shutter* remake, 123, 124n5

Jaws (Steven Spielberg, 1975), 35
Jolokay Phii Sing (Rit Ti Narong, 1993), 55
Ju-On (Hideo Nakata, 2002), 121, 122

Kendara, Kong, 102
Khang Lang Phap/Behind the Painting (Cherd Songsri, 2001), 68, 72, 75
Khao Chue Karn (Chatrichalerm Yukol, 1973), 48
Khmer culture, 97–103
Khon Lok Chit/Distortion (Nonzee Nimibutr, 2012), 157
khwan, 19, 22, 23
Kitiarsa, Pattana, 19, 59–60
Kog, 22
Kon Hen Pee/The Eyes Diary (Chukiat Sakwirakun, 2014), 155
Korean Wave, 152–3
Krasue: Inhuman Kiss (Sittisiri Mongkolsiri, 2019), 183
Krasue Valentine/Ghost of Valentine (Yuthlert Sippapak, 2006), 111
Kristeva, Julia, 6
Kuan Meun Ho/Hello Stranger (Banjong Pisanthankun, 2010), 152, 166n1
Kung Fu Pocong Perawan (Yoyok Subagyo, 2012), 173
Kuntilanak (Rizal Mantovani, 2018), 173
Kwai, Wise, 174–5

La May Tren Bau Troi Ai Do (Thanadet Pradit, 2022), 179
Laa Thaa Phii see *Ghost Game*
Laddaland (Sophon Sakdaphisit, 2011), 155–6, 158, 161, 162, 169, 182
Laos, 17, 90, 98, 99, 168
Le, Nguyen, 173
Le, Troy, 179
Li Hui, 91–2
Lin Yu, 97
literature, 35–6, 41
Localism, 69, 70–1, 73–4, 92, 111
 and vengeful ghost, 110, 115
Loke Thang Bai Hai Nai khon diaw/Romantic Blues (Rashane Limtrakul, 1995), 66–7
Long Duan, 92
Long Jamnam/Pawn Shop (Rphan Rangsee, 2013), 155, 158, 161
Long Khong see *Art of the Devil 2/Long Khong*
Long Tor Tai/The Coffin (Ekachai Uekrongtham, 2008), 169
Love Sud Jin Fin Sugoi (Thanwarin Sukhaphsit, 2014), 166n1
lowbrow horror, 32–4, 42
lower-classes, 10, 11, 88–9, 138–40, 184
 and 16mm era, 17, 23–4, 42
 and Heritage films, 73
 and *Nang Nak*, 80
 and politics, 160–1
 and supernatural, 18
 and viewing scenario, 37–8
 and women, 44–5, 60, 61
 see also provincial audience; rural village; vengeful ghost films; working-classes
Luang Phii Teng/Holy Man (Note Chermyim, 2005), 140, 142
Lumière Brothers, 16

MacRae, Henry, 16
Mae Nak, 19, 21
Mae Nak Prakanong (Rangsir Tasanapayak, 1959), 19, 21, 25, 31
 and *Nang Nak*, 72, 79–80
 and temple fair, 93
magic, 85
Maid, The (Lee Thongkham, 2020), 181, 183
Mak, 72–3, 74, 75, 76, 80–2, 83, 85–6
 and *Pee Mak*, 169–70
Mak Tae/Lucky Loser (Adisorn Tresirikasem, 2006), 90
Malaysia, 98, 151, 173, 176
 and belief systems, 172
 and film industry, 171, 188n3, 192
 and Thai horror films, 167, 168, 169, 170
Man With The Golden Gun, The (Guy Hamilton, 1974), 7, 185

INDEX

marginalisation, 138–40
masculinity, 153
masked drama, 41
Matching Motion Pictures Co. Ltd., 95
Mathayompak ma tha Mae Nak (Poj Arnon, 2014), 173
Meak, My, 102
Medium, The/Rang Song (Banjong Pisanthanakun, 2021), 183, 187
mediums, 19, 22–3
melodrama, 27, 29, 31, 32, 55–6
men, 21–2, 153; *see also* patriarchy
middle-classes, 13, 149–56, 160–6, 176
Midsommar (Ari Aster, 2019), 182
migration, 19–20, 23, 77
military rule, 45, 46, 117
Mills, Mary Beth, 23, 59
Mo 6/5 pak ma tha phi/Make Me Shudder (Poj Arnon, 2013), 173
mobility, 19–20, 21–2, 61
modernity, 10, 13, 154
    and Americanisation, 151–2
    and Southeast Asia, 175–7
    and supernatural, 23, 130–1
    and trauma, 84
    and viewing scenario, 39
    and women, 20, 59, 61
Moh Lum Phii Pha (healing method), 22
Momok The Movie (M. Jamil, 2009), 171
Mongkut of Thailand, King, 33
Monrak Luktung (Rangsi Thatsana Payak, 1970), 45
Monrak Transistor/Transistor Love Story (Pen-Ek Ratanaruang 2001), 93, 128
monstrous female, 6, 10, 18–19, 20–1, 76–7
Muay-Thai boxing films, 168
multiculturalism, 4–5
Mulvey, Laura, 5
music, 45, 49, 66–7, 80
Myanmar, 89–90, 98, 99, 168

Na Songkhla, Pornchita, 141
Nak, 72–3, 74, 75, 76, 79, 80–2, 83, 85–6
nam nao, 32–3, 50

Nang Nak (Nonzee Nimibutr, 1999), 11, 64–5, 68, 72–7, 86–7
    and authenticity, 95, 191
    and Buddhism, 172
    and elites, 142
    and film form, 77–84
    and international audience, 119, 179–80
    and Localism, 141
    and *mise-en-scène*, 122
    and natural law, 84–6
    and patriarchy, 111, 112
    and romance, 182
Nang Prai Taa Nii (Nakarin, 1967), 18, 21, 25, 28–9, 53
Nang Re touring cinemas, 52
Nang Sao Sawan/Miss Suwanna of Siam (MacRae, 1923), 16
Nang Sayong Kwan ('scary movies'), 157
narrative, 28–9, 30–1, 32, 35, 42
    and *Baan Phii Pop*, 52–3, 55–6
    and *The Promise*, 156–8, 159, 161–2, 164–5
    and provincial audience films, 144–6
    and (self-)reflexivity, 132–3, 134–5
    and revenge, 58, 63n10
    and *Tone*, 47, 49
    and vengeful ghost films, 113–19, 121
    and viewing scenario, 39
    and *Zee Oui*, 104–5
nationalism, 6, 11, 91, 99
    and Heritage films, 68–9, 71, 74–5, 79
    and vengeful ghost films, 113
    and *Zee Oui*, 92, 93
    see also Localism
natural law, 5, 11, 84–6
    and supernatural, 24–5, 129, 130
Neale, Steve, 2–3
Netflix, 180, 181, 186
New Thai film, 1, 3, 6, 11–12, 64–5
    and international growth, 179–81, 191–2
    and the Other, 90–1
    and provincial audience, 138–48
    and (self-)reflexivity, 125–9, 131–6
    and Southeast Asia, 167–75
    and technology, 129–31

New Thai film (*cont.*)
  and urbanism, 150–1
  see also *Ghost Game*; Heritage films; vengeful ghost films; *Zee Oui*
Newin Chidchob, 99
Ngangkung (Ismail Bob Hasim, 2010), 173
Nguu Phii (Saet Thaa Phak Dee, 1966), 18, 21, 22, 25, 28–9, 39
non-Thai viewers, 78–9, 119–22
Noodle Boxer (Rerkchai Paungpetch, 2006), 142
normality, 89–90, 92
North, Erika, 186
nostalgia, 67–70, 77, 79, 80, 143
novels, 35–6
numbers concept, 5, 13, 28–32, 42
  and B-grade films, 55–6
  and *Nang Nak*, 79–81, 82–3
  and provincial audience films, 145–6
  and teen cycle, 66
  and vengeful ghost films, 119

Oan Hon (Troy Le, 2015), 179
October 1973 revolution, 46
Omen, The (Richard Donner, 1976), 4
onryou figure, 58, 122, 123, 124n5
open-air screens, 51, 63n5
oppression, 23, 45, 61, 141
oral commentary, 40, 41
orientalism, 7–9, 185
O. T. The Movie/OT Phii Overtime (Issara Nadee, 2014), 155
Othering, 6, 11, 76, 88–91
  and *Ghost Game*, 97–103, 106–7
  and Korean horror, 158
  and monstrous female, 111
  and *Zee Oui*, 91–7, 104–5, 108
OTT ('Over-The-Top') platforms, 180–1

Pa, 18
PAD ('People's Alliance for Democracy'), 140, 146
Pajee, Parinyaporn, 104
Paranormal Activity (Oren Peli, 2007), 127
Parivudhiphong, Alongkorn, 1

parody, 66
patriarchy, 6, 10, 12, 58, 59
  and Buddhism, 23
  and economics, 20, 21
  and monstrous females, 19, 111
  and *Nang Nak*, 77
  and the Other, 89
  and (self-)reflexivity, 134
  and vengeful ghost, 112–13, 115
peasantry, 69–70
Pee Mak (Banjong Pisanthanakun, 2013), 13, 182
  and Southeast Asia, 168, 169–70, 174–5, 177, 188
performance, 35, 49
Pestonji, Ratana, 44, 49–50, 62
Phap Su Mu/Blind Shaman (Minh Thang Ly, 2019), 173
Phenomena Motion Pictures, 120
Phii, 18, 20, 22, 24, 25; see also *Baan Phii Pop*
Phii Chong Air/The Sisters (Tiwa Moeithaisong, 2004), 111, 113
Phii Ha Ayotya/Black Death (Chalermchatri Yukol, 2015), 157
Phii Saat Meng Mum Sao (Wan Chana, 1990), 55
Phii Saht Sen Haa (Pan Kam, 1969), 18–19, 22, 25, 28–9
  and emotion, 31–2
  and length, 39
  and provincial audience films, 143
Phii Sam (Nai Gaay, 1990), 60
Philippines, the, 151, 167, 171
Phongpaichit, Pasuk, 51, 99
Phromyothi, Parichat, 15–16
Phuan/Friends (Apitchaat Pothipiroj, 1986), 66
Phutthinan, Rewat, 66
Phuu Ti Sa Ney Haa (Supasith, 1987), 60
pirate videos, 138–9
Pisanthankun, Banjong, 175
Pocong Minta Kawin (Harry Dagoe, Suharyadi, Chiska Doppert, 2011), 173
point-of-view (POV) shots, 35, 42, 47
police, 46

politics, 5, 13, 18, 146
  and middle-classes, 160–1
  and oppression, 45, 46
  and TRT, 139–40
  and women, 58–61
Poolvoralaks, Visute, 65
pop music, 66–7
popular culture, 13, 33, 166n1, 168
  and USA, 45, 46, 47, 66
pornography, 28, 32
possession, 22–3
post-war era *see* 16mm era
poverty, 48
Praai Phitsawat (Chaluay Sri Rattana, 1968), 22, 39
Prae Dam/Black Silk (Pestonji, 1961), 50, 63n4
Preah Vihear temple, 101
prior-known stories, 81–2
profit, 2, 33
Promise, The (Sophon Sakdaphisit, 2017), 13, 149, 155, 156–9, 161–3, 164–6
  and modernity, 184
  and trauma, 182
propaganda, 16
prostitution, 48
provincial audience, 138–48
Psycho (Alfred Hitchcock, 1960), 4
puppetry, 41

Rab Nong Sayong Kwan/Scared (Pakhpoom Wonjinda, 2005), 157
racism, 6, 89–91, 97–103, 106–8; *see also* anti-Chinese-ness
radio, 41
Rak Luang Lon/The Couple (Talent 1 Team, 2014), 155
rape revenge, 58
Ratchaiboon, Buranee, 95, 104
REC (Jaume Balagueró and Paco Plaza, 2007), 127
Red Bike Story/Chakkrayan Si Daeng (Euthana Mukdasanit, 1997), 66
Red Gaur organisation, 46
red shirt movement, 140, 141, 146
reflexivity *see* (self-)reflexivity

religion, 18, 20, 27; *see also* Buddhism
repression, 5, 6, 11, 89, 134
Reside/Singsu (Wisit Sasanatieng, 2018), 183
revenge films, 58, 63n10; *see also* vengeful ghost films
Ring, The (Gore Verbinski, 2002), 58
Ringu (Hideo Nakata, 1998), 58, 121, 122
Rithdee, Kong, 7, 50, 105
  and folk horror, 184–5, 187
  and Southeast Asia, 172, 174
river bathing, 53, 56
Roh (Emir Ezwan, 2021), 172
romance, 55–6, 79
romantic comedy, 152, 153–4, 159, 179
Rorng Ta Lap Phlap (Prachya Pinkaew, 1992), 66
Running Man (Paul Michael Glaser, 1987), 98
rural village, 10, 11, 15, 22
  and 16mm era, 17
  and *Baan Phii Pop*, 52–3, 54
  and Heritage films, 71–2
  and Localism, 69–71
  and *Monrak Luktung*, 45
  and *Nang Nak*, 72–4, 75, 80–1, 82–3
  and provincial audience films, 142–8
  and Southeast Asia, 176
  and supernatural, 18, 24, 25
  and US development, 19–20
  and vengeful ghost films, 115–16
  and viewing scenario, 37, 40, 42
  and women, 59, 60, 61
Ruth, Richard A., 19, 20

sacrifice, 73–5
Sangkapreecha, Saharat, 66
Sarit Thanarat, Field Marshall, 45, 62n1
Sars Wars/Khunkrabiihiiroh (Taweewat Wantha, 2004), 126, 172–3
Sasanatieng, Wisit, 2, 128
Satrusayang, Cod, 187
Scott, Sir George, 8
Screen at Kamchanod/Pee Chang Nang (Songsak Mongkolthong, 2007), 126, 132–5

See How They Run (Jaturong Mokjok, 2006), 142
(self-)reflexivity, 12, 125–36, 191
Series 7: The Contenders (Daniel Minahan, 2001), 98
sex scenes, 86
sexuality *see* female sexuality
shamanism, 22–3, 100
shared pleasure (*sanuk*), 37–8, 40–1, 42
Shutter (Banjong Pisanthanakun/Parkpoom Wongpoom, 2004), 2, 12, 110–11, 155, 168, 169
  and Buddhism, 172
  and elites, 142
  and horror-comedy, 173
  and international audience, 119, 120–3
  and (self-)reflexivity, 126
  and spirits, 182
  and urbanism, 141
  and vengeful ghost, 113, 114–15, 116–18
Shutter (Masayuki Ochiai, 2008), 122–3, 124n5
Si Phraeng/4bia see *4bia/Si Phraeng* (Youngyooth Thongkonthun, Banjong Pisanthanakun, Parkpoom Wongpoom, Paween Purijitpanya, 2008)
Siam, 8
silent era *see* 16mm era
Singapore, 51, 151, 168–9, 171
Sitthisaman, Nattanee, 52
siwilai (civilisation), 33–4
slapstick comedy, 12, 31, 53, 122, 126, 186
  and *Baan Phii Pop*, 55, 57
  and provincial audience, 137, 140, 141, 144–5
  and Southeast Asia, 173, 174, 184
soap opera, 187
social inequality, 5, 6, 12–13, 17, 48, 52, 64–5
  and Heritage films, 73–4, 75
  and middle-classes, 160–1, 163–5
  and *The Promise*, 161–2
  and vengeful ghost films, 112–13, 117
  and women, 61

social media, 180
Social Problem films, 4, 45, 48, 63n3
Somdej Toh, 82, 87n5
Sondhi Lim, 146
Sophon Sakdaphisit, 155
sound, 17, 40, 45; *see also* music
South Korea, 13, 29, 122, 158
  and modernisation, 151–3, 154, 160
Southeast Asia, 13, 19, 22, 167–75, 188
  and ASEAN identity, 177–9, 192
  and colonialism, 98–9
  and middle-classes, 150
  and modernity, 151–2, 154, 160, 175–7
  and women, 74–5
spectacle, 10, 27, 29, 30–1, 39, 49
  and lowbrow, 32, 42
spectatorship *see* audience
spirits, 10, 12, 13, 42, 182–3
  and female sexuality, 19
  and rural society, 18
  and Southeast Asia, 171–2
  and women, 22–3, 59
Stranded, The (Sophon Sakdahisit, 2019), 181, 185, 186, 187
streaming platforms, 13, 180–1
Suam Noi Noikalon Mak Noi (Wataleela and Jitnukul, 1985), 65, 66
Sudasna, Nida, 95, 104
Suicide Circle (Shion Sono, 2001), 122
Sukawong, Dome, 26, 28, 29, 35, 40
Sungsri, Patsorn, 15, 26, 32
Supab Burut Suatai/Thai Gentleman Bandit (M. C. Sukrawandit Ditsakul/Tae Prakartwutisan, 1949), 17
supernatural, 1, 10, 11–12
  and authenticity, 184–5
  and Cambodia, 99–100
  and *Nang Nak*, 84–6
  and natural law, 24–5
  and politics, 146
  and rural audience, 18
  and technology, 129–36
  and women, 58, 59–60, 61
  and *Zee Oui*, 105–6
  see also ghosts; monstrous female; spirits

superstition, 18
Suriyothai (Chatrichalerm Yukol, 2001), 68, 71, 75, 79, 95
  and Localism, 141
  and the Other, 89–90
  and patriarchy, 111, 112
suspense, 5, 26, 35
Suwanlert, Sangun, 18, 22, 23
Swimmers, The/Fak wai nai gai thoe (Sopon Sukdapisit, 2014), 155, 158, 169, 182
Syndromes and a Century/Saeng Satawat (Apichatpong Weerasethakul, 2006), 129

Tai Entertainment Production Company, 65
Taiwan, 151–2
Talad Phromajaree (Sakka Jarujinda, 1973), 48
Tale of Two Sisters, A (Kim Jew-woon, 2003), 122, 158
Tears of the Black Tiger/Fa Thalai Chon (Wisit Sasanatieng, 2000), 128
technology, 57, 85, 127, 129–36; see also digital technology
teen cycle, 64, 65–7
television, 41
temple fairs, 92–3, 142
Texas Chain Saw Massacre, The (Tobe Hooper, 1974), 4, 107
Thai cinema see 16mm era; B-grade films; horror genre; New Thai film; teen cycle
Thai elites see elites
Thai-ness, 11, 74, 90–1, 92
  and Cambodia, 101, 102, 106–8
Thailand, 7, 98, 185
  and Cambodia, 100–1
  and Chinese community, 95–7
  and culture, 27–8
  and economics, 51–2, 60, 75, 149, 154–5
  and female sexuality, 19
  and gender roles, 58–9, 77
  and inferiority constructions, 33–4, 42
  and Localism, 69–71
  and middle-classes, 149–53, 160–1
  and military rule, 45, 46, 117
  and modernity, 84, 131
  and the Northeast, 134
  and orientalism, 7–9
  and politics, 139–40, 146
  and supernatural beliefs, 22–3, 85
  see also Bangkok; provincial audience; rural village; social inequality; Thai-ness
Thaksin Shinawatra, 99, 139–40, 146, 160–1
Tham Tu Hen Ry/Detective Hen Ry (Tan Beo, 2015), 173
Thang Máy (Peter Mourougaya, 2020), 179
theatre, 41
Tone (Piak Poster, 1970), 44, 45, 46–8, 49, 51, 52, 62
  and capitalism, 58
torture-porn, 29
tourism, 7–8
trauma, 3, 6, 12, 29, 44–5
  and Cambodia, 102
  and Heritage films, 77–8
  and horror genre, 176, 182, 191
  and modernity, 84
  and monstrous female, 10
  and *Nang Nak*, 86
  and patriarchy, 21
  and racism, 94
  and women, 58, 59, 60, 62
Trink, Bernard, 34
Tropical Malady/Sat Pralat (Apichatpon Weerasethakul, 2004), 129
Troy (Wolfgang Petersen, 2004), 120
TRT ('Thai Rak Thai') party, 139–40
Tudor, Andrew, 3
Tuol Sleng Khmer Rouge prison, 103

Uabumrungjit, Chalida, 15, 45, 50
Udo, Seiji, 27–8
Uncle Boonmee Who Can Recall His Past Lives/Loong Boonmee Raluek Chat (Apichatpong Weerasethakul, 2009), 129
UNESCO, 33

Ungpakorn, Giles Ji, 139
Uninvited (Lee Soo-yeon, 2003), 158
United States of America (USA), 17,
    19–20, 38, 154
  and popular culture, 45, 46, 47, 66
  see also Hollywood
Unseeable, The (Wisit Sasanatieng,
    2006), 2, 111
urbanism, 83, 84, 85, 151–3, 176–7; *see
    also* Bangkok; middle-classes

vengeful ghost films, 11–12, 110–17,
    134, 191
  and 16mm era characteristics, 117–23
Vengeful Heart (Qua Tim Mau, 2014),
    171
Vichit-Vadakan, Juree, 37–8
Victim, The/Phii Khon Pen (Monthon
    Arayangkoon, 2006), 126
video rental, 51, 138–9; *see also* DVDs
Vietnam, 17, 99, 168, 170, 173
  and belief systems, 172
  and censorship, 176
  and film industry, 171, 178–9, 192
  and Thai Film Festival, 169
viewers *see* audience; communal viewing
voyeurism, 5, 53

Weerasetakul, Apichatpong, 128–9, 134
West, the, 7–9, 24–5; *see also*
    Eurocentrism; international audience
Western genre, 3, 89
Whole Truth, The/Pritnarulon (Wisit
    Sasanatieng, 2021), 183, 187

'widow ghost phenomena', 23, 59
Williams, Linda, 28, 32, 36
Winichakul, Thongchai, 8, 33, 34
women, 11–12, 21–2, 47
  and abuse, 44–5, 58–61, 62
  and bathing, 53, 56
  and Final Girl, 107–8
  and historical figures, 74–5
  and romantic comedy, 153
  and supernatural, 22–3, 76–7
  see also monstrous female; vengeful
    ghost films
Wood, Robin, 20, 89
Wor Mah Ba Mahasanook (Bunjong
    Sinthanamongkolkul, 2008), 140,
    142–3, 144–6, 147–8
working-classes, 162–3
World Bank, 51–2, 151
wounds, 6, 21, 176

Yongchaiyut, Chaovalit, 96
Yort Gaen (Amnuai Kalatnimi, 1968),
    21–2
Young, Tata, 66
youth culture, 45–6, 47–8, 163–4, 165;
    see also teen cycle

Zee Oui (Nida Sudasna/Buranee
    Ratchaiboon, 2004), 11, 88–9,
    103–6, 108–9, 191
  and anti-Chinese-ness, 91–7
*Zombi kampong Pisang/Zombies from
    Banana Village* (Mamat Khalid,
    2008), 173

EU representative:
Easy Access System Europe
Mustamäe tee 50, 10621 Tallinn, Estonia
Gpsr.requests@easproject.com

www.ingramcontent.com/pod-product-compliance
Lightning Source LLC
Chambersburg PA
CBHW071714160426
43195CB00012B/1681